Social Networking and
Impression Management

Social Networking and Impression Management

Self-Presentation in the Digital Age

Edited by Carolyn Cunningham

LEXINGTON BOOKS
Lanham • Boulder • New York • Toronto • Plymouth, UK

Published by Lexington Books
A wholly owned subsidiary of The Rowman & Littlefield Publishing Group, Inc.
4501 Forbes Boulevard, Suite 200, Lanham, Maryland 20706
www.rowman.com

10 Thornbury Road, Plymouth PL6 7PP, United Kingdom

British Library Cataloguing in Publication Information Available

Library of Congress Cataloging-in-Publication Data
Social networking and impression management : self-presentation in the digital age /
edited by Carolyn Cunningham.
    p. cm.
  Includes bibliographical references and index.
  ISBN 978-0-7391-7811-9 (cloth : alk. paper) — ISBN 978-0-7391-7812-6 (electronic)
1. Impression formation (Psychology) 2. Self-presentation. 3. Social networks. I.
Cunningham, Carolyn, 1973–
  HM1081.S63 2013
  302.3—dc23   2012038971

⊖™ The paper used in this publication meets the minimum requirements of American
National Standard for Information Sciences—Permanence of Paper for Printed Library
Materials, ANSI/NISO Z39.48-1992.

Printed in the United States of America

Contents

Acknowledgments

Putting together this edited collection was a rewarding process, one that I could not have accomplished without the help of several people. First, I would like to thank Lenore Lautigar and Johnnie Simpson from Lexington Books for their support of the project. Thanks to the authors for their important contributions to the field. My colleagues in the Masters Program in Communication and Leadership Studies at Gonzaga University provided an encouraging environment that helped me complete this undertaking. I want to especially acknowledge Kathy Gustafson for her willingness to assist in finding resources and offering advice about logistics. She is a talented woman whom I admire greatly. Heather Wallace, my graduate research assistant, was instrumental in formatting the book. It was a pleasure working with her, especially because of her attention to detail and creative problem-solving. Despite helping twins complete driver's ed. classes and an injury during a climb up Mt. Adams, she worked hard to ensure the book was completed. I am grateful to members of my writing group, especially Rebecca Stephanis, Rebecca Marquis, Elizabeth Goldstein, Anastasia Wendlinder, and Lisa Davis who always provide such thoughtful suggestions on my work. Heather Crandall is an extraordinary colleague who provided invaluable insight and thought about the framework and approach to the book. I learn so much from her sharp mind and quick wit and look forward to sharing more accomplishments with her. Finally, thanks to John, Jack, and Scarlett, who not only support my endeavors, but provide such a happy and loving place to come home to.

Introduction

Carolyn Cunningham

Three months ago, I received a friend request on Facebook from my mother. The picture depicted a younger woman, about thirty-five, and the profile information matched my mother's biography. Studied at Duke University. Lives in Chapel Hill, North Carolina. From Atlantic City, New Jersey. While the information mimicked my mother's real-life profile, it was so impersonal that I questioned whether someone was posing as my mom to gain access to my information. Her only status update read, "I will not be checking Facebook often so please contact me via email if you require a response." This statement seemed antithetical to why one might use Facebook, i.e., to connect with others to form community and share information about one's likes, interests, and life happenings. Knowing that my mother is bed ridden with multiple sclerosis, going blind, and has lost the use of her hands, I wondered who created this profile and for what purpose. Turns out, my father put together this profile as a way for my mom to keep in touch with friends and family. Since her diagnosis fifteen years ago, she has felt isolated and lonely as she deals with her progressively debilitating disease. However, the way my father crafted her profile, highlighting her professional accomplishments and using an outdated picture, makes we wonder how successful she will be at creating a social network that will fulfill her needs. To date, she has five friends, including me.

1

Social networking sites (SNS) have been around since 1997, but didn't hit the mainstream until 2003.[1] SNS such as Facebook, LinkedIn, BlackPlanet, and Twitter, provide users with an online space to construct an image of themselves, create designated networks, and communicate with others. As evidenced from the example of my mother, self-presentation becomes a strategic negotiation of how one presents one's self to audiences. The architecture of SNS provide opportunities for users to ask questions such as who am I; what matters to me; and, how do I want others to perceive me. Some argue that the presentation of online identity is key to success or failure in the information age, especially because SNS are increasingly becoming the dominant form of communication among Internet users.[2]

Communication scholars have been interested in computer-mediated communication (CMC) since the early 1990s.[3] CMC research is cross-disciplinary, of interest to scholars of psychology, sociology, and cultural studies. Within the field of communication, CMC research is integrated into a number of subdisciplines, such as health communication and organizational communication. Early studies of CMC focused on email communication, instant messaging, bulletin boards, and chat rooms, as questions arose about the impact of CMC on identity formation, relationship maintenance, and interpersonal communication. Overall, scholars have been interested in how users navigate the different social context cues in CMC versus FtF (FtF) interactions. For example, scholars such as Sproull and Kiesler found that the CMC form of communication can lead to more uninhibited behavior, increase the amount of disclosure online, and lead to nonconforming behavior.[4] Others argue that CMC can lead to more "authentic" interpersonal relationships.[5]

Research on SNS continues in this tradition. In general, SNS allow users to construct a profile within a "bounded system," connect to others to share information, and have access to other connections within this system.[6] As boyd and Ellison argue, the uniqueness of SNS is that they enable users to construct and manage their own social networks.[7]

SNS transcend virtual space. They allow for a series of "networked publics" which create an "imagined collective that emerges as a result of the intersection of people, technology, and practice."[8] The architecture of SNS structures public and private space and participation within this space. Thus networked publics are "simultaneously a space and a collection of people."[9]

Similar to research on CMC, this collection of current research takes both an optimistic and pessimistic view of the social impacts of SNS. On the one hand, users often strategically present different aspects of their "selves" to increase their social capital, form new personal relationships, and acquire jobs.[10] Scholars have also praised the medium for offering opportunities for social change and allowing for the creation of communities of interest. On the other hand, there are concerns about the negative impacts of SNS, such as the commercialization of identity, privacy, harassment, and promotion of anti-social behaviors where FtF relationships are replaced with virtual ones.

The conflicting impacts of SNS can be understood through the trajectory of Sherry Turkle's work. Turkle's early work on performances of online identity studied how the medium of the computer provided a venue for users to explore and experiment with new ways of understanding relationships, sexuality, and identity.[11] In her research, she found that people could create and navigate multiple identities and have productive virtual relationships. Her early work presented a positive view of technology because it seemed to allow users to have a freedom of identity that was different than what was possible in "real-life." Fifteen years later, Turkle extended this work in *Alone Together: Why We Expect More from Technology and Less from Each Other*. Here, Turkle presents a dystopian view of SNS as adolescents are more interested in communicating with friends through texting and Facebook than actual physical interactions.[12] Turkle argues that our online world does not provide the same amount of liberation as in the 1990s. The way she sees it, both identity and forms of expression are increasingly constrained by the medium. In other words, rather than giving us more control over our "selves," the technology controls who we are and who we can become. She writes, "over time, such performances of identity may feel like identity itself."[13] As she laments, "we are increasingly connected to each other but oddly more alone."[14]

These questions of how SNS are impacting our personal and professional lives are of central concern to this book. One way to look at these pressing social issues is through the multiple ways in which identity is constructed, deconstructed, performed, and perceived on SNS.

Performing the Self Online

Self-presentation and identity management have always been key concerns for communication scholars, particularly those interested in the social and psychological impacts of public identity.[15] Self-presentation is a complex process of selecting which aspects of one's self to disclose, hide, or fake in order to create a positive impression on the audience. This form of inquiry is influenced by the work of Erving Goffman, a sociologist who brought attention to the study of human interaction. Goffman's ethnographic approach shed light on the nuances that occurred in social settings. In his classic text, *The Presentation of Self in Everyday Life*, Goffman likened impression management to a stage performance, where human interaction becomes a strategic negotiation between the individual and the audience.[16] Interactions, Goffman argues, are shaped by both the environment and the audience. As Goffman writes, "when an individual enters the presence of others, they commonly seek to acquire information about him or to bring into play information about him already possessed."[17] Individuals seek out this information to better understand the context of the interaction and to define expectations of behavior. Human interaction includes two different kinds of activity: expressions *given* (performance cues through verbal and nonverbal forms of communication) and expressions *given off* (translation of cues by the audiences).

Goffman uses the conceptual framework of a theatrical performance to make a convincing case that we can study interactions on both the "front" and "back" stage. Goffman argues that there is a "front" stage where the performance of identity occurs.[18] The "front" stage defines the situation for those present observing the performance. The front includes both verbal and nonverbal communication, such as one's clothing, sex, age, or expressions. During the performance, individuals may have several motives for trying to control their own impression when appearing before others. They may want to fit in, gain employment, be invited to join a social circle, or become romantic partners. The "back" stage is where individuals can drop their guard and be more authentic.

Goffman's conceptual framework, or what he calls a "dramaturgical analysis," has been influential for the study of SNS since SNS provide a platform for the management of identity to multiple audiences. Both users and audiences participate in the production and maintenance of individual identity, since users are connected to each other and each other's networks. As Zizi Papacharissi writes, "self-presentation is a process that becomes an ever-changing cycle through which individual identity is presented, compared, adjusted, or defended against a constellation of social, cultural, economic, or political realities."[19] Performances of identity occur on the "front" stage and can be displayed through a number of technological strategies, such as connections with friends, comments people make on updates, and tastes as represented through activities such as "liking" other pages. Papacharissi calls this type of identity a "networked self" which becomes actualized through the ways in which identity is performed through the use of multimedia tools.[20]

The architecture of SNS is an important consideration of how identities are produced and perceived. Identity is not simply performed by the profile, but also through friends lists, public commenting tools, and status updates. SNS are both a private and public space. As such, users can experience what Marwick and boyd call a "context collapse" causing users to develop different strategies for communicating one's self than they would in FtF communication.[21] How users navigate these many issues is the subject of this book.

Organization of the Book

The chapters in this edited collection use a variety of qualitative and quantitative methods to explore the central questions of impression management and CMC such as: what are the different strategies used for impression management on different social media platforms; how does race, class, gender, and sexuality impact these different strategies; how do audiences perceive users of SNS; and, what are the psychological impacts of identity construction on SNS.

Part 1, "Impression Management Strategies" contains three chapters that look at the motivations and strategies that individuals have for identity performance based on Goffman's "front" stage. The collection of chapters asks questions such as what constitutes successful online identities, how users negotiate the complexities of the network, and how users present multiple selves to multiple audiences.

In the fifteen years since SNS have emerged, the medium has matured in offering a variety of services that users seek out for different purposes. Why might one choose to use one SNS over another? And, how does self-presentation differ in different mediums? These questions are taken up in chapter 1 by Jeffrey Kuznekoff. In his research, Kuznekoff analyzes impression management strategies across different social media platforms, including Facebook, online support groups, and first-person shooter (FPS) games. Using a quantitative study, he found significant differences among the impression management strategies in these mediums. This study has multiple implications for design and promotion of different social media. For example, one can imagine that this research is helpful for learning how users learn to navigate the norms of different SNS to achieve desired results.

In addition to across medium strategies, it is important to consider specific strategies that users employ in specific mediums. How do we create a profile on SNS that balances both professional and social goals? Knowing that these performances are public, how do we manage multiple performances? The question of differences between how users want to present themselves and their actual behavior is explored in chapter 2. In "Looking Good and Playing the Part," Judith Rosenbaum, Benjamin Johnson, Peter Stepman, and Koos Nuijten design a mixed-methods study to examine user practices. They found several important differences between perceived and actual behavior suggesting the need for further study about how we might ideally want to navigate SNS compared with FtF interactions. For example, while users are aware that they should be concerned about their privacy settings, why don't more people actually customize those settings?

Performance of identity on the "front" stage is complicated because there are a number of goals users may have as they navigate this space. In chapter 3, "Face-Off," Daniel Davis, Jessica Tougas, Margaeux Lippman, and Timothy Morris look at identity privileging and self-disclosure. Their central research question asks what differences might exist between male and female users. Operationalizing gender differences through the lens of social presence and social identity, they found that females tended to disclose more information on SNS and use the medium to meet their communication needs. This chapter extends work on gender differences in CMC, which suggests that male and female users use CMC for different purposes. Female users have been labeled "power communicators" using the medium of the computer to keep in touch and maintain relationships. Male users, on the other hand, tend to use CMC for more instrumental purposes. The findings of this chapter offer several fruitful suggestions for future research on gender differences and SNS.

Part 2, "Identity in Professional Contexts" looks at how the workplace has influenced impression management. As Marwick and boyd found, SNS users create networks that include members from a variety of professional and social contexts.[22] The blurring of the boundaries between family, friends, and the workplace offers a rich area for critical inquiry. This section investigates questions about how the workplace impacts self-presentation, the similarities and differences between how individuals try to brand themselves on SNS and how corporations brand themselves, and how successful corporations are at using SNS.

Returning to the theme of positive and negative aspects of SNS, Bree McEwan and Jennifer Mease (chapter 4) draw attention to the ways in which the concept of "work" can determine how individuals perform identities on SNS. Their argument is both structural and technological. On the one hand, users must consider the long-term impacts SNS have on their ability to obtain and maintain employment. On the other hand, there are technical limits to the ways in which users can perform identities online. Thus, individuals must make strategic choices about which identities to privilege over others. But what factors determine which identities are privileged? In their case studies of popular media stories of workers penalized for their private SNS activity, McEwan and Mease argue that powerful discourse communities, including the government and corporations, are causing users to self-regulate, creating a virtual panopticon.

College students increasingly are concerned about capitalizing on SNS to obtain employment. Corey Liberman (chapter 5) uses a qualitative study to research how college students present themselves on LinkedIn and Facebook. He found that on both platforms students aimed to brand themselves similar to the ways that companies brand a product. Additionally, students joined networks based on how successful others branded themselves. This study draws attention to the many ways in which corporate identity intersects with personal identity.

Moving from individual identity to corporate identity, Binod Sundararajan and Malavika Sundararajan (chapter 6) ask if corporations are successfully making use of Facebook and Twitter for impression management. Drawing comparisons between those companies that are ranked highest on social responsibility lists and those companies that utilize SNS, Sundararajan and Sundararajan argue that the social media can be vital for maintaining a company's positive identity, especially in times of crisis. This chapter offers avenues for future research on organizational communication and SNS.

Part 3, "Managing Intersectionality" considers how users negotiate the multiple intersections of identity online. Research on SNS show how race, class, gender, and sexuality impact self-presentation and audience perception. Yet, this continues to be a rich area for further investigation. Two common themes in this section are questions of who owns identity and how power is enacted online.

The multiple audiences that we try to present ourselves to may make it hard to "hide" different aspects of our identity. This can be especially tricky for lesbian, gay, bisexual, transgendered, and queer (LGBTQ) users who may want to remain in the "closet." Bruce Drushel (chapter 7) argues that while SNS facilitate multiple identities, these identities are harder to maintain because identity is produced by so many other users in one's network. Even if one might want to remain "in the closet," the architecture of SNS may lead to others' assumptions about one's true identity, "outing" some who don't want to be out. Findings such as these give rise to questions about the technological limitations of SNS for offering an emancipatory space for users to perform identities of their choosing.

The question of who owns identity is taken up in chapter 8 by Amber Johnson in her case study of Antoine Dodson, a poor, gay, African American man. Dodson was interviewed on a local television network after an attempted assault on his sister. The interview went viral and Dodson's likeness was re-mixed multiple times transforming him into a caricature that reinforced negative stereotypes about race, class, and sexuality. Dodson also participated in impression management by strategically exploiting various social media forms. While the viral nature of social media may make it difficult for individuals to control how information is spread, Johnson argues that it may allow users to insert their own stories and offer more complex versions of themselves in the process.

Among marginalized groups such as those who are LGBTQ, community can be vital to one's personal well-being. In the literature on SNS, many cite the importance of community formation as key to understanding social impacts. In chapter 9, Sara Green-Hamann and John Sherblom look at how transgendered individuals' participation in the virtual community Second Life influences their self-concept. They argue that SNS can facilitate and enhance both weak tie and strong-tie networks. SNS can allow people to form personal connections with others, while also providing access to valuable information.

Part 4, "The Dark and Light Side of Impression Management" offers insight into the social and psychological impacts of SNS. As Goffman reminds us, performances of identity are dependent on context and audiences. Thus, we may not be able to control how we are perceived, no matter how hard we try.

Research on self-presentation tends to assume that users aim to make a positive impression on the audience. However, as Nicholas Brody and Jorge Peña (chapter 10) argue, little attention is paid to negative impressions held by audiences despite supposed positive performances by SNS users. This study asks how the topics in messages affect audience perceptions. The findings help illuminate the paradox of what messages make someone less socially attractive, even if the message is intended to promote a positive "face."

Do SNS offer users a chance to feel better about themselves? Catalina Toma addresses this question in chapter 11, looking at how SNS self-presentation can provide a venue for self-affirmation and can affect how users view themselves in the world. Toma reviews three important studies that showed the impact of viewing one's SNS profile on increasing one's self-esteem and alleviating stress. Given the pessimistic outlook provided by Turkle, this chapter suggests that SNS may offer positive psychological benefits. In other words, there may be underlying reasons why we are migrating to SNS over FtF communication.

Finally, Jeffrey Hall and Natalie Pennington (chapter 12) ask the question of how audiences perceive users based on profile information. Hall and Pennington designed an experimental study to research how users estimated others' personalities based on information contained in SNS profiles. They investigated which Facebook cues are most useful for judging a user's personality. Utilizing a mini meta-analysis, they found that certain aspects of users' profiles could predict a user's self-reported personality. This study provides interesting avenues for future research, not only in its innovative research design, but also for how we may use SNS to better convey our "true" selves.

Together, this work furthers the conversation on self-presentation and impression management on SNS. It may act as a heuristic for questions to ponder as we become more comfortable with identity negotiation online. The chapters offer insight into both the positive and negative implications of SNS and CMC, providing new theoretical frameworks and an intriguing array of research designs.

To return to the important questions that Turkle raises about the platform, this collection may offer some insight into why users such as my mom (and dad) may feel constrained by SNS and feel more "alone together." In the end, the chapters in this collection offer some direction on how to move forward in the field and further areas to explore such as privacy implications of SNS, long-term impacts of the commercialization of identity on SNS, and designing SNS architectures that address some of the limitations of the medium.

Notes

1. danah boyd, and Nicole B. Ellison, "Social Network Sites: Definition, History, and Scholarship," *Journal of Computer Mediated Communication* 13, no. 1 (October 2007): 210–30.

2. Kaiser Family Foundation, "Daily Media Use Among Children Trends Up Dramatically From Five Years Ago, last modified January 20, 2010, accessed August 4, 2012, http://www.kff.org/entmedia/entmedia012010nr.cfm; Zizi Papacharissi, "The Virtual Sphere: The Internet as a Public Sphere," *New Media and Society* 4, no. 1 (February 2002): 9–27.

3. See for example Susan C. Herring, "Introduction" in *Computer-Mediated Communication*, ed. Susan C. Herring (Philadelphia, PA: John Benjamins Publishing Company, 1996), 1–13.

4. Lee Sproull and Sara Kielser, "Reducing Social Context Cues: Electronic Mail in Organizational Communication," *Management Science* 32, no. 11 (November 1996): 1492–1512.

5. Joseph B. Walther, "Interpersonal Effects in Computer-Mediated Interaction: A Relational Perspective," *Communication Research* 19, no. 1 (February 1992): 52–90; Joseph B. Walther, "Computer-Mediated Communication: Imper-

sonal, Interpersonal, and Hyperpersonal Interaction," *Communication Research* 23, no. 1 (February 1996): 3–43.

6. boyd and Ellison, "Social Network Sites," 210.

7. boyd and Ellison, "Social Network Sites."

8. danah boyd, "Social Network Sites as Networked Publics: Affordances, Dynamics, and Implications," in *A Networked Self: Identity, Community, and Culture on Social Network Sites*, ed. Zizi Papacharissi (New York: Routledge, 2011), 38.

9. danah boyd, "Social Network Sites as Networked Publics," 41.

10. boyd and Ellison, "Social Network Sites."

11. Sherry Turkle, *Life on the Screen: Identity in the Age of the Internet* (New York: Simon and Schuster, 1995).

12. Sherry Turkle, *Alone Together: Why We Expect More from Technology and Less From Each Other* (New York: Basic Books, 2011).

13. Turkle, *Alone Together*, 12.

14. Turkle, *Alone Together*, 19.

15. See for example Edward E. Jones and Thane S. Pittman, "Toward a General Theory of Strategic Self-Presentation," in *Psychological Perspectives on the Self*, ed. Jerry M. Suls (Hillsdale, NJ: Erlbaum, 1982), 231–62; Barry R. Schlenker, "Self-Presentation," in *Handbook of Self and Identity*, eds. Mark R. Leary and June Tangney (New York: Guilford Press, 2003): 492–519.

16. Erving Goffman, *The Presentation of Self in Everyday Life* (New York: Anchor Books, 1959).

17. Goffman, *The Presentation of Self*, 1.

18. Goffman, *The Presentation of Self*, 22.

19. Zizi Papacharissi, "Conclusion: A Networked Self," in *A Networked Self: Identity, Community, and Culture on Social Network Sites*, ed. Zizi Papacharissi (New York: Routledge, 2011), 304.

20. Papacharissi, "Conclusion: A Networked Self," 307.

21. Alice Marwick and danah boyd, "I Tweet Honestly, I Tweet Passionately: Twitter Users, Context Collapse, and the Imagined Audience," *New Media and Society* 13, no. 1 (February 2011): 114–33.

22. Marwick and boyd, "I Tweet Honestly, I Tweet Passiionately."

Part 1

Impression Management Strategies

Chapter 1

Comparing Impression Management Strategies across Social Media Platforms

Jeffrey H. Kuznekoff

Introduction

Without a doubt, the everyday, social lives of billions of people around the world have become intertwined and perhaps somewhat dependent on modern communication technology. These communication technologies take a variety of forms and can include something as simple as a mobile phone or something as complex as a virtual world. Regardless of the channel of mediated communication, the fact that new communication technology, or computer-mediated communication (CMC), has become so pervasive and popular in usage, across the globe, indicates that we are seeing a change in the way that people interact with others. Certainly, we still have FtF (FtF) communication and this remains the cornerstone of human communication; however, interactions facilitated and perhaps enhanced by CMC remain an important area to study.

Along those lines, this chapter examines the theoretical concept of impression management, or the presentation of self, and how people engage in impression management online. Furthermore, this chapter analyzes differences in the use of impression management strategies between three different social media platforms. By understanding how impression management differs based on the social media platform, we can come to a better understanding of how people continue to engage in the presentation of self through social media.

One way of understanding the interactions that take place online is by examining online impression management and how the impression management strategies employed by users of online systems differ between these systems. Originally introduced by Erving Goffman, the study of impression management or self-presentation (the terms are used interchangeably in this chapter) have been taken up by a variety of scholars in a multitude of fields.[1] We already know that the presentation of self plays an important role in our everyday, FtF interactions.[2] We also know that this presentation or performance of self occurs in CMC contexts and that communicators can use advantages available to them, by the medium, to selectively present themselves.[3] Past scholars have examined how people form online identities and engage in self-presentation online; however, much of this research is based on technology available in the 1990s.[4] Modern day communication technologies like Facebook, YouTube, online multiplayer video games, and virtual environments still maintain much of the communicative abilities of their text-based forerunners; however, these modern CMC contexts also present new challenges to the presentation of self and these challenges have yet to be thoroughly examined.

Goffman's Presentation of Self

In his work, Erving Goffman uses the metaphor of an actor performing a role in a play to explain how individuals communicate or express messages to an audience.[5] Goffman notes, "the very structure of the self can be seen in terms of how we arrange for such performances."[6] In other words, individuals are actively engaged in performing a role, the self, and this performance is put on for the outside world, the audience, who interprets the meaning associated with this performance. Correctly or incorrectly, the audience attempts to interpret the messages the performer generates, through their performance, and come to an understanding of who the performer is.

In the context of CMC, individuals give a performance through their interactions with other people. For example, one's Facebook page is essentially a performance of self. This page functions to communicate messages about the user to others and to portray a certain image of the person. This self-performance could be given to one's friends or perhaps anyone with an Internet connection. Beyond Facebook, any CMC context in which a person interacts with another human being is an opportunity for the presentation of self and for that person to engage in impression management.

According to Goffman, the performer has a certain level of control over his or her performance.[7] For example, the performer may intentionally portray an idealized version of him or herself, in order for the audience to react favorably to them. The actor or performer may accomplish this by highlighting certain aspects of his performance to help support this image. In general, "when the individual presents himself before others, his performances will tend to incorporate and exemplify the officially accredited values of the society, more so, in fact, than does his behavior as a whole."[8] Through careful manipulation of verbal and nonverbal cues, the actor can exert a degree of control over the messages he communicates and, in turn, portray an idealized version of him or herself.

Goffman's notion of an actor portraying an idealized version of him or herself is certainly present in CMC contexts.[9] On social networking sites (SNS) users may only disclose that information which supports a positive portrayal of the user. For example, on LinkedIn a user may only post that information that portrays the individual or forms the impression of being professional. On the same token, the users would likely hide the content that would negatively impact this performance.

These performances, metaphorically, take place in an area called the front. This area could be considered, as Goffman defines it, "the expressive equipment of a standard kind intentionally or unwittingly employed by the individual during his performance."[10] This front is made up of two main parts: the setting and the personal front. The setting is made up of all the background elements that help the audience to understand the context of the performance, while the personal front is the characteristics of the performer. For example, age, sex, and physical appearance are all characteristics of the personal front and many of these characteristics are unchanging.[11] The audience makes use of the setting and personal front to make sense of the actor's performance.

Although much of the activity of the performance is portrayed in the front, Goffman posits that another area, the backstage, exists.[12] This backstage is the area that is typically unseen by the audience, it is an area in which the performer "can relax; he can drop his front, forgo speaking his lines, and step out of character."[13] This area is typically off limits to the audience, as such it exists as an area in which the performer can be him or herself, without the audience observing.

In the context of CMC, we can certainly see aspects of front and backstage being present. For example, the postings a user makes to Facebook would be self-presentations occurring in the front. These are the messages that are viewable by a wide audience and intentionally communicated by the performer. However, the private messages the user sends and receives with friends, or the content they choose to label as private, would likely exist in the backstage area. These backstage communications are all the messages that the user wants to remain hidden, not viewable by the audience.

Impression Management

The majority of Goffman's book, *The Presentation of Self in Everyday Life*, is devoted to explaining the different attributes that construct the performance of self.[14] However, in the later part of this book, Goffman brings together these attributes by formally introducing impression management, which has been a fruitful area of research for a variety of scholars.[15] Leary defines impression management as "the process of controlling how one is perceived by other people,"[16] while Tedeschi and Riess define impression management as "any behavior by a person that has the purpose of controlling or manipulating the attributions and impressions formed of that person by others."[17] Although impression management is certainly not a new concept, Leary notes that the study of self-presentation began with Goffman and spread to other disciplines shortly after his work.[18]

Past Research on Impression Management

In the communication discipline, as well as others, impression management has productively been used as the theoretical foundation of a number of studies. For example, O'Sullivan developed an impression management model that examined the strategic use of CMC channels in order to attain certain self-presentational goals.[19] Ultimately, this model helps to explain why people use CMC channels to manage impressions with certain self-presentation goals in mind. In another CMC example, Chen compares impression management strategies in popular blogs in both Taiwan and the United States.[20] Using the impression management strategies identified by Jones and Pittman, Chen compared differences in impression management between the blogs in the different countries.[21] In particular, the study found that Taiwanese bloggers engaged in more self-promotion strategies than American bloggers did.

In the mid-1990s, Turkle examined identity and the presentation of self in Multi-User Dungeons (MUD), which were forerunners to contemporary, online multiplayer games.[22] In her research, Turkle interviewed users of MUD to help understand how people develop an identity or sense of self in these online environments. In particular, Turkle identified several tensions or themes that emerged from her interview data and these include: boundaries between playing a virtual game and real life, issues of interpersonal intimacy via CMC, and lastly anonymity.[23] Beyond Turkle's work, scholars have examined impression management in more modern CMC contexts.[24]

Becker and Stamp studied impression management in chat rooms and note that "most impression management research focuses on FtF (FtF) interaction. However, impression management behaviors are not confined to FtF social interaction."[25] Specifically, the authors posit that impression management can, and does, occur through CMC channels and this influences how people communicate while online. Using grounded theory, Becker and Stamp created a model that explains the connection between impression management motivations, impression management strategies in chat rooms, and goals related to this process. Allen and Caillouet also studied impression management, but in the context of organizational communication, specifically how impression management strategies were employed by organizations in crisis.[26]

Perhaps the greatest contribution other scholars have added to Goffman's original work is the study of the different strategies people use to engage in self-presentation or impression management. Although a full list of the different tactics individuals use in impression management is beyond the scope of this chapter, Leary explains several of these tactics in more detail. The important consideration is that, by examining tactics or strategies used in self-presentation, we can better understand how people engage in identity management.[27]

Strategies

In response to a lack of theoretical framework for studying self-presentation, Jones and Pittman developed a taxonomy that identified self-presentation strategies.[28] This taxonomy identified five self-presentational strategies that individuals could use when engaging in impression management. The five strategies include: ingratiation, intimidation, self-promotion, exemplification, and supplication.

Ingratiation

The first strategy, ingratiation, is noted as being "the most ubiquitous of all self presentational phenomena."[29] This strategy is concerned, first and foremost, with the notion that others like us or hold favorable impressions of us. Put another way, an individual (the actor) implementing the ingratiation strategy would engage in a self-presentation that would have others attribute the notion of being likable to the actor.

Intimidation

The second strategy, intimidation, is nearly the opposite of ingratiation. With the intimidation strategy, the actor "tries to convince a target person that he is *dangerous*. . . the intimidator typically disdains any real interest in being liked; he wants to be feared, to be believed."[30] In essence, while the ingratiation strategy aims for the individual to be liked by others, the intimidation strategy aims for the individual to be considered dangerous or to be feared by others.

Self-Promotion

The third self-presentational strategy identified by Jones and Pittman is the strategy of self-promotion.[31] According to these scholars "we speak of the actor as 'self promoting' when he seeks the attribution of competence, whether with reference to general ability level (intelligence, athletic ability) or to a specific skill (typing excellence, flute-playing ability)."[32] Although self-promotion is related to the first two strategies, the authors note that self-promotion is still a unique strategy. In regards to ingratiation, self-promotion is more concerned with others attributing the concept of competence to us, instead of likeability. Again with intimidation, self-promotion is focused on competence and, as Jones and Pittman note, "we can convince others of our competence without threatening them or striking fear in their hearts."[33]

Exemplification

The fourth strategy, exemplification, is similar to the self-promotion strategy in that in both strategies the person wants other people to respect them; however, differences between the two strategies do exist. According to Jones and Pittman, "whereas the self promoter wants to be seen as competent, masterful, olympian, the exemplifier seeks to project *integrity and moral worthiness*."[34] Clearly many individuals would want to be viewed as likeable (ingratiation) and competent (self-promotion); however, Jones and Pittman argue that exemplification has strategic qualities that make it distinct from the strategies of ingratiation or self-promotion.

Supplication

The final strategy, supplication, can occur when an individual is unable to use or lacks the resources needed for the other four strategies. In essence, supplication is "the strategy of advertising one's dependence to solicit help."[35] For example, someone might proclaim that they do not know how to fix a problem they are having with a computer and use this lack of knowledge to ask for help. Jones and Pittman give the gendered example of a woman, who is unable to change a tire, employs the supplication strategy to get a man, who apparently can change a tire, to solve the problem for her. These authors explain, "she accomplishes this at the small cost of being considered totally incompetent by her vain and dedicated husband or suitor."[36] Although this example, provided by Jones and Pittman, is clearly based on gender stereotypes, it does demonstrate how the supplication strategy could be employed.

Cumulatively, the five self-presentation strategies identified by Jones and Pittman offer a way of studying self-presentation or impression management by offering a theoretical framework from which to work from.[37] By measuring these strategies in different social media platforms, we may be able to more thoroughly understand how people use these strategies to manage their self-presentation and engage in impression management. Furthermore, we can extend this study of impression management by measuring impression management strategies in online contexts or across different social media platforms. This approach to data collection diverges from past research (e.g., Turkle) that has used ethnography and interviews to collect data about impression management.[38]

Social Media Platforms

The three social media platforms examined in this chapter are Facebook, online first-person shooter (FPS) games, and online social support sites. These platforms or CMC contexts were chosen for two main reasons. First, and perhaps foremost, each context should differ in many if not all of the impression management strategies. Second, each context is widely used by a large population, some even number in the hundreds of millions, thus results from research into these contexts can help us to understand the ways in which large number of users interact and communicate in each context.

Facebook is one of the most popular SNS currently available. By 2012, Facebook had over 900 million users and half of those users logged into Facebook every day.[39] Using Facebook, virtually anyone can keep in contact with their friends, regardless of geographic location. Furthermore, users cannot only post updates about what is going on in their lives, but also comment on the posts or updates of others, regardless of how trivial that information might be. Users also have the ability of uploading digital photos and videos, and identifying which of their friends are present in that content. Because of the richness and connectivity afforded by Facebook, users can engage in impression management by posting comments to their Facebook timeline, posting on their friend's posts/comments, or even by sharing posts/content with others.

The second social media platform discussed in this chapter is multiplayer FPS games. Put simply, FPS games allow gamers to experience a virtual environment through the perspective of their character. Often, FPS games are violent nature and involve the player engaging in gameplay with other players through the Internet.[40] Past research has even linked game play of some types of video games with aggressive behavior; however, little research has examined impression management in FPS games.[41]

One important feature of many contemporary FPS games is multiplayer gameplay. Through subscription services, like Xbox LIVE, gamers can play with or against several other people and typically can communicate with those players in real time using their voices. Video games, which certainly include FPS games, are rather popular, with 97 percent of young people (ages twelve to seventeen) in the United States reporting that they play video games.[42] By itself, the FPS game Halo 3 sold an estimated $170 million within twenty-four hours of being released and within eighteen months 1 billion multiplayer matches had been played online.[43] Through the real-time voice capabilities of many modern FPS games, gamers can engage in impression management by engaging in conversation with other, similar to how impression management is carried out in FtF interactions.

The last social media platform examined in this chapter is online social support websites. Such websites are generally online communities where groups of people can discuss issues important to them. Black, Bute, and Russell explain that social support sites can include the following, "expressions of encouragement or validation, advice or feedback about behaviors, sharing of information, and offers of tangible assistance."[44] Often, social support websites focus on medical conditions or diseases and offer users a way to talk with others about the issues they are facing. One such social support website is FatSecret, which is an online community that focuses on weight loss.[45] According to the FatSecret website, "FatSecret is a **new** online diet, nutrition and weight loss community that harnesses the collective contributions of our members to generate practical and motivating information so that you can make better decisions to achieve your goals."[46] On social support web-sites, such as FatSecret, users can engage in impression management by interacting with other users through discussion boards, private messages, and even by journaling.

Given the different goals of these three social media platforms, the question then becomes how do people engage in impression management differently between each context?

RQ: What are, if any, the differences in the use of impression manage-ment between the three contexts?

Measuring Impression Management Strategies

One way of studying impression management strategies between differ-ent social media platforms is by asking users of these platforms to com-plete a survey that asks questions about their use of impression manage-ment in that particular context. Bolino and Turnley developed a measure of impression management behaviors in organizations and based this measure on a taxonomy proposed by Jones and Pittman.[47] Bolino and Turnley developed this measure in an attempt to overcome shortcomings with other impression management scales and research methods.[48] To accomplish this, the scholars used Jones and Pittman's taxonomy of im-pression management behaviors, which includes self-promotion, ingratia-tion, exemplification, intimidation, and supplication, as the basis for sur-vey items that measure these strategies.[49]

The impression management scale is made up of twenty-two items, broken down into five subscales, each subscale representing a different strategy identified by Jones and Pittman. Each item on the subscales is measured on a five-point scale. Participants respond to each item by in-dicating how often they behave in the way noted on that item. The an-chors for this scale include the following: (1) *never behave this way*, (2) *very rarely behave this way*, (3) *occasionally behave this way*, (4) *some-times behave this way*, and (5) *often behave this way*.[50] Thus, higher scores indicate that the participant engages in that strategy more fre-quently and lower scores indicate that the participant does not use that strategy regularly. In general, the subscales for this measure of impres-sion management have demonstrated excellent reliability and the following alpha reliabilities, for each subscale, were found: self-promotion 0.82, ingratiation 0.83, exemplification 0.73, intimidation 0.89, and supplication 0.84.

To study differences in impression management strategies between these three social media platforms, 171 people were recruited from these contexts to complete a survey that asked about their use of impression management in that particular context. A total of sixty-two people participated in the survey asking about their use of Facebook. In this group the average age was 35.38 and the majority (68.8 percent) were female while the remaining participants were male (31.3 percent). By far, the majority of the participants reported their race as being Caucasian (93.8 percent), followed by African American (4.2 percent), and Pacific Islander (2.1 percent). For the online social support sites, thirty-two people responded to the online social support survey. Of the participants of this survey, the majority were female (68 percent) while the remaining participants were male (32 percent). The average age of participants in this survey was 34.32 years old. Again, the majority of participants were White or Caucasian (96 percent) while the remaining participants reported their race as being other (4 percent). Lastly, seventy-seven people participated in the survey focusing on FPS games. For this group the average age was 19.16 years old, with the majority being male (77.3 percent) and the remaining participants being female (22.7 percent). Again, the majority of participants were Caucasian (90.7 percent), followed by African American (5.3 percent), Hispanic (1.3 percent), Asian (1.3 percent), or other (1.3 percent). The only difference in the surveys between the different social media platforms was noun usage in each question, in order to be consistent with each context, and minor changes to wording, again to be consistent.

Differences in Impression Management Strategies

To determine if the use of each impression management strategy differs based on the social media platform, or CMC context, an ANOVA was run for each strategy. Each ANOVA examined the mean score for each strategy by each context. No statistically significant differences were detected for the self-promotion or supplication strategies; however,

a statistically significant difference was found for ingratiation scores between the three groups $F(2, 149) = 22.83, p < .05, \eta^2 = 0.24$. Tukey post-
hoc comparisons indicate that the FPS group ($M = 2.13, SD = 1.02$) differed from the Facebook group ($M = 3.06, SD = 0.94$) and online social
support group ($M = 3.45, SD = 1.01$). The FPS group used ingratiation
strategies significantly less than the other two groups and social support
used ingratiation significantly more than FPS users.

For the exemplification strategy, a statistically significant difference
was found amongst the three groups $F(2, 147) = 5.75, p < .05, \eta^2 = 0.07$.
Post-hoc testing using Tukey indicates that the social support group ($M = 2.26, SD = 1.13$) differs significantly from the Facebook ($M = 1.64, SD = 0.84$) and FPS groups ($M = 1.60, SD = 0.82$). It appears as though the
social support group uses higher levels of exemplification than Facebook
users or FPS users.

Finally, a statistically significant difference in intimidation strategy
was found amongst the three groups $F(2, 146) = 25.06, p < .05, \eta^2 = 0.26$. Tukey post-hoc tests indicate that FPS users ($M = 2.58, SD = 1.15$)
differed significantly from the Facebook ($M = 1.33, SD = 0.65$) and
online social support ($M = 1.63, SD = 1.07$) groups. Results indicate that
FPS users use more intimidation strategies in their CMC interactions
than Facebook or online social support users (see Table 1.).

Table 1.1. CMC Impression Management Means Comparison by Group

		Facebook	FPS	Social Support
Self-promotion	M	2.43	2.45	2.52
	SD	0.86	1.14	1.08
	n	49	75	26
Ingratiation*	M	3.06_a	2.13_{ab}	3.45_b
	SD	0.94	1.02	1.01
	n	49	75	26
Exemplification*	M	1.64_c	1.60_d	2.26_{cd}
	SD	0.84	0.82	1.13

	n	49	75	26
Intimidation*	M	1.33_e	2.58_{ef}	1.63_f
	SD	0.65	1.14	1.07
	n	48	75	26
Supplication	M	1.60	1.71	1.97
	SD	0.65	0.79	1.00
	n	48	75	26

Note: Common subscripts indicate a statistically significant difference between groups *p<.05

Discussion

The results reported in this chapter indicate that the use of three of the five impression management strategies (ingratiation, exemplification, and intimidation) do seem to differ between the three social media platforms identified in this chapter. In particular, social support users engaged in more frequent use of ingratiation than the FPS group and relatively comparable levels of ingratiation compared to the Facebook group. In the case of this finding, 24 percent of the variance in ingratiation can be accounted for based on the social media platform. Bolino and Turnley, as well as Jones and Pittman, note that ingratiation is used when an individual wants to appear likeable by others and that individuals might use flattery or favors to form that impression.[51] Given this explanation, it would make sense that social support and Facebook users would differ from FPS users in the use of ingratiation. One explanation is that Facebook and social support users are likely involved in more interpersonal than impersonal communication within that context, thus appearing likeable might be socially beneficial. Furthermore, appearing unlikeable, or perhaps using greater amounts of intimidation in Facebook or social support sites, may have a negative effect on that user's social standing within the group and likely would serve to inhibit other user's social interaction with that user. Within the context of social support sites, appearing more likeable or friendly would likely benefit the user and provide a more appropriate fit with the specific goals of social support sites.[52] However, in many FPS games, we would not expect users to perform favors or use flattery to appear likeable. Instead, it might make more sense for FPS users to engage in more intimidation, perhaps as a tactical advantage, and the results from this chapter support that conclusion.

For intimidation, the FPS users engaged in significantly more frequent use of intimidation than Facebook or social support users and 7 percent of this variance can be accounted for based on the social media platform. Arguably, intimidation could provide a strategic advantage to the person engaging in this strategy. For example, we know from Jones and Pittman that users engaging in intimidation want to be feared or viewed as being dangerous.[53] In the context of an FPS game, this might make other players weary or afraid to attack or approach that intimidating player. Past research has demonstrated that video games are often violent in nature and that game play of some video games may have a link with aggressive behavior.[54] Given past research, and the combative and violent nature of many FPS games, intimidation likely serves a practical purpose in the game, yet juxtaposed to either Facebook or social support sites, intimidation would likely be viewed as anti-social behavior. In the context of social support websites in particular, intimidation likely accomplishes the opposite of the goals of such sites.[55] Instead of appearing intimidating, social support users would likely want to avoid this strategy and engage in other forms of impression management and this appears to be the case.

For exemplification, social support users appeared to use this strategy significantly more than the other two groups and 26 percent of this variance in usage can be accounted for by social media platform. As noted earlier, exemplification is essentially the individual demonstrating that they possess integrity and/or morality.[56] Bolino and Turnley expand on this by explaining that exemplification is portrayed when "people self-sacrifice or go above and beyond the call of duty in order to gain the attribution of dedication from observers."[57] In the case of online social support, the goal of which is to provide "expressions of encouragement or validation, advice or feedback about behaviors, sharing of information, and offers of tangible assistance," it would make sense that users engage in more exemplification than the other two contexts.[58]

In the case of this chapter, we do see differences in how users of three different social media platforms engage in impression management strategies differently depending on the context. Goffman would likely tell us that the individuals (or actors) in each context are portraying a particular role for that context (or audience).[59] We could also argue that the actors might be portraying an idealized performance of self, or portraying a role that upholds the socially acceptable standards of behavior for that context. Another explanation is that users of each social media platform engage in impression management that roughly corresponds to the goals of that particular platform. FPS users engage in more intimidation because intimidation serves a practical purpose in that context. Put another way, appearing as someone who is powerful, in the eyes of one's competitors, may provide users with a tangible benefit in the context of FPS video games. Social support and Facebook users engage in more ingratiation than FPS users because appearing likeable may prove to be socially beneficial in those two contexts. Lastly, social support users engaged in more exemplification than the other two groups because appearing dedicated or self-sacrificing helps to support the overall goal of online social support.

Implications and Conclusion

Perhaps the most important implication for research stemming from this chapter is providing a starting point for studying impression management across different social media platforms. In some cases, past research has examined how two different groups engage in certain impression management strategies differently.[60] However, this chapter extends this approach by expanding the study of impression management to three different social media platforms. Continuing this expansion, by examining other popular social media sites like Twitter, foursquare, Pinterest, LinkedIn, or Google+ would help the scholarly community to more fully understand how users engage in impression management in contemporary CMC contexts.

Another implication or area for future research is to examine how online impression management differs between different contexts and FtF self-presentation. For example, it could be that these social media platforms allow users to engage in radically different forms of impression management than their FtF lives. Examining this potential difference, and perhaps what characteristics of the social media platforms can account for this difference, will likely help impression management scholars more thoroughly understand and explain impression management in contemporary CMC contexts. Understanding these differences may even help developers of social media platforms to more thoroughly understand how their user base utilizes their particular platform to interact with others.

One specific contribution from this study is the inclusion of FPS games as one context in which additional study of impression management should be conducted. FPS games are unique from other social media platforms in that gamers likely have a low expectation of future interaction. For example, in several modern FPS games, users are automatically paired up with competitors, yet after the game is over those users may not be likely to encounter each other again. This is staunchly different from social media platforms like Facebook or social support sites in which users are likely to interact with same users again. Future research should examine how this expectation of future interaction impacts impression management.

Perhaps the main contribution of this chapter is the comparison of three different social media platforms. This chapter provides more information about the use of impression management strategies in modern day CMC by situating the research in these contemporary contexts (i.e., Facebook, FPS, social support sites). By providing more information about how users engage in impression management, in these contemporary online contexts, this chapter can provide the scholarly community with additional information about impression management online. In addition, this chapter can also serve as a starting point for additional research into online impression management to help further our understanding of how people engage in the presentation of self while online.

From the standpoint of Goffman's presentation of self, the goal of this chapter was to examine differences in the use of five impression management strategies among three different social media platforms.[61] When we compared the use of impression management strategies between different social media platforms, we found that users tended to engage in impression management differently, depending on the platform. In particular, FPS users engaged in more intimidation than the other two groups and social support users engaged in more ingratiation and exemplification than the both Facebook and FPS users. Findings indicate that users of these contexts do differ in three of the five strategies and these differences likely can be attributed to the specific goals or atmosphere of each context.

Notes

1. Erving Goffman, *The Presentation of Self in Everyday Life* (New York: Anchor Books, 1959).

2. Goffman, *The Presentation of Self*.

3. Joseph B. Walther, "Computer-Mediated Communication: Impersonal, Interpersonal, and Hyperpersonal Interaction," *Communication Research* 23, no. 3 (February 1996): 3–43.

4. Sherry Turkle, *Life on the Screen: Identity in the Age of the Internet* (New York: Simon and Schuster, 1995).

5. Goffman, *The Presentation of Self*.

6. Goffman, *The Presentation of Self*, 252.

7. Goffman, *The Presentation of Self*.

8. Goffman, *The Presentation of Self*, 35.

9. Goffman, *The Presentation of Self*.

10. Goffman, *The Presentation of Self*, 22.

11. Goffman, *The Presentation of Self*.

12. Goffman, *The Presentation of Self*.

13. Goffman, *The Presentation of Self*, 112.

14. Goffman, *The Presentation of Self*.

15. Mark R. Leary, *Self-Presentation: Impression Management and Interpersonal Behavior* (Madison, WI: Brown and Benchmark, 1996).

16. Leary, *Self-Presentation*, 2.

17. James T. Tedeschi and Marc Riess, "Identities, the Phenomenal Self, and Laboratory Research," in *Impression Management Theory and Social Psychological Research*, ed. James T. Tedeschi (New York: Academic Press, 1981), 3.

18. Leary, *Self-Presentation*.

19. Patrick B. O'Sullivan, "What You Don't Know Won't Hurt Me: Impression Management Functions of Communication Channels in Relationships," *Human Communication Research* 26, no. 3 (July 2000): 403–31.

20. Yi-Ning Katherine Chen, "Examining the Presentation of Self in Popular Blogs: A Cultural Perspective." *Chinese Journal of Communication* 3, no. 1 (March 2010): 28–41.

21. Edward E. Jones and Thane S. Pittman, "Toward a General Theory of Strategic Self-Presentation," in *Psychological Perspectives on the Self*, ed. Jerry M. Suls (Hillsdale, NJ: Erlbaum, 1982), 231–61.

22. Turkle, *Life on the Screen*.

23. Turkle, *Life on the Screen*.

24. Turkle, *Life on the Screen*.

25. Jennifer A. Becker and Glen H. Stamp, "Impression Management in Chat Rooms: A Grounded Theory Model," *Communication Studies* 56, no. 3 (September 2005): 244.

26. Myria W. Allen and Rachel H. Caillouet, "Legitimation Endeavors: Impression Management Strategies Used by an Organization in Crisis," *Communication Monographs* 61, no. 1 (March 1994): 44–62.

27. Leary, *Self-Presentation*.

28. Jones and Pittman, "Toward a General Theory."

29. Jones and Pittman, "Toward a General Theory," 235.

30. Jones and Pittman, "Toward a General Theory," 238.

31. Jones and Pittman, "Toward a General Theory."

32. Jones and Pittman, "Toward a General Theory," 241.

33. Jones and Pittman, "Toward a General Theory," 241.

34. Jones and Pittman, "Toward a General Theory," 245.

35. Jones and Pittman, "Toward a General Theory," 247.

36. Jones and Pittman, "Toward a General Theory," 248.

37. Jones and Pittman, "Toward a General Theory."

38. Turkle, *Life on the Screen*.

39. Facebook, "Statistics," *Facebook Statistics* 2012, accessed June 21, 2012, http://newsroom.fb.com/Key-Facts/Statistics-8b.aspx.

40. Nicholas L. Carnagey, Craig A. Anderson, and Brad J. Bushman, "The Effect of Video Game Violence on Physiological Desensitization to Real-Life Violence," *Journal of Experimental Social Psychology* 43, no. 3 (May 2007): 489–96; Vincent Cicchirillo and Rebecca M. Chory-Assad, "Effects of Affective Orientation and Video Game Play on Aggressive Thoughts and Behaviors," *Journal of Broadcasting and Electronic Media* 49, no. 4 (December 2005): 435–49; Stacy L. Smith, Ken Lachlan, and Ron Tamborini, "Popular Video Games: Quantifying the Presentation of Violence and Its Context," *Journal of Broadcasting and Electronic Media* 47, no. 1 (March 2003): 59–76.

41. Craig A. Anderson and Brad J. Bushman, "Effects of Violent Video Games on Aggressive Behavior, Aggressive Cognition, Aggressive Affect, Physiological Arousal, and Prosocial Behavior: A Meta-Analytic Review of the Scientific Literature," *Psychological Science* 12, no. 5 (September 2001): 353–59; Mary E. Ballard and J. Rose Wiest, "Mortal Kombat ™: The Effects of Violent Video Game Play on Males' Hostility and Cardiovascular Responding," *Journal of Applied Social Psychology* 26, no. 8 (April 1996): 717–30; Joel

Cooper and Diane Mackie, "Video Games and Aggression in Children," *Journal of Applied Social Psychology* 16, no. 8 (1986): 726–44; Matthew S. Eastin, "Video Game Violence and the Female Game Player: Self and Opponent Gender Effects on Presence and Aggressive Thoughts," *Human Communication Research* 32, no. 3 (July 2006): 351–72.

42. Associated Press, "Survey: 97 Percent of American Youth Play Video Games," *CNN*, 2008, accessed September 16, 2008, http://www.cnn.com/2008/TECH/ptech/09/16/videogames.survey.ap/index.html.

43. Reuters, "Microsoft's Halo 3 Registers Biggest Day in US Entertainment History with $170 Million in Sales," last modified 2007, accessed June 20, 2012, www.reuters.com/article/2007/09/27/idUSIN20070927063131 MSFT20070927; "One Billion Served and Counting," Bungie 2009, accessed June 20, 2012, http://www.bungie.net/news/content.aspx?type=topnews&link= CGHV33KGD2R9D3W9V4QY7MF9Q.

44. Laura W. Black, Jennifer J. Bute, and Laura D. Russell, "'The Secret Is Out!': Supporting Weight Loss through Online Interaction," in *Cases on Online Discussion and Interaction: Experiences and Outcomes*, ed. Leonard Shedletsky and Joan E. Aiken (Hershey, PA: IGI Global, 2010), 354.

45. FatSecret, "About Us," *FatSecret*, accessed June 20, 2012, www.fatsecret.com/Default.aspx?pa=a.

46. FatSecret, "About Us," 1.

47. Mark C. Bolino and William H. Turnley, "Measuring Impression Management in Organizations: A Scale Development Based on the Jones and Pittman Taxonomy," *Organizational Research Methods* 2, no. 187 (April 1999): 187–206; Jones and Pittman, "Toward a General Theory."

48. Bolino and Turnley, "Measuring Impression Management."

49. Jones and Pittman, "Toward a General Theory."

50. Bolino and Turnley, "Measuring Impression Management."

51. Bolino and Turnley, "Measuring Impression Management"; Jones and Pittman, "Toward a General Theory."

52. Black, Bute, and Russell, "The Secret Is Out."

53. Jones and Pittman, "Toward a General Theory."

54. Carnagey, Anderson, and Bushman, "The Effect of Video Game"; Cicchirillo and Chory-Assad, "Effects of Affective Orientation"; Smith, Lachlan, and Tamborini, *Popular Video Games*; Anderson and Bushman, *Effects of Violent Video*; Ballard and West, *Mortal Kombat*; Cooper and Mackie, *Video Games and Aggression*; Eastin, *Video Game Violence*.

55. Black, Bute, and Russell, "The Secret Is Out."

56. Jones and Pittman, "Toward a General Theory."

57. Bolino and Turnley, "Measuring Impression Management, "190.

58. Black, Bute, and Russell, "The Secret Is Out," 354.

59. Goffman, *The Presentation of Self.*
60. Chen, "Examining the Presentation."
61. Goffman, *The Presentation of Self.*

Chapter 2

"Looking the Part" and "Staying True": Balancing Impression Management on Facebook

Judith E. Rosenbaum, Benjamin K. Johnson,
Peter A. Stepman, and Koos C. M. Nuijten

The social networking site Facebook has grown dramatically since its original incarnation as a site specifically for college students. The site now has over 900 million active members,[1] while social media constitute a large portion of people's daily media usage.[2]

Social networking sites (SNS) like Facebook have attracted much scholarly interest, including the fast-growing area of inquiry focused on how people engage in self-presentation in an SNS environment.[3] This chapter adds to the growing literature on social networking site self-presentation by offering an exploratory analysis of self-presentation on Facebook through the juxtaposition of focus groups conducted with African American college-aged users against a content analysis of status updates collected from the "newsfeeds" and "walls" of a convenience sample of the same population.

This chapter will investigate the behaviors and motivations of Facebook users through a qualitative analysis of a convenience sample drawn from a historically black university. Reports from the Pew Research Center show that blacks and other racial minorities in the United States are well represented on SNS and are more likely than whites to use the micro-blogging service Twitter.[4] It is important to note, however, that the absence of a balanced, representative sample, along with the use of qualitative methods, preclude this study from drawing any conclusions about differences in SNS use along demographic or cultural lines. But since most studies into computer-mediated communication (CMC) and SNS use mainly rely on samples of predominantly white college students (with some valuable exceptions), the present study could aid in providing a more diverse understanding of participants' viewpoints.[5]

Self-Presentation

Goffman characterizes self-presentation (also known as impression management) behavior using a dramaturgical analogy where people act out roles and present a managed "face" to others in their various social settings.[6] Building on Goffman's paradigm, later researchers conceptualized self-presentation as a two-step process that consists of impression motivation and impression construction.[7]

The first step, motivations for managing other's impressions, includes identity development, self-enhancement, influencing others, and obtaining credit and avoiding blame for actions.[8] Secondly, impression management entails specific strategies, which have been characterized as focused on the self (agency or proself orientation) or cooperation with others (communion or prosocial orientation).[9]

Maintaining authenticity appears to be key to effective impression management. When designing their self-presentation, people can feel pressured to present a self that is consistent with existing reputations or likely future actions.[10] A greater preoccupation with one's social image fosters an emphasis on consistency rather than on a positive image.[11] As social rewards are obtained through pleasing the audience, people are more likely to use positive presentations when interacting with strangers, while self-presentation with friends tends to be more modest and vulnerable.[12]

Self-Presentation in CMC

Research in the area of (CMC) focuses on how people engage in self-presentation through mediated channels such as chat, email, and social media. This research has focused on two core issues: cues available for transmitting extra-verbal information, and the control that users have through self-editing and other technological affordances.[13] Since traditional cues such as nonverbal communication are absent from CMC, message recipients will attend to other cues instead, such as the number of friends a person has and how those friends look and behave.[14] Additionally, research has found that the self-presentation of information relevant to social attractiveness will be more effective when the message is less susceptible to manipulation.[15] For example, statements about a person made by credible others and the use of photos may carry more warrant.[16]

Research specifically oriented toward SNS self-presentation has assessed various aspects of impression management. For starters, demographics and individual differences play a role. Both female and younger users changed their profile pictures more frequently, while younger users and those motivated to use a SNS for friends or networking (as opposed to romantic relationships) disclosed more information.[17] Personality traits such as narcissism and self-efficacy predicted sharing more information.[18]

The distinction between disclosure and privacy control is important when it comes to self-presentation. SNS users are motivated to control information about themselves in order to project a "socially desirable self."[19] Christofides et al. came to the conclusion that disclosure and privacy control are not "two ends of the same spectrum," but are instead independent.[20] Interestingly, although Gross and Acquisti found users unlikely to utilize available privacy options despite a desire for privacy, more recent studies showed that SNS users who desired privacy still disclosed information rather than withholding it, preferring to use privacy settings to restrict access.[21]

Information control in social media is important when the self-presentation involves communicating to multiple audiences in the "context collapse" of a single space such as Facebook.[22] When engaging distinct audiences, such as friends, family, and coworkers, with possibly discrepant expectations and norms, in a single social setting, users may target specific segments of the audience, and conceal and misinform when needed.[23] However, privacy boundaries are often unclear, leading to frustration when private information becomes public or discrete audiences are collapsed into one.[24]

In addition to hiding and editing information, SNS users also face the challenge of selecting the best information about themselves and putting that positive face forward to others. However, evidence is accumulating that online self-presentation requires a healthy dose of authenticity, or at least a balance of self-promotion and accuracy, and that Facebook profiles better match the users' actual personalities than their idealized selves.[25]

If Facebook users must balance disclosure, control, positivity, and authenticity, how effective are they at these self-presentation acrobatics? Impression management in unmediated settings generally involves discrete social spaces, allowing for what Goffman characterizes as frontstage settings, where we actively self-present by playing a role, and backstage settings, where, alone or in the company of intimidates, we "turn off" the performance.[26] In largely open SNS, the private becomes public, and social settings may blur as users communicate openly with heterogeneous groups, making impression management even more challenging.[27] Additionally, the finding that MySpace wall comments primarily consisted of quick exchanges used to either establish or maintain contact suggests that the challenge of effective self-presentation may be such that active or elaborate impression management is the exception to the rule of superficial and easy social grooming.[28]

Current Study

While self-presentation has been an essential part of theorizing about CMC, at least as far back as the hyperpersonal model and empirical evidence continues to accumulate, the fact remains that SNS are new and evolving social settings, which may have implications for self-presentation practices.[29] Hence, the conceptual frameworks presented thus far may not fully describe and explain behaviors in these altered settings. For example, although much of the initial SNS impression management research has focused on profile features and simple indicators, like photos, interpersonal interaction is increasingly becoming the core of SNS like Facebook and Twitter, and as such, requires study.

Additionally, some research is beginning to ask how effective individuals are at managing impressions on SNS and what divergence may exist between goals, norms, and actual behavior.[30] There is also the question of how proficient users are at managing their privacy.[31] Utilizing two data sets, one of Facebook user self-reports, and the other of actual behavior on the site, allows us to assess possible discrepancies between reported activities and actual behavior.

To explore these issues, and to approach the subject as broadly and inductively as possible, we used a grounded theory approach to qualitatively analyze data. Grounded theory appeared to be the most relevant method for our study, as although there is a considerable body of research on social networking and self-presentation, a clear conceptual framework is still a work in progress. Moreover, the reiterative categorization process of the constant-comparative technique allowed us to inductively capture diverse expressions and ideas in our data that could help us further clarify self-presentation in SNS. Subsequently, we pose the following research questions:

RQ1:   What do Facebook users say about their self-presentation motivations and activities?

RQ2:   What self-presentation activities are evident from the status updates and comments of Facebook users and their friends?

RQ3:   In what ways do reported self-presentation activities correspond with the activities observed in status updates and comments?

RQ4:   In what ways do reported self-presentation activities differ from the activities observed in status updates and comments?

Method

As the goal of our study was to compare how respondents discussed self-presentation with the actual self-presentation behavior observed on Facebook, our methods entailed both content analysis and focus groups.

Data Collection

The starting point for our study was a series of focus group interviews on Facebook usage.[32] This technique is especially suitable for studying behavior that takes place in a group, such as interacting with Facebook friends, and allows for a deeper understanding of what respondents' answers mean.[33]

We carried out three focus group interviews (each approximately ninety minutes; three to six participants each) with eighteen to twenty-five year-old Facebook users who were all African American college students. The focus groups were carried out with students at a medium-sized, public, historically black university in the southeastern United States. The participants were recruited through flyers posted on campus. As theoretical saturation was apparent upon conclusion of the third session, i.e., we did not uncover any new statements and conceptual categories, three focus groups were deemed to be a sufficient dataset.

Before the start of the focus group, all respondents were asked to print out their newsfeed and wall for their own reference. The focus group discussion was guided by a topic list, which covered many aspects of Facebook usage, from selecting friends to posting updates to the use of private messages.

To further explore Facebook users' behaviors, and to provide a point of comparison, we also carried out a content analysis of Facebook newsfeeds and walls, which utilized a convenience sample of seventeen college students, aged eighteen to twenty-five. This specific group was selected because they comprise Facebook's original target audience and make up the bulk of the network's users.[34] The participants came from a medium-sized, public, historically black university and a medium-sized, public, community college in the southeastern United States. As students were asked to participate in both the focus groups and the content analysis, there was some overlap between the respondents in both studies. As with the focus groups, theoretical saturation was apparent during the initial phase of analysis, suggesting a satisfactory sample for grounded theory analysis.[35]

After logging into their accounts, the participants were asked to display all comments and include posts hidden under "older posts," print out their wall, newsfeed, and personal profile, and render all identifying information invisible using a marker. There was some variation in the amount of time covered by each individual's timeline, ranging from a few days to a few months. The number of status updates and wall posts collected per user varied from 38 to 278, with an average of 67 posts. In total, we collected 676 newsfeed posts, 465 wall posts, and 660 comments.

Analysis

Both the data collected from the content analysis and the focus groups were analyzed using grounded theory's constant comparative technique.[36] After close readings of both the transcript data collected from the focus groups as well as the walls and newsfeeds, we constructed categories to reflect the types of self-presentation activities that were described by participants or could be observed in the newsfeeds. A reiterative process was used to compare, incorporate, and revise the different categories. As material was grouped into categories, two authors assessed each category to see if adjustments or revisions were needed. They compared their findings and synthesized any changes in the categorization until reaching consensus on the final categorization.

Regarding the content analysis, as we focused solely on self-presentation through interpersonal interaction, we did not analyze profile pages, application results, or other Facebook components, as they are outside the scope of this study, though they certainly play a role in impression management.

Results

Focus Groups: Reported Self-Presentation

Analysis of focus group transcripts identified three categories for the roles that the Facebook user can adopt: poster, reader, and reactant. After this first categorization, each fragment was analyzed for reference to any aspect of self-presentation. Fragments that appeared to refer to similar aspects were grouped together and used to identify specific behavioral strategies. These strategies were then categorized into groups of strategies that served specific goals, thus answering the first research question regarding self-reported self-presentation motivations and activities on Facebook. We identified five goals, of which the first three were considered major: more prevalent and mentioned from the perspective of poster, reader, and reactant. Conversely, the last two goals were considered minor, since, while significant, they were only discussed from two of three perspectives.

Major Goal 1: Creating an Authentic Self-Presentation

The majority of the participants in this study viewed constructing an authentic image as a vital aspect of self-presentation on Facebook. As one respondent put it, "nobody wants to misrepresent themselves." The participants also invoked authenticity when judging others' self-presentation tactics and cultivated images. They felt that inauthentic presentations hurt credibility, especially if the presenter was well-known in other settings, and the image they created on Facebook did not correspond to how the respondents knew them in real life.

> D: I have a person who I know was just a geek in high school, and the next thing they're doing, they're on their Facebook with guns or rags or something.
> E: I've seen that, too. It's really. . . I laugh at it.
> D: I laugh too. You in high school, you ain't in no gang.

Reported strategies for ensuring an authentic self-presentation included making sure that one's profile content was an accurate and current reflection of their interests, using an honest profile photo, sharing candid photos, and writing status updates that are up-to-date, insightful, and reflect who the respondents feel they really are. An interesting observation was that not all the respondents agreed on how vulnerable or frank one should be in their status updates or pictures. One respondent, while disapproving of friends who had posted pictures of themselves drinking and partying, did note that "I think they're just being themselves." Another respondent clearly indicated that he would not put bad feelings on Facebook too often, for a fear of being perceived as a "sad guy," while other respondents claimed to be very honest in their status updates. There was general consensus, however, that exaggerated or contrived attempts at impression management were undesirable in others. Respondents reported critiquing friends for unrealistic or inappropriate status updates. Finally, when discussing self-presentation as reactants, the respondents also mentioned that Facebook users should ensure that all their comments are meaningful. This dislike for meaningless comments included the "like" button, but extended to simple or mundane comments like "hi."

Major Goal 2: Creating a Professional, Positive, and Current Self-Presentation

While impression management needs grounding in reality, the focus group participants also stressed the need for creating an image that emphasizes admirable aspects of the self, by being positive, current, and professional. According to the respondents, timeliness can be achieved through strategies like posting daily, ensuring that photos and profile information are up-to-date, and responding to comments and wall posts. The focus group participants disliked friends who were overly negative in the way they expressed themselves, and who were reckless or offensive in their posts and content.

> B: I have this one friend from high school and every time she is on status she is talking about somebody or "I am hating her"—she is always up in negative. . . . So it goes through my head like "why are you bringing up like this negative. . ." basically like negatively presenting yourself, being a negative person.

Content that was considered mundane, vague, or meaningless was also reported to be annoying, and harmful to anyone's self-presentation.

> K: I have a lot of friends who write a lot of craziness. . . . I guess they be bored. . . and they write stupid questions. . . . I guess some people just like to write for attention or whatever.

There was an awareness that profiles are public and that audiences like families and future employers were watching on Facebook, requiring that self-presentation be appropriate for diverse audiences. One respondent captured this sentiment well when he said:

> D: The thing that keeps me from, like, putting all my pictures and stuff on Facebook would be a level of professionalism. And I care about my parents seeing some of them, and I care about employers seeing some of the pictures I've got.

Finally, participants mentioned that they also monitored their own walls for inappropriate content from friends, which leads us to the third goal, controlling information.

Major Goal 3: Controlling Information

The two goals discussed previously seemingly include controlling information as one of their strategies; monitoring and deleting wall posts is, for instance, a strategy for controlling information. The goal that will be discussed in this section, however, refers specifically to a need to control who can access one's information.

The Facebook users in our focus groups spoke about privacy needs extensively. One participant mentioned that she went so far as to use multiple profiles, one for college friends, and one for family. Other participants spoke about using strategies like censoring what they say in status updates or what they put on their profiles, and making use of Facebook's privacy settings.

> B: I try to keep it pretty straight to the point, because I do know there are some people that I have as friends that I don't know but just go to my school, though, so I just accepted them. I don't want them to know too much of that.

Most of the respondents indicated that they were apprehensive about sharing phone numbers and romantic relationship information online, while some individuals expressed a tendency to "lay low" and avoid drawing attention to themselves, as a way of preserving their privacy and control. Additional control strategies were to monitor one's wall for offensive or revealing wall posts, deleting them if necessary. Furthermore, all respondents kept track of when they were "tagged" in photos, to ensure they would not be linked to unflattering images of themselves.

Minor Goal 1: Receiving Recognition

Feeling appreciated and receiving recognition was a goal that was raised both from the perspective of the poster, as well as from the perspective of the reader. One respondent even indicated that this is his main activity when on Facebook:

> G: I just go on and see just really who thought about me.

Participants tried to solicit recognition from others by writing status updates to garner attention, which they indicated were usually funny or controversial statements (e.g., "This itchin' ain't stopping"). In their discussion about comments, the respondents made it clear that they valued, and often expected, feedback and attention from others. Moreover, respondents indicated that they would often write updates asking for advice or support from their friends. Feedback also had to be significant; participants preferred detailed or meaningful comments on their posts, as opposed to use of the "like" button or other low-information responses.

Minor Goal 2: Presenting Oneself as Socially Literate

The desire to come across as someone who adheres to existing social norms is a goal that was mentioned both from the perspective of the poster, as well as from the perspective of the reactant. Our Facebook users wanted to come across as polite, courteous, and social. They felt pressure to wish other people "happy birthday" on their walls, and to reciprocate with gratitude when others wished them a happy birthday, or requested support or feedback. They reported expectations for complimenting friends' new profile pictures, trying to say hi to someone they hadn't talked to in a while, and avoiding embarrassing or hurtful wall posts.

Content Analysis: Observed Self-Presentation

The second research question concerned the self-presentation activities that could be observed from Facebook users' status updates and comments and was answered using content analysis of the participants' feeds. After analyzing the content of the Facebook walls and newsfeeds for the different types of behaviors people exhibit online when interacting with others, we categorized the different expressions (e.g., updates, comments, and likes) into groups of similar behaviors, or practices. Since some of the practices identified in the posts and comments shared common purposes, we grouped related practices into three orientations: relationship-oriented, self-oriented, and maintaining proper communication.

Orientation 1: Relationship-Oriented

The three groups of behaviors, or practices, which were grouped into this category, are all focused on interacting, helping, reciprocating, and collaborating with other Facebook users. The first practice, "maintaining relationships," was carried out through various expressions, such as paying one's friends compliments and encouraging them, as exemplified by this wall post:

I think ur phone pics is cute, despite watcha say! Keep smiling!

Other expressions were asking concrete questions about specific situations in someone's life, "affirming a relationship," and "touching base." Affirming a relationship referred to posts and updates that indicated affection for a specific person ("miss ya, love ya"), while touching base referred to wall posts which contained little more than a short note to friend's ("Hey [friend's name], how's life?") to see how they were doing. Comments on posts were also used to maintain relationships, often offering support in response to a statement, or occasionally expressing affection for the original poster.

The second practice could be best described as "consulting and collaborating," that is, asking or giving specific advice. Expressions that were categorized with this practice were "prompting opinions," e.g., "It's Earth Day! What did you do?," posting advice, and asking for help, advice, and opinions. Comments in response to these types of posts would often share opinions or similar experiences.

The third and final practice that shared the social orientation was about setting social boundaries: establishing who one's friends are, what types of behavior are acceptable or not, and ascertaining whether one's friends still like you. One form of expression that fit into this specific class of behavior was writing posts that expressed judgment of certain type of behavior (both on- and offline), such as:

> My neighbor definitely woke up me up this morning and seeing as im possibly sick . . . that's not a nice move

Two final types of expressions are expressing solidarity with people's actions and reducing uncertainty about their friends' opinion of them and their relationship. The latter entailed posting detailed questions on friends' walls to find out what they were doing or how they had handled a specific situation.

Orientation 2: Self-Oriented

Practices that were grouped into this category focused on projecting a certain image to one's Facebook friends: what the posters are doing, who they are, or who they want their friends to think they are. This distinction, between how one wants to be seen and who one really is, is fundamental to impression management on SNS. Although this study did not allow for the assessment of "actual" selves and how they related to the images projected to friends, the analysis did reveal a distinction between posts that appeared to show the poster in a more vulnerable, at times, negative, manner, and posts that appeared more positive, superficial, and even boastful.[37] This distinction was captured by the practices in this orientation.

The first practice grouped under self-orientation was "looking the part," and includes expressions that allow posters to present themselves in the most current, positive, and interesting manner possible. Expressions included stating one's opinion about an issue, or a person, or an event, sharing anecdotes and interesting facts, expressing a positive mood or gratitude ("is sooo blessed to have a wonderful love like [boyfriend's name]! I love him soooo much"), and expressing goals in life. Moreover, Facebook users in this sample posted pictures, shared links, and boasted about accomplishments:

Awesome . . . we won conference in track

The two additional expressions, "describing values" and "sharing quotations or aphorisms," were focused on sharing philosophical thoughts about one's life, excerpts from texts important to the poster, or personal truths, such as:

Is turning obstacles into opportunities

Although, at first glance, these posts come across as candid, they all mainly consisted of well-known platitudes and were always upbeat. Finally, posters also used self-deprecation, where the posts would appear to be honest and in line with the next practice, "staying true," but would then often negate or ridicule whatever honesty the poster had just shown.

The second practice, which, in our set of newsfeeds and walls, appeared to be far less popular than the first, focused on staying true to one's self. The expressions that were used in conjunction with this practice were marked by a certain vulnerability; the posters did not hesitate to be honest, negative, or mundane, and post in a manner that could possibly be condemned as not socially acceptable. Specific expressions included expressing negative emotions:

Is feeling so tired and kind of stressed about the situation she's in . . . feels like her once beautiful happy world is slowly falling apart . . . sigh. . .

Additionally, this practice included expressing a need for something or someone, examining one's actions, and educating one's self (i.e., asking how someone did something so the poster could learn to do it too). An interesting final expression, "reflection," could be argued to be the counterpart to the describing values expression identified in the previous practice. While when describing values, posters remain superficial and upbeat, posts that were coded as reflection were more personal and, at times, negative. These posts focused on the poster's emotional life, their thoughts and feelings, and appeared to be largely uncensored:

Is still trying in some challenges, but others are just down for the count.

A third practice that was linked to the creation of a personal image was the expression of consumer affiliations. This practice entails presenting oneself as a consumer or fan of certain choice products, events, and groups. The analysis revealed two main expressions, namely marketing (inviting people to, asking for support of, or indicating participation in) an event, and expressing a preference for a specific product ("will be updating my iphone on June 17. U should do the same!"). This practice was also carried out through the sharing of links, video, and other media intended to reflect the poster's taste and cultural values.

The final practice in this category is to keep one's friends updated about one's activities, to make sure that the impression people have is current. The expressions that respondents utilized in the content analysis were notifying their friends of their current activity and expressing anticipation about future events:

Is up feeding my son . . .watching his father talk in his sleep . . . watching saved by the bell . . .

Orientation 3: Maintaining Proper Communication

This orientation refers to acting in a socially literate manner, making sure everyone understands what one is trying to say, and observing proper online etiquette. Maintaining proper communication is characterized by two practices: adhering to socially acceptable forms of communication, and coordinating relational communication.

The first practice includes expressions that reflected an understanding of basic social norms. The expressions that we observed included, for instance, wishing people a happy birthday, and thanking people when appropriate through posts or comments. Some comment-specific social conventions included showing appreciation of humorous or insightful posts, joking with the original poster, or poking fun at their status update.

Second, Facebook users in this study wanted to facilitate online communication as much as possible. The expressions they employed to achieve this were, among other things, to point out proper etiquette if someone threatened to deviate from it:

> People please quit writing/copying and pasting these insane comments and messages in my honesty box ...

Other expressions used were requests for details or clarification if a post was unclear, as well as meta-discussions about Facebook and other online communication. Many comments that appeared on posts requested either details or asked for clarification about a statement made in a status update. Coordination across other channels like SMS text and FtF interaction was also apparent in the content analysis:

> My phone is completely dead, so if you want to get in contact with me, hit me up on Facebook

Comparing Results: Convergence

To answer the third research question, in what ways reported self-presentation activities corresponded to the activities observed on Facebook, we compared the findings from the focus groups with the findings from the content analysis. This juxtaposition revealed several similarities.

First of all, consistent with existing literature into the nature of online presentations, presenting a positive, current, and professional self is clearly evident on Facebook pages, as indicated by the "looking the part" practice.[38] For example, the focus group finding that respondents liked to use Facebook for professional activities like promoting on-campus organizations was corroborated by the content analysis.

Although authenticity, and the challenges associated with it will be addressed next, one common "authenticity" theme was the need for meaningfulness in people's updates and comments, as identified in the focus groups. Although both posts and comments exhibited great variety in their tone and content, "meaningful" posts and comments were evident, and many comments asked for clarification or details, requesting more "meaning" from the original post.

Third, the desire to keep people abreast of one's life became apparent through the focus groups, where the second major goal focused in part on creating a current self-presentation, and was also reflected in the content analysis, where many of the posts centered on updating one's friends and pictures. Interestingly, although not tested in this chapter, previous research found that this tendency was related to a user's level of narcissism.[39]

Controlling information, an important aspect of self-presentation on SNS, was the third major goal of self-presentation described by the focus groups.[40] In the content analysis it was, of course, impossible to see what information people did not share, or remove. We were, however, able to ascertain that a number of posts requested friends to message their number (as opposed to asking for their number to be posted on Facebook), showing the same need for privacy as expressed in the focus groups.

Furthermore, the communion approach to self-presentation was reflected in both the focus groups as well as the content analysis.[41] The "consulting and collaborating" practice uncovered through the content analysis reflected the claim made during the focus groups that asking for advice or support is a considerable part of one's activities on Facebook. The respondents in the focus groups also claimed to write funny or controversial updates to garner attention, which was confirmed by the content analysis, where many of the updates were classified as humorous. It could also be argued that "touching base" (i.e., leaving short comments on people's walls) is yet another way to receive (and give) attention.

Finally, the desire to present oneself as socially literate was echoed by the findings from the content analysis, which identified numerous birthday wishes, thank-yous, and wishing people a good day (see "adhering to socially acceptable forms of communication"), and can be tied to previous research showing people's desire to receive social approval.[42]

Comparing Results: Divergence

To answer the fourth research question, which asked in what ways reported self-presentation activities differed from the activities observed on Facebook, we also compared the focus group findings with the findings from the content analysis. We uncovered the following differences.

The first issue raised by the juxtaposition between the two sets of results is the need to be authentic. The difficulty underlying this need has been captured in previous research, which found that self-presenters are expected to self-promote, be modest and accurate, all while striking a coherent, consistent persona.[43] The focus groups results first hinted at a discrepancy within this need, when respondents discussed the first major goal, the need to be "authentic" and disagreed on how honest one should be in one's updates. This discrepancy is further underlined with the second major goal that emerged from the focus groups, which included the need to remain professional and positive, even if it meant being less than authentic. The results from the content analysis point to this tension as well. We found various posts that could be described as authentic, but in distinctly different ways. Some posts (the ones that fell under "looking the part") seemed to be an attempt to selectively present interesting and positive aspects of one's self, while others (which belonged to the practice known as "staying true"), made the poster appear vulnerable, mundane, or even negative. So although "being yourself" is seen as an important aspect of self-presentation on Facebook, this dichotomy between being interesting and positive, versus negative and vulnerable, raises the question of what the respondents meant when they talked about the need to be authentic. Does being authentic mean showing all aspects of oneself, as implied by the first goal identified in the focus groups? Or did the focus group respondents interpret authenticity as a strategy to appear honest, but control enough information to retain a positive image, as captured by the second and third goals from the focus groups? Obviously, a content analysis cannot indicate the relative authenticity of given expressions, but the focus group results point to the challenges and complexities associated with conveying authenticity.

The need for authenticity in self-presentation also includes the notion of meaningfulness. During the focus groups, one of the themes that emerged was the need for meaningful comments and updates, i.e., more than a just a "hi." Yet, in line with previous research, the content analysis revealed that "touching base," or quick and simple forms of social maintenance are a prominent practice on Facebook.[44] So although respondents claim to prefer meaningful content, the need to make sure that one's friends know one is thinking of them appears more important. This is further underlined by the discovery in the content analysis that the much disliked "like" button, as well as other comments low in information (such as "lol"), were in fact used quite often.

On a similar note, during the focus groups, the respondents also expressed a dislike for posts that were negative or contained what they perceived to be inappropriate presentations, and instead stressed the need for maintaining a positive image. In spite of this attitude, the content analysis revealed a number of negative posts (such as those categorized under "staying true"), as well as provocative posts, indicating that, in spite of what the respondents told us about norms regarding professionalism and appropriateness, they did push the envelope at times, perhaps because, as noted in previous studies they were focused on conveying their "true selves" in the context of being with friends.[45]

When discussing the desire to keep people abreast of one's life, the focus group respondents also mentioned how a continuous stream of updates, especially if they were dull or meaningless, from a friend could become annoying. This would suggest that the most updates found in the content analysis would be vivid and entertaining. Conversely, the vast majority of the notification updates were very mundane, which is in keeping with previous content analyses of SNS posts, and with findings that modesty is common in self-presentation to friends.[46]

Another theme that became apparent from the comparison of the two sets of results is the desire for interaction. During the focus groups, the respondents indicated that responding to people's wall posts and comments was an important aspect of maintaining a current self-presentation. In spite of this, however, a lot of updates and comments never received any feedback, and many wall posts went unanswered. Interaction and feedback are essential elements of CMC, but remain understudied.[47] The discrepancy between self-reports and actual feedback behavior found in this study underlines the importance of investigating this specific aspect of CMC.

Controlling information was the third major goal of self-presentation according to the focus groups. The content analysis revealed that several people did share their phone number on people's walls, and had no problems sharing their relationship status or new developments in their relationships; in other words, disclosure seemed valued.[48]

Conclusion

A qualitative, exploratory analysis of both Facebook newsfeeds and walls, and the statements from the focus group participants regarding self-presentation, provided answers to our four research questions, and revealed a complex and nuanced negotiation of the impression management process. This study showed that although there were some similarities between self-presentation as discussed in the focus groups and observed through content analysis, there was sufficient divergence to point to a need for further research.

It is important to note that this qualitative and exploratory investigation of a small sample of Facebook users may not necessarily allow for generalizations, and the discrepancies between what people say they do and actually do on Facebook could possibly have some origin in the limitations of self-report and content analysis. Despite this, our results do align with existing CMC self-presentation findings, and suggest the following areas in need of further scrutiny.

First of all, the nature of "authenticity." Although Facebook users claim that authenticity is an important aspect of self-presentation, both the focus groups and content analysis reveal that authenticity is not a straightforward concept, an idea further underlined by previous research into this aspect of self-presentation.[49] As evidenced by the focus group discussions, and by the distinction between the practices "looking the part" and "staying true," authenticity can be positive and upbeat or vulnerable and negative. The finding that authenticity is a multifaceted concept implies that, when deciding on their performance, SNS users face two choices. Not only do they have to decide whether they will enhance their presentation (act positive and upbeat), or show vulnerability, but they also need to choose between an unfiltered authentic presentation, or one that is more selective and contrived. We speculate that self-enhancement and vulnerability are two ends of the same dimension; that is self-presentation strategies and goals will vary on a spectrum ranging from positive and bolstering to negative and humble. The second dimension of performance is made up by the extent to which the users desire to be authentic, which can vary from unfiltered presentations of one's actual persona to highly managed presentations, whether contrived or selective. As these two dimensions intersect, presentations can consist of any combination of authenticity, selectivity, vulnerability, and enhancement. Our findings show a tension within and between these different dimensions of self-presentation, and it seems that Facebook users work to balance these demands, which are further complicated by the context collapse, which forces people to please different audiences in the same space.[50]

Second, our study demonstrates the value of investigating the wide range of interactions used in SNS impression management. Not only do these behaviors play an important role in the self-presentation as a whole, they also point to the tensions and challenges that users face. For example, respondents in the focus groups mentioned the importance of meaningfulness in self-presentation, while at the same time, the content analysis revealed that a lot of the posts were simple "hi's" or "lol's" and did not contain the depth that the respondents seemed to expect. However, it could be argued that these posts and comments are not as meaningless as the focus group participants might think, but instead are an example of communion-based strategies used to enhance social relationships and maintain audiences.[51]

The dynamics between authenticity, selectivity, vulnerability, and enhancement, as well as the networks' rich conversations and interactions deserve further examination, as evidenced by recent research that has begun to examine the role of linguistic devices in both impression management and impression formation online.[52] In addition, research on SNS self-presentation will benefit from further emphasis on the many communicative strategies employed by users, with the all the complexity and nuance that entails. Finally, in an area that has largely been experiment and survey oriented, future research should attempt to utilize qualitative analysis to better understand self-presentation practices.

In conclusion, our findings suggest that interaction is an important part of self-presentation, and just as vital as the construction of one's image, which appears to be a balancing act between enhancement and vulnerability, and between authenticity and selectivity, all of which is complicated by audience heterogeneity. Moreover, strategic self-presentation is an ongoing, dynamic process that requires the negotiation of multiple goals that often fall in conflict with each other, placing demands on the SNS user.

Notes

1. Facebook, "Key Facts," accessed May 4, 2012, http://newsroom.fb com/content/default.aspx?NewsAreaId=22.

2. Kaiser Family Foundation, "Daily Media Use among Children and Teens Up Dramatically from Five Years Ago," last modified January 20, 2010, accessed May 14, 2012, http://www.kff.org/entmedia/entmedia012010nr.cfm;

Nielsen Wire, "Social Media Report: Spending Time, Money, and Going Mobile," last modified September 11, 2011, accessed May 14, 2012, http://blog. nielsen.com/nielsenwire/online_mobile/social-media-report-spending-time-money-and-going-mobile/.

3. Joan Morris DiMicco and David R. Millen, "Identity Management: Multiple Presentations of Self in Facebook," in *Proceedings of the ACM Conference on Supporting Group Work* (New York: ACM, 2007), 383–86; Elza Dunkels, Gun-Marie Frånberg, and Camilla Hällgren, *Youth Culture and Net Culture: Online Social Practices* (Hershey, PA: Information Science Reference, 2011); Shangyang Zhao, Sherri Grasmuck, and Jason Martin, "Identity Construction on Facebook: Digital Empowerment in Anchored Relationships," *Computers in Human Behavior* 24, no. 5 (March 2008): 1816–36.

4. Keith Hampton, Lauren Sessions Goulet, Lee Rainie, and Kristen Purcell, "Social Networking Sites and Our Lives," Pew Internet & American Life Project, last modified June 16, 2011, accessed June 6, 2012, http://www .pewinternet.org/Reports/2011/Technology-and-social-networks.aspx; Aaron Smith and Joanna Brenner, "Twitter use 2012," Pew Internet & American Life Project, accessed June 6, 2012, http://pewinternet.org/Reports/2012/Twitter-Use-2012.aspx.

5. Sheana S. Bull, Lindsey T. Breslin, Erin E. Wright, Sandra R. Black, Deborah Levine, and John S. Santelli, "Case Study: An Ethics Case Study of HIV Prevention Research on Facebook: The Just/Us Study," *Journal of Pediatric Psychology* 36, no. 10 (November/December 2011): 1082–92; Dara N. Byrne, "Public Discourse, Community Concerns, and Civic Engagement: Exploring Black Social Networking Traditions on BlackPlanet.com," *Journal of Computer-Mediated Communication* 13, no. 1 (October 2007): 319–40; Sherri Grasmuck, Jason Martin, and Shanyang Zhao, "Ethno-Racial Identity Displays on Facebook," *Journal of Computer-Mediated Communication* 15, no. 1 (October 2009): 158–88.

6. Erving Goffman, *The Presentation of Self in Everyday Life* (Garden City, NY: Doubleday, 1959).

7. Mark R. Leary and Robin M. Kowalski, "Impression Management: A Literature Review and Two-Component Model," *Psychological Bulletin* 107, no. 1 (January 1990): 34–47.

8. Leary and Kowalski, "Impression Management"; James T. Tedeschi and Marc Riess, "Identities, the Phenomenal Self, and Laboratory Research," in *Impression Management Theory and Social Psychological Research,* ed. James T. Tedeschi (New York: Academic Press, 1981), 3–22; Roy F. Baumeister, "A Self-Presentational View of Social Phenomena," *Psychological Bulletin* 91, no. 1 (January 1982): 3–26.

9. Delroy L. Paulhus and Paul D. Trapnell, "Self-Presentation of Personality: An Agency-Communion Framework," in *Handbook of Personality,* ed. Oliver P. John, Richard W. Robins, and Lawrence A. Pervin (New York: The Guil-

ford Press, 2008), 492–517; Jurjen Iedema and Matthijs Poppe, "The Effect of Self-Presentation on Social Value Orientation," *The Journal of Social Psychology* 134, no. 6 (1994): 771–82.

10. Baumeister, "A Self-Presentational View"; Roy F. Baumeister, "Self-Esteem, Self-Presentation, and Future Interaction: A Dilemma of Reputation," *Journal of Personality* 50, no. 1 (March 1982): 29–45.

11. Kevin Doherty and Barry R. Schlenker, "Self-Consciousness and Strategic Self-Presentation," *Journal of Personality* 59, no. 1 (March 1991): 1–18.

12. Baumeister, "A Self-Presentational View"; Dianne M. Tice, Jennifer L. Butler, Mark B. Muraven, and Arlene M. Stillwell, "When Modesty Prevails: Differential Favorability of Self-Presentation to Friends and Strangers," *Journal of Personality and Social Psychology* 69, no. 6 (December 1995): 1120–38.

13. Joseph B. Walther, "Selective Self-Presentation in Computer-Mediated Communication: Hyperpersonal Dimensions of Technology, Language, and Cognition," *Computers in Human Behavior* 23, no. 5 (September 2007): 2538–57.

14. Nicole B. Ellison, Rebecca Heino, and Jennifer Gibbs, "Managing Impressions Online: Self-Presentation Processes in the Online Dating Environment," *Journal of Computer-Mediated Communication* 11, no. 2 (January 2006): 415–41; Cliff Lampe, Nicole B. Ellison, and Charles Steinfield,"A Familiar Face(book): Profile Elements as Signals in an Online Social Network," in *Proceedings of the 2007 ACM Conference on Human Factors in Computing* (New York: ACM, 2007) 435–44; Joseph B. Walther, Brandon Van Der Heide, Sang-Yeon Kim, David Westerman, and Stephanie Tom Tong, "The Role of Friends' Appearance and Behavior on Evaluations of Individuals on Facebook: Are We Known by the Company We Keep?" *Human Communication Research* 34, no. 1 (January 2008): 28–49.

15. Sonja Utz, "Show Me Your Friends and I Will Tell You What Type of Person You Are: How One's Profile, Number of Friends, and Type of Friends Influence Impression Formation on Social Network Sites," *Journal of Computer-Mediated Communication* 15, no. 2 (January 2010): 314–35.

16. Joseph B. Walther, Brandon Van Der Heide, Lauren M. Hamel, and Hilary C. Shulman, "Self-Generated Versus Other-Generated Statements and Impressions in Computer-Mediated Communication: A Test of Warranting Theory Using Facebook," *Communication Research* 36, no. 2 (April 2009): 229–53; Brandon Van Der Heide, Jonathan D. D'Angelo, and Erin M. Schumaker, "The Effects of Verbal vs. Photographic Self-Presentation on Impression Formation in Facebook," *Journal of Communication* 62, no. 1 (February 2012): 98–116.

17. Michele M. Strano, "User Descriptions and Interpretations of Self-Presentation through Facebook Profile Images," *Cyberpsychology: Journal of Psychosocial Research on Cyberspace* 2, no. 2 (2008): article 1, http://cyberpsychology.eu/view.php?cisloclanku=2008110402&article=1; Strano, "User Descriptions"; Kris Boyle and Thomas J. Johnson, "MySpace Is Your

Space? Examining Self-Presentation of MySpace Users," *Computers in Human Behavior* 26, no. 6 (November 2010): 1392–99; Boyle and Johnson, "MySpace Is Your Space."

18. Emily Christofides, Amy Muise, and Serge Desmarais, "Information Disclosure and Control on Facebook: Are They Two Sides of the Same Coin or Two Diffeent Processes?"*Cyberpsychologyand Behavior* 12, no. 3 (2009): 341–45; Nicole C. Krämer and Stephan Winter, "Impression Management 2.0: The Relationships of Self-Esteem, Extraversion, Self-Efficacy, and Self-Presentation within Social Networking Sites," *Journal of Media Psychology* 20, no. 3 (2008): 106–16; Soraya Mehdizadeh, "Self-Presentation 2.0: Narcissism and Self-Esteem on Facebook," *Cyberpsychology, Behavior, and Social Networking* 13, no. 4 (August 2010): 357–64; Eileen Y. L. Ong, Rebecca P. Ang, Jim C. M. Ho, Joylynn C. Y. Lim, Dion H. Goh, Chei Sian Lee, and Alton Y. K. Chua, "Narcissism, Extraversion, and Adolescents' Self-Presentation on Facebook," *Personality and Individual Differences* 50, no. 2 (January 2011): 180–85; Sonja Utz and Nicole Krämer, "The Privacy Paradox on Social Network Sites Revisited: The Role of Individual Characteristics and Group Norms," *Cyberpsychology: Journal of Psychosocial Research on Cyberspace* 3, no. 2 (2009): article 1, http://www.cyberpsychology.eu/view.php?cisloclanku=2009111001.

19. Shangyang Zhao, Sherri Grasmuck, and Jason Martin, "Identity Construction on Facebook: Digital Empowerment in Anchored Relationships," in *Computers in Human Behavior* 24, no. 5 (March 2008): 1816–36.

20. Christofides, Muise, and Desmarais, "Information Disclosure"; Zeynep Tufekci, "Can You See Me Now? Audience and Disclosure Management in Online Social Network Sites," *Bulletin of Science, Technology, and Society* 28, no. 1 (February 2008): 20–36.

21. Susan B. Barnes, "A Privacy Paradox: Social Networking in the United States," *First Monday* 11, no. 9 (September 4, 2006): article 5, http://firstmonday.org/htbin/cgiwrap/bin/ojs/index.php/fm/article/view/1394/1312; Ralph Gross and Alessandro Acquisti, "Information Revelation and Privacy in Online Social Networks," in *Proceedings of the 2005 ACM Workshop on Privacy in the Electronic Society* (New York: ACM, 2005), 71–80.

22. Alice E. Marwick and danah boyd, "I Tweet Honestly, I Tweet Passionately: Twitter Users, Context Collapse, and the Imagined Audience," *New Media and Society* 13, no. 1 (February 2011):114–33.

23. Marwick and boyd, "I Tweet Honestly."

24. Barnes, "A Privacy Paradox"; Gross and Acquisti, "Information Revelation."

25. Ellison, Heino, and Gibbs, "Managing Impressions Online"; Mitja D. Back, Juliane M. Stopfer, Simine Vazire, Sam Gaddis, Stefan C. Schmukle, Boris Egloff, and Samuel D. Gosling, "Facebook Profiles Reflect Actual Personali-

ty, Not Self-Idealization," *Psychological Science* 21, no. 3 (March 2010): 372–74.

26. Goffman, *The Presentation of Self in Everyday Life.*

27. DiMicco and Millen, "Identity Management"; Marwick and boyd, "I Tweet Honestly"; Erika Pearson, "All the World Wide Web's a Stage: The Performance of Identity in Online Social Networks," *First Monday* 14, no. 3 (March 2009): article 5, http://firstmonday.org/htbin/cgiwrap/bin/ojs/index.php/fm/article/view/2162/2127; Vladimir Barash, Nicolas Ducheneaut, Ellen Isaacs, and Victoria Bellotti, "Faceplant: Impression (Mis)management in Facebook Status Updates," in *Proceedings of the 4th International AAAI Conference on Weblogs and Social Media* (New York: ACM, 2010), 207–10.

28. Mike Thelwall and David Wilkinson, "Public Dialogs in Social Network Sites: What Is Their Purpose?" *Journal of the American Society for Information Science and Technology* 61, no. 2 (2009): 392–404; Tiffany A. Pempek, Yevdokiya A. Yermolayeva, and Sandra L. Calvert, "College Students' Social Networking Experiences on Facebook," *Journal of Applied Developmental Psychology* 30 (2009): 227–38.

29. Walther, "Selective Self-Presentation"; Joseph B. Walther, "Computer-Mediated Communication: Impersonal, Interpersonal, and Hyperpersonal Interaction," *Communication Research* 23, no. 1 (February 1996): 3–43; Lampe, Ellison and Steinfeld, "A Familiar (Face)book"; Kramer and Winter, "Impression Management 2.0"; Ong et al., "Narcissism, Extraversion"; Barash et al., "Faceplant: Impression (Mis)management."

30. Barash et al., "Faceplant: Impression (Mis)management."

31. Pempek, Yermolayeva, Calvert, "College Students" Social Networking"; Barash et al., "Faceplant: Impression (Mis)management."

32. Judith E. Rosenbaum, Benjamin K. Johnson, Peter A. Stepman, and Koos C. M. Nuijten, "Just Being Themselves? Goals and Strategies for Self-Presentation on Facebook" (paper presented at the 80th Annual Conference of the Southern States Communication Association, Memphis, TN, April 2010).

33. Monique M. Hennink, *International Focus Group Research: A Handbook for the Health and Social Sciences* (Cambridge, UK: Cambridge University Press, 2007); Thomas L. Greenbaum, *Moderating Focus Groups. A Practical Guide for Group Facilitation* (Thousand Oaks, CA: Sage, 2000).

34. Justin Smith, "College Students" Facebook Use Easing up over Summer, While Parents Logging on in Record Numbers," last modified July 6, 2009, accessed May 14, 2012, http://www.insidefacebook.com/2009/07/06/college-students-facebook-use-easing-up-over-the-summer-while-parents-logging-on-in-record-numbers/.

35. Kathy Charmaz, *Constructing Grounded Theory: A Practical Guide through Qualitative Analysis* (Thousand Oaks, CA: Sage, 2006).

36. Rosenbaum et al., "Just Being Themselves?"; Barney G. Glaser, "The Constant Comparative Method of Qualitative Analysis," *Social Problems* 12, no. 4 (1965): 436–45.

37. Back et al., "Facebook Profiles Reflect Actual Personality," 372–74.

38. Doherty and Schlenker, "Self-Consciousness"; Zhao, Grasmuck, and Martin, "Identity Construction."

39. Ong et al., "Narcissism, Extraversion"; Barashet al., "Faceplant: Impression (Mis)management."

40. Christofides, Muise, and Desmarais, "Information Disclosure"; Tufekci, "Can You See Me Now?"

41. Paulhus and Trapnell, "Self-Presentation of Personality"; Iedema and Poppe, "The Effect of Self-Presentation."

42. Doherty and Schlenker, "Self-Consciousness"; Zhao, Grasmuck, and Martin, "Identity Construction on Facebook."

43. Tice et al., "When Modesty Prevails"; Ellison, Heino, and Gibbs, "Managing Impressions Online"; Baumeister, "A Self-Presentational View"; Doherty and Schlenker, "Self-Consciousness."

44. Thelwall and Wilkinson, "Public Dialogs"; Pempek, Yermolayeva, and Calvert, "College Students" Social Networking."

45. Tice et al., "When Modesty Prevails"; Back et al., "Facebook Profiles Reflect."

46. Thelwall and Wilkinson, "Public Dialogs"; Pempek, Yermolayeva, and Calvert, "College Students" Social Networking"; Tice, et al., "When Modesty Prevails."

47. Walther, "Computer-Mediated Communication."

48. Christofides, Muise, and Desmarais, "Information Disclosure"; Tufekci, "Can You See Me Now?"

49. Baumeister, "A Self-Presentational View", Baumeister, "Self-Esteem"; Doherty and Schlenker, "Self-Consciousness"; Tice et al., "When Modesty Prevails"; Ellison, Heino, and Gibbs, "Managing Impressions Online"; Zhao, Grasmuck, and Martin, "Identity Construction."

50. DiMicco and Millen, "Identity Management"; Marwick and boyd, "I Tweet Honestly"; Pearson, "All the World Wide Web," article 5.

51. Paulhus and Trapnell, "Self-Presentation of Personality."

52. Catalina L. Toma and Jeffrey T. Hancock, "What Lies Beneath: The Linguistic Traces of Deception in Online Dating Profiles," *Journal of Communication* 62, no. 1 (February 2012): 78–97.

Chapter 3

Face-Off: Different Ways Identity Is Privileged through Facebook

Daniel C. Davis, Margeaux B. Lippman,
Timothy W. Morris, and Jessica A. Tougas

Existing research suggests a growing relationship between social presence and social identity when using social networking sites.[1] In ever increasing numbers, males and females are using social networking sites such as Facebook which extended beyond its original development as a networking tool for college students to recruit users via pools of high school students, professors, corporations, governments, and even celebrities.[2] On Facebook, people are able to leave messages for friends, make new friends at their college or high school before ever setting foot on the campus, and keep in touch with friends they no longer see face to face.

Research also shows a difference in the way males and females use social networks, as well as computer-mediated communication. Computer-mediated communication (CMC) is "tentatively defined as any human symbolic text-based interaction conducted or facilitated through digitally-based technologies."[3] Initially comprised mostly of text descriptors of individuals, many aspects of Facebook were prime examples of CMC modes. Aragon defines "social presence" as "the degree of salience of the other person in the interaction and the consequent salience of the interpersonal relationship."[4] In other words, social presence is the degree to which one communicator in a relationship perceives the other.

More specifically, Facebook is an area of social networking offering high potential for studying identity management issues, as the information disclosed by a particular user is often edited/controlled or reality-*based*, rather than blatant reality itself. Sites like Facebook even have privacy settings controlling who can see certain aspects of personal information.[5] Self-disclosure through CMC differs greatly from self-disclosure in face to face (FtF) communication. Merkle and Richardson explain that since FtF relationships lack anonymity, individuals tend to reveal very little about themselves to another person at first.[6] However, one's disclosure increases as she gets more comfortable with other individuals. The Internet typically allows for a certain mystery about one's persona, so one can choose to post whatever is more comfortable for them to disclose. Oblinger and Hawkins explain how one student noticed that his friend had written things in his own Facebook profile making himself sound like a wild partier when, in fact, he was more similar to an academic individual, providing a useful example of altering one's Internet identity.[7]

Yet, because the Internet can often provide a deep history of one's activities, and this is especially true in the case of Facebook, the amount of information disclosed on the Internet is likely to include *more* than what can be said in FtF, because in FtF situations information is typically disclosed in private or to one particular person.[8] Finally, many earlier forms of CMC provided high degrees of anonymity among individuals as a virtual medium. However, Facebook greatly decreases this anonymity as, for example, individuals on a college campus pass each other on a daily basis, and the photograph feature allows one to present their physical self as well as text descriptors. Additionally, Facebook's "timeline," previous posts by the users' friends and other components, allow participants to view users' past activities "in perpetuity," and even users' photo-deleting efforts can be thwarted by the very electronic architecture facilitating access to multiple users.[9] The amount of information inadvertently made available to others by Facebook users is so large and problematic, in 2009, the United States' military began issuing administrative directives banning the use of military networks for accessing such sites as Facebook, Twitter, and MySpace.[10] This decrease in anonymity may have an impact on trends of self-disclosure and identity privileging yet to be studied.

As such, the present study examines identity privileging and self-disclosure patterns employed by different groups. The first of these examinations looks toward differences in Facebook use among females and males. The second looks at use differences in college class levels (i.e., freshmen, sophomores, juniors, and seniors).

The Rise of Social Networking Websites

In an attempt to keep in touch with and meet other people, many individuals now use the Internet for social networking purposes.[11] With the growing number of college students going away to school, social networking is becoming especially vital to students wanting to maintain ties with home area relationships, as well as facilitating the formation of new bonds with their college peers.

The social networking website Facebook was launched in 2004 and had over 12 million users located in over 40,000 networks by 2006.[12] Due to its widespread popularity, Facebook actually tied with beer for second place among the things college students use most, demonstrating the importance of Facebook for college students.[13] In the time since, it has grown even more pervasive and integrated into people's lives.[14]

The question remains as to why social networking websites, like Facebook, have grown to be so popular. The widely accepted reason is that social networking websites allow an "opportunity to build new relationships through existing friends."[15] However, some worry about an increased dependence on Facebook as a social tool. Although that may be an ongoing debate, Facebook is clearly used to interact in a social manner with others, increasing the formation of social ties due to the amount of social contact involved.[16] Yet, even early on, Bell and others suggested that social networking sites (like Facebook) could allow users to create online personas or "avatars" of themselves.[17] These types of platforms allow users a level of control in editing out the parts of their lives and background they don't wish others to see, or highlighting certain aspects of their lives. In this sense, what a user presents is a reality-*based* impression of themselves, rather than the blatant reality. Of course, this may and does create a higher desirability for the user among the particular social network she belongs to, which is the point of impression management in this sense.

Unfortunately, though, this desirability can lead to stalking and other invasions of users' privacy unless the disclosure is carefully controlled by the user.[18] At one point, Facebook added controversial features to its network such as the "News Feed" component which displayed everything a user's friends have done recently on the site, and a program called "instant personalization" that drew information from participants' profiles to customize other sites the person might visit.[19] Due to bad reviews by users, including being called a "stalking tool," the Facebook staff added privacy settings allowing a user to control how much information about their lives their friends can see on the News Feed. Though prompted by user feedback, the end result of these changes was a shift in disclosure from "public or private" to "a much more sophisticated understanding of privacy that's more like what real people have in real life."[20] That is, people generally share some aspects of their lives with specific groups of people, and other aspects with other groups. The more recent privacy settings allow participants to segment their social networks in more of this way.

Blogs as a Form of Social Networking

Web logs, herein "blogs," are clearly becoming an integral part of the online community. A blog is a close relative of the web journal, a place where people can share their innermost thoughts with their online community. Blogs are maintained by all sorts of individuals, such as politicians, celebrities, athletes, and the general public. Most social networking sites include a blog or "notes" feature, allowing users to post their thoughts, interests, and experiences on the Internet. Finneran writes that blogs are self-centered and self-indulgent, and they are also independent.[21]This is, in part, due to blogs being written in the first person. Blogs, according to Johnson and Kaye "are a growing phenomenon, increasing from an estimated 30,000 in 1998 to at least three million by the beginning of 2004."[22] The increase in users also reveals the growing positive sentiment toward using blogs. Blogs are important in allowing users the freedom to write about whatever they feel without limitations. Plutchak states "this is certainly the case with blogs, particularly those which attempt to track the news of the day."[23] The type of lawlessness this brings is favored by journalists who, under their strict codes of ethics, cannot necessarily write freely or insert their opinions into their professional pieces.

The recent addition of a blog-type feature to Facebook is integral to the understanding of privileged identity characteristics, as it allows the owner of the blog to express pieces of their self on a public forum that may not have been expressed before. Skiba reveals that blogs are a part of Web 2.0, which is a comparison of the past and present in Internet features and products, and also shows that blogs are effectively an upgrade to personal and social networking sites.[24]

Social Presence

One of the most basic goals and desires of human beings is to be perceived as a viable person in the social sphere. This aspect ties nicely into the concept of "social presence," first introduced by Short, Williams, and Christie in 1976.[25] A simple explanation of "social presence" is the concept of one communicator being aware of with whom she is communicating.[26] This enables a conceptualization of the other person's identity and a growing comfort with the environment around the individual. Thus, "social presence" is about putting one's self out into a social atmosphere, ostensibly to meet others not necessarily just on the electronic realm. That is, "Facebook users engage in 'searching' for people with whom they have an offline connection more than they 'browse' for complete strangers to meet."[27] To this same end, Aragon states the goal of creating social presence is the ability to create comfort levels between people.[28] In traditional FtF interactions, this can be achieved through social cues such as dress and facial expression. As such, social presence theory has ties to "media richness" theory, stating that the degree of "richness" of communication hinges on the ability of the medium to analyze and process ambiguous communication.[29] This media theory says that "FtF communication is considered to be the richest, while other media are thought to be leaner since they have fewer contextual cues and slower feedback compared to face-to-face."[30]

Social Presence and the Internet

Since the Internet was historically simply a collection of cables, screens and binary code, those engaging in social activity via the Internet were at a disadvantage due to a lack of visual cues associated with typical FtF interactions. Tidwell and Walther state "the most obvious disadvantage of using the Internet to communicate is that the written medium precludes the exchange of nonverbal cues that accompany FtF speech."[31] Without interacting in person, nonverbal cues such as eye contact and body language cannot be viewed by each communicator. Also, Tidwell and Walther include that these differences have suggested that impressions and relational development might be thwarted in CMC, rendering it a "relatively impersonal medium."[32] Some people even felt as though CMC did not leave room for people to build interpersonal relationships with one another.

Bargh and McKenna explain that there are three separate models of CMC: first, the *filter model* which views CMC as reduced in social cues with a negative affect on social interaction; second, the *engineering model*, which views individuals as the determiners of the overall outcome of the communication situation; and third, an approach which places the utmost importance on the social context of an Internet social interaction.[33] Although the Internet historically lacked the nonverbal and visual cues perceived necessary for social presence, there is a growing base of evidence claiming that social presence can be achieved without displaying physical aspects. Rogers and Lea state that "it is possible that one can experience physical presence without a corresponding level of social presence, and conversely one can experience social presence in the absence of physical presence."[34] Thus, a person is able to create social presence without revealing who she physically is. This speaks to the heart of an edited identity, and the essence of how social networking allows users to carefully disclose specific social cues to others. However, Rogers and Lea proceed to note that "social influence in computer mediated environments is restricted to the extent that interpersonal contact is constrained within that environment, i.e. the social is equated with the interpersonal."[35] As Facebook quickly evolved to provide visual forums to represent different aspects of one's life (e.g., party side, kooky and playful side, athletic side), much of the former constraints limiting CMC's social presence fell away, providing viewers of a user's pages of photographs to form impressions of that individual *based on* what was presented to them. Thus, social networking allowed CMC to move toward acting as a tool for social impression management and, in doing so, also a tool for users to participate in identity management. Yet, not all users approached CMC's power for identity management similarly. Early teens routinely show a lack of awareness regarding problematic disclosure and interactions with online persons who may not be what they seem.[36] As such, individuals younger than thirteen are not supposed to participate on Facebook, nor have their own Facebook profile. Yet, Horn recently revealed that some 7.5 *million* Facebook users are actually under the minimum age.[37] This naturally raises the question of age differences in communicative disclosure behaviors across participants, and even the possibility of class differences (i.e., freshmen, sophomores, juniors, and seniors) within college participants. Beyond age, different sexes experience social networks differently.

Sex Differences

Research shows that males and females use networks differently, thereby achieving different levels of social presence while on a network. Gefen and Straub show that females perceive online discourse as displaying higher social presence than males.[38] That is, females feel a greater presence with the other person when communicating online in a social setting. Gefen and Straub also explain that females appear to rely more on using ways of communicating via the Internet, and females were using the Internet more than males to have their communication needs met.[39]

More recently, Punyanunt-Carter indicates that, among college students, females and males have different trends of self-disclosure.[40] Females self-reported that they freely disclose information about themselves on the Internet, while males reported disclosing far less.

Identity and the Internet

In light of the way in which the Internet functions, it is important to note how it can be manipulated to privilege certain aspects of one's identity. Indeed, early on, Turkle even discussed how the Internet's higher levels of anonymity actually *facilitated* people experimenting with different versions of themselves, playing out identities, even portraying themselves as different sexes, without fears of being disapproved of by their nonmediated social circle.[41]

Even using one's actual sex, social information, and accurate background, a person's identity is affected by using networks on the Internet. Joinson shows that people disclose more personal information while on the Internet.[42] However, what they may disclose is not always pertinent to who they truly are in person. Sharing information can result in tensions distorting what information is shared and how it becomes shared.[43] Some people may feel uncomfortable disclosing certain information in person, but may feel free to disclose anything while on the Internet. The latest exemplar of this trend comes from the 2009 incoming Britain Secret Intelligence Service (SIS, a.k.a., "MI6") chief's wife posting family pictures and exposing details of where the couple live and take their holidays and who their friends and relatives are, potentially compromising the safety of their family and friends by revealing this information to terrorists or "hostile foreign powers."[44]

Lee shows that "due to [these] characteristics of CMC, such as technologically induced anonymity and minimal social feedback, participants' objective self-awareness decreases and thus they are more likely to act upon impulses that would normally be inhibited."[45] These impulses may lead to testing out new identities over the Internet. Teenagers are able to experiment with different identities on web pages via the Internet.[46] They may be able to see the reaction of others with a new identity and may receive confirming messages. Lonely and unhappy teens may be more dissatisfied with how groups and other individuals view themselves.[47]

People also take into consideration how *other* individuals or groups act, and build self-constructs for themselves over the Internet based off of those considerations. Postmes, Spears, and Lea state that "the self not only encompasses one's individual identity, but also comprises social identities associated with valued group membership."[48] The group's traits eventually override the person's unique traits and mold them. Markovits, Benenson, and White state that "individuals of both sexes can be primed to incorporate either individuals or groups into their self-construals."[49] Thus, the projected identity becomes some combination of both one's own characteristics, and traits of the group.

Self-Presentation and Self-Disclosure

Self-disclosure can best be defined as the revealing of information about the self to other individuals. When on the Internet, this is especially true as "CMC and general Internet-based behavior can be characterized as having high levels of self-disclosure."[50] As a result of this disclosure, one can form an identity over the Internet.

When online, it is easier for people to change or distort the type of person they are. A person can omit or embellish personal attributes. Some individuals may even become a whole new person altogether. Thus, the way in which people represent themselves online may not always be who they really are. In fact, the lack of nonverbal cues on the Internet may result in "selective self-presentation."[51] This means that positive aspects of a person are more likely to be disclosed over true personal characteristics.[52]

In FtF contact, the ways in which people interact also affect disclosure. A greeting with a certain tone can even have the ability to affect a person.[53] People are also found to enhance their views while online as a result of interacting with others online. They tend to exaggerate traits of masculinity and femininity while using the Internet to portray an identity for others.[54]

People who go online to meet others experience different processes of disclosing information than those who meet FtF. They may try to go through measures to reduce uncertainty with the person that they are speaking.[55] One way they may try to attain the aforementioned reduction is by revealing things about themselves. It is much easier to disclose information online than in person because of the lack of specific problems that may occur when meeting FtF.[56]

Ellison, Steinfeld, and Lampe state that "pressures to highlight one's positive attributes are experienced in tandem with the need to present one's true self to others, specifically in relationships."[57] Two equal, opposite, forces push a person's ability to present a true picture of one's self, and much of the time specific aspects may be slightly exaggerated in the result. A person may lose their individual sense of self when not revealing their identity via communicating online.[58] Individuals have the ability to be whoever they would like to be through the Internet, use of profiles, and various other outlets allowing people to portray information contributing to an identity. This ability also occurs while in groups. In order to fulfill a need to be social via the Internet, people have a tendency to join and identify with groups, such as provided by the large-scale social network of Facebook. Douglas and McGarty indicate that "people are motivated to act in a manner that is consistent with group norms when they are identifiable to an in-group audience."[59] People are at risk of being influenced by group norms to change themselves into a completely different person.

Adolescents are able to act in different ways and be placed in different social circles while on the Internet, whereas FtF communication might not allow them such access.[60] Teenagers can alter their identity to fit with different groups online easier than they would FtF in school. Thus, self-constructs may affect one's ability to enter a group and, as such, an individual may alter their portrayed self in order to fit into a particular desired group. The challenge, of course, is that one's collective self-disclosures can also often undermine one's attempt to change one's image, or the impression one makes on others.[61] This is especially the case in the Facebook era, when one's online history is presented to those willing to dig through weeks, months, or even years' worth of posts and pictures.[62]

Summary

In sum, the Internet is a medium upon which self-disclosure is made easier due to the anonymity granted by sitting in front of a computer screen, rather than directly facing another human, and the ability to present a reality-based image of one's self and one's life. By studying communicative differences between computer-mediated and FtF self-disclosures across identities, the relationships between the Internet, social presence, and identity formation can be more easily discerned.

Hypotheses

H₁: Females are more likely to self-disclose identity privileging characteristics via social networking sites than males.

H₂: Freshmen are more likely to include identifying characteristics on their Facebook user profiles than users in other class years.

General Methodology

Two studies were used to test the hypotheses of this chapter. Study #1 was a content analysis of 200 Facebook profiles to determine the amount of self-disclosure put forth by individuals. Study #2 was the distribution and analysis of 200 survey questionnaires, also to discern the amount of self-disclosure put forth by individuals.

Methodology: Study #1

Setting
Study #1 was conducted on Facebook user profiles of students at a small, liberal arts college in the northeastern United States. Content analyses were performed on individual profiles via the Internet.

Participants
In study #1, the researchers engaged in convenience sampling of 200 individuals (Male = 100, Female = 100) on Facebook. After 100 male profiles were analyzed through convenience sampling, there was a targeted search conducted through convenience sampling to fill the remainder of the female quota in order to achieve a balanced sample. Content analysis was conducted to see how many individuals had up photographs and the amount thereof, a phone number, an address at which they could be reached and if they had any "notes" postings.

The Facebook analysis was done discretely, with no notification to the participant because of the open access of Facebook. Users determine the disclosure level of their information themselves. No identifying information was taken about those participants, with the only data collected being a "yes" or "no" regarding if they had certain sections of the site filled out and the number of photographs on the profile.

Analysis
Scales were constructed to determine the amount of disclosure provided by individuals. If the phone number, address, or notes sections were not filled out, the respective section was given a score of 1. Conversely, if the section was filled out, a score of 2 was given. Disclosure via photographs was ranked on a scale of 1 through 26. This scale started with 1 being profiles with 1–50 photographs, 2 being 51–100 photographs, and so on. The lowest score attainable on this scale was a 3, while the highest was a 26. Data for this study were analyzed through SPSS version 12.0.1. An ANOVA was performed, where the independent variable was participant sex and the dependent variable was the scale disclosure score described above.

Results

ANOVA results indicated statistically significant differences ($F_{1,198}$ = 26.98, $p < 0.001$, $eta^2 = 0.130$) between males and females. The overall mean disclosure score was 7.03 for the content analysis with a standard deviation of 2.67, with the mean for males (n = 100) being 6.07 (SD = 1.98), and the mean for females (n = 100) being 7.99 (SD = 2.92).

Methodology: Study #2

Setting

Study #2 was conducted on the campus of a small, liberal arts college in the northeastern United States. Participants were surveyed on public areas of the campus in the fall of 2006. A survey questionnaire was developed to ascertain participants' comfort levels in disclosing personal or private information, and the types of information most likely to be disclosed. This information was embedded within other questions to be used in another research study, but also to diminish the obviousness of this study's purpose to participants. The questionnaires were distributed between the hours of 10:00 am and 9:00 pm on the campus using a convenience sampling method, surveying individuals as they walked past various points on the campus.

Participants

In study #2, a total of 200 participants engaged. All participants in the survey were informed of the voluntary nature of their participation and consent.

Analysis

Similar to Study #1's methodology, a similar scale of disclosure was used to further test the findings of Study #1, as well as extend forward and test Study #2's hypothesis (i.e., Hypothesis 2). As such, the same scale was utilized for areas of disclosure involving what classes the individual was taking, the class sections of the individual, and what clubs the individual was in. The highest attainable score was a six. An ANOVA test was performed, with sex and class year of the participants as the independent variables, and scale of disclosure again serving as the dependent variable.

Results

ANOVA results ($F_{1,190}$= 1.41, p = 0.236, eta^2 = 0.007) indicate non-significant findings and accounting for less than 1 percent of variance), suggesting that males and females disclosure some, but not all, personal information areas differently. The overall mean disclosure score for participants (n = 191) was 4.15 (SD = 1.1), with the mean for males (89) being 4.04 (SD = 1.14), and the mean for females (102) being 4.24 (SD = 1.07).

Results broken down by class standing indicate differences approaching statistical significance ($F_{3,192}$= 2.16, p = 0.094, eta^2 = 0.033), but only accounting for approximately 3 percent of the overall data's variance). The overall mean for participants (n = 193) was 4.16 (SD = 1.1). The mean for freshmen (48) on the scale of disclosure was 4.19 (SD = 1.2), the mean for sophomores (67) was 4.39 (SD = 1.14), the mean for juniors (45) was 3.89 (SD = 0.93), and the mean for seniors (33) was 4.0 (SD = 1.0).

Discussion

Two hypotheses were tested by these studies. Study #1 specifically tested Hypothesis 1, while study #2 tested both Hypothesis 1 and Hypothesis 2.

Hypothesis 1:

As demonstrated through study #1, there is a very significant relationship between the privileging of identity information and sex, thus supporting the hypothesis. Study #2 indicates a lesser, nonstatistically significant level. This will be addressed later in this section.

In study #1, the mean scores of the scale of disclosure varied greatly between males and females. Males had a mean score of 6.07 while females had a mean of 7.99. This is a difference of 1.92 points on the scale. Additionally, with a probability of error of less than 0.001, the chance of a false positive being found from study #1 is very low.

These numbers have many implications that support the hypothesis. First, the sharp contrast in mean value of the scale of disclosure between the sexes is indicative of a higher degree of self-disclosure and identity privileging on behalf of females through Facebook. This supports the hypothesis by implying that females self-disclose more through Facebook than males, despite the decreased amount of anonymity that Facebook provides in contrast to other forms of CMC.

Study #2, however, causes some small problems for the support of the hypothesis. Unlike the significant result yielded from study #1's comparison of means, the difference in means in study #2 was less drastic. The mean on the 6-point scale for males was 4.044 and the mean for females was 4.235. This is only a 0.191 difference in scores between the sexes. Additionally, this is not a significant statistic, as the significance of the data came in at 0.236.

This is not meant, however, to discount the findings of study #1 and negate Hypothesis 1. There are many reasons for this to not negate the entirety of the findings. For instance, content analysis proves to be a much more accurate depiction of the areas which individuals fill out on Facebook profiles as opposed to self-reporting through surveys. It is not always easy to remember what sections of a user profile one fills out, thus accounting for the lack of significance on study #2. Additionally, there may be issues with the difference between privileging identifying information in regards to academics and the privileging of other identifying characteristics. This plays a role because study #2 concentrated on privileging aspects of academic identity, such as class sections and extracurricular involvement. Regardless of the significance factor, the slight difference in means on study #2 should be taken into account as indicative of a trend of increased disclosure.

The findings of these studies indicate that there is a significant relationship between self-disclosure of identity characteristics and sex. This study is in line with the findings of past research detailed in this chapter's literature review in regards to CMC, as there is a high degree of disclosure on behalf of both sexes as demonstrated by the scale in both study #1 and #2.

Hypothesis 2:

The findings of study #2 failed to support Hypothesis 2, set forth earlier in this paper. The means of the disclosure scale for each individual class year were far different than were expected. Seeing as the upperclass students at the college have already established themselves socially, it was expected that the freshman class would privilege more identity characteristics in order to connect with other individuals on the campus who they have yet to socialize with. As demonstrated by the results of the study, this was not the case.

Two instances specifically disprove this point. First, the sophomores in the study had a higher mean disclosure score than the freshmen surveyed. Additionally, scores were fairly evenly distributed throughout the four class years. Although the sample size was small, this is indicative of how, in future studies or examinations, there may be little or no specific increase in disclosure on behalf of college freshmen as opposed to the rest of the undergraduate population.

Since this hypothesis was investigative in nature, there is no prior research to compare this to. However, this may provide a basis upon which future studies of the connection between age and disclosure can be built upon.

General Discussion

Overall, these studies gave credence to claims that males and females put forth a different amount of information via the Internet. However, it discredited the concept of class status in college having any impact on the same sort of disclosure. The comparison of the two separate groups' disclosure trends is important because it shows specific trends that can be attributed to one qualifying characteristic (in this case, the sex of the study's participants) of an individual. Otherwise, questions would remain as to what individual characteristic the trend is connected to.

Additionally, these studies help to support many theories found within the field of computer-mediated communication and social presence. There are three specific theories that this study supports. These theories are set forth in the work of Punyanunt-Carter, Tidwell and Walther, and Joinson.[63]

The findings of study #1 support the work done by Punyanunt-Carter in the field of self-disclosure on a grander scale.[64] While Punyanunt-Carter relied on a basic Likert scale, the content analysis conducted by this study on the use of a specific mechanism for self-disclosure by both males and females provides greater insight into one of the many facets of self-disclosure.[65]

The theory regarding selective self-presentation set forth by Tidwell and Walther is supported by the content analysis conducted by study #1, with the added benefit of exposing differences in utilization by males and females.[66] When posting photographs on Facebook, individuals choose specific aspects of their lives to the social network that they belong to. The sheer number of photographs displayed by college students as a whole shows that they can pick from many possible representations of the self and post it for a captive audience. In showing that more females than males pick from different aspects of their social realms to post online, this study can help to discern trends in self-representation through photographs by males and females.

The theory of self-disclosure of Joinson is supported by this study on the whole.[67] Both study #1 and study #2 display trends in self-disclosure through an under-researched social networking mechanism. Mean scores of disclosure by all groups involved were on the high side of the scale, thus displaying that Facebook is used for self-disclosure purposes by members of both sexes. Research done by Joinson can be supplemented by this study as it displays a difference in use by males and females.[68]

Limitations and Implications for Future Research

The errors made in self-reporting and the limitations of survey gathering played a large role in this study. The sample lacked diversity due to the specific small private college setting of the study: Over 80 percent of the students attending this specific institution could ethnically be described as "Anglo-American," and belonging to a similar social economic strata. A more accurate depiction of disclosure-identity trends may be found at a public university, at schools outside of the northeastern United States, and certainly through replication on a national scale. Similarly, the sample size for study #2's testing of Hypothesis 2 may be problematic. With a sample of only 200 individuals overall, there should have been a better balance in class year. The freshman class comprised close to one-fourth of the total sample (n = 48). While this is an accurate base, the senior class only comprised 33 out of 200 of the sample population. Trends may be discovered with a larger sample size with a more balanced distribution of class years. Thus, a greater emphasis could be put on surveys to off-campus and upper-class students so that the emphasis on those students could balance out the amount of underclass students presently surveyed. Future researchers could also draw data from all-female or all-male colleges to compare trends in disclosure.

When told to self-report, individuals may often fail to accurately portray a situation. This can be best represented by the difference between the data gathered on the content analysis and via the surveys. Although the mean on study #2 for females was higher than that of males, the gap between the two means was minute and failed to be statistically significant. In situations such as this, it may be better to rely on content analysis than self-reported survey data as the depiction given through the hard content data is more accurate, possibly reflecting deeper consideration of information disclosure when crafting one's electronic profile than filling out a campus survey within a few minutes while FtF with one of the study's researchers. Yet, this situation may actually present a potential vein of research to pursue in terms of social presence and disclosure patterns: Do people disclose less when in FtF situations than when in reality-edited situations? Since individuals possess greater levels of control when crafting their electronic profile, they may feel more comfortable disclosing personal information in these situations. Additionally, individuals possess the ability to disclosure specific content within each area of disclosure (interests, hobbies, favorite books, etc.), thereby constructing a particular electronic identity that may, or may not, mirror their FtF identity. That is, individuals have the power to "edit" their online identity, presenting a somewhat to potentially radically different persona to others. The implications this has for issues of social presence within electronic spaces should be further investigated by future scholars.

Indeed, these studies provide a good basis upon which future studies about trends in identity privileging and self-disclosure can be built upon. Research could be done to see if individual choice in major or membership in athletic/academic clubs had an effect on the likelihood of disclosure in socially identifying characteristics on Facebook. Personality traits could also be studied to see if different personalities were more likely to privilege social identity.

Additionally, much work could be done when relating identity privileging to relationship formation via Facebook. Future researchers can look toward trends in the formation of meaningful relationships (e.g., close friendships or intimate contacts) solely over Facebook and determine how it varies across sex.

Finally, although the current study focused on identity privileging via the highlighting or disclosure of specific information, the concept of "identity performance" should also be acknowledged, where individuals have become hyperaware of the possibilities for digital recording and sharing of their activities that they actually perform in accordance with their online portrayed identity; as such, they *become* who they portray themselves to be, in a type of self-perpetuating prophecy identity.[69] Clearly, this represents another interesting line of research to pursue.

Notes

1. Adam N. Joinson, "Self-Disclosure in Computer-Mediated Communication: The Role of Self-Awareness and Visual Anonymity," *European Journal of Social Psychology* 31, no. 2 (March/April 2001): 177–92.

2. Rachel E. Dubrofsky, "Surveillance on Reality Television and Facebook: From Authenticity to Flowing Data," *Communication Theory* 21, no. 2 (May 2011): 111–29.

3. Brian H. Spitzberg, "Preliminary Development of a Model and Measure of Computer-Mediated Communication (CMC) Competence," *Journal of Computer-Mediated Communication* 11, no. 2 (January 2006): 630.

4. Steven R. Aragon, "Creating Social Presence in Online Environments," *New Directions for Adult and Continuing Education* 100 (Winter 2003): 59.

5. Tony Bradley, "Facebook Privacy Is a Balancing Act," *PC World*, accessed May 17, 2010, http://www.pcworld.com/businesscecnter/article/196431/Facebook_privacy_is_a_balancing_act.html.

6. Erich Merkle and Rhonda Richardson, "Digital Dating and Virtual Relating: Conceptualizing Computer-Mediated Romantic Relationships," *Family Relations: An Interdisciplinary Journal of Applied Family Studies* 49, no. 2 (April 2000): 187–92.

7. Diana Oblinger and Brian Hawkins, "The Myth about Putting Information Online," *EDUCAUSE Review* 41, no. 5 (September/October 2006): 14–15.

8. Samual Axon, "Five Ways Facebook Changed Dating (for the Worse)," *Mashable.com*, accessed April 10, 2010, http://mashable.com/2010/04/10/Facebook-dating/.

9. Dubrofsky, "Surveillance on Reality Television and Facebook," 117; Christopher Null, "No Such Thing as 'Deleted' on the Internet," *Christopher Null: The Working Guy*, accessed May 22, 2009, http://www.anahuactexasindependence.com/NoSuchThingAsDeletedOnInternet.htm.

10. Pauline Jelinek "Pentagon Reviews Social Networking on Computers," *Associated Press Wire,* accessed August 4, 2009, http://www.azcentral.com/news/articles/2009/08/04/20090804pentagon-internet04-ON.html.

11. Cliff Lampe, Nicole Ellison, and Charles Steinfield, "A Face(book) in the Crowd: Social Searching vs. Social Browsing," *Proceedings of the 2006*

20th Anniversary Conference on Computer Supported Cooperative Work (New York: ACM Press, 2006), 167–70.

12. Mark Zuckerberg, "About Facebook" (Msg 1), accessed June 28, 2012, Message posted to http://www.Facebook.com/about.php.

13. Oblinger and Hawkins, "The Myth."

14. Dubrofsky, "Surveillance on Reality Television."

15. Josef Kolbitsch and Hermann Maurer, "The Transformation of the Web: How Emerging Communities Shape the Information We Consume," *Journal of Universal Computer Science* 12, no. 2 (February 2006): 202.

16. Shanyang Zhao, "Do Internet Users Have More Social Ties? A Call for Differentiated Analyses of Internet Use," *Journal of Computer-Mediated Communication* 11, no. 3 (April 2006): 844–62.

17. David Bell, *An Introduction to Cybercultures* (London: Routledge, 2001); Alessandra Talamo and Beatrice Ligorio, "Strategic Identities in Cyberspace," *Cyberpsychology and Behavior* 4, no. 1 (February 2001): 109–22.

18. Don Thompson, "California Man Used Facebook to Hack Women's Emails," *Associated Press Wire*, January 14, 2011.

19. Barbara Ortutay, "Facebook Adjusts Privacy Controls after Complaints," *Associated Press Wire*, May 26, 2010.

20. Marshall Kirkpatrick, "A Closer Look at Facebook's New Privacy Options," *ReadWriteWeb*, June 29, 2009, accessed June 20, 2012, http://www.readwriteweb.com/archives/a_closer_look_at_Facebooks_new_priv acy_options.php.

21. Kevin Finneran, "To Blog, or Not to Blog," *Issues in Science and Technology* 22, no. 2 (2006): 23–24.

22. Thomas J. Johnson and Barbara K. Kaye, "Wag the Blog: How Reliance on Traditional Media and the Internet Influence Credibility Perceptions of Weblogs among Blog Users," *Journalism and Mass Communication Quarterly* 81, no. 3 (September 2004): 622.

23. Scott T. Plutchak, "I See Blog People," *Journal of the Medical Library Association* 93, no. 3 (July 2005): 305.

24. Diane J. Skiba, "WEB 2.0: Next Great Thing or Just Marketing Hype?" *Nursing Education Perspectives* 27, no. 4 (2006): 212–14.

25. John A. Short, Ederyn Williams, and Bruce Christie, *The Social Psychology of Telecommunications* (London: John Wiley & Sons, 1976).

26. Paul Rogers and Martin Lea, "Social Presence in Distributed Group Environments: The Role of Social Identity," *Behavior and Information Technology* 24, no. 2 (2005): 151–58.

27. Nicole Ellison, Charles Steinfield, and Cliff Lampe, "The Benefits of Facebook 'Friends': Social Capital and College Students' Use of Online Social Network Sites," *Journal of Computer-Mediated Communication* 12, no. 4 (July 2007): 1144; Cliff Lampe, Nicole Ellison, and Charles Steinfield, "A Face(book) in the Crowd."

28. Aragon, "Creating Social Presence."

29. Richard L. Daft and Robert H. Lengel, "Information Richness: A New Approach to Managerial Behavior and Organizational Design," in *Research in Organizational Behavior* Vol. 6, ed. Larry L. Cummings, and Barry M. Staw (Greenwich, CT: JAI Press), 191–233.

30. Yun-Jo An and Theodore Frick, "Student Perceptions of Asynchronous Computer-Mediated Communication in FtF Courses," *Journal of Computer-Mediated Communication* 11, no. 2 (January 2006): 486.

31. Lisa Collins Tidwell and Joseph B. Walther, "Computer-Mediated Communication Effects on Disclosure, Impressions, and Interpersonal Evaluations: Getting to Know One Another a Bit at a Time," *Human Communication Research* 28, no. 3 (July 2002): 318.

32. Tidwell and Walther, "Computer-Mediated Communications," 318.

33. John A. Bargh and Katelyn Y. A. McKenna, "The Internet and Social Life," *Annual Review of Psychology* 55 (January 2004): 573–90.

34. Rogers and Lea, "Social Presence," 151.

35. Rogers and Lea, "Social Presence," 152.

36. Martins Evans, "Sex Predator May Have Groomed Over 1,000 School-girls," *The Daily Telegraph* (London), May 19, 2012, 1.

37. Leslie Horn, "7.5 Million Facebook Users Are Below the Minimum Age," *PC Magazine*, accessed May 10, 2011, http://www.pcmag.com/article2/0,2817,2385122,00.asp.

38. David Gefen and Detmar W. Straub, "Gender Differences in the Perception and Use of E-mail." *MIS Quarterly* 21, no. 4 (December 1997): 389–400.

39. Gefen and Straub, "Gender Differences."

40. Narissra Maria Punyanunt-Carter, "An Analysis of College Students' Self-Disclosure Behaviors on the Internet," *College Student Journal* 40, no. 2 (June 2006): 329–31.

41. Sherry Turkle, *Life on the Screen: Identity in the Age of the Internet*, (New York: Simon & Schuster, 1995); Bargh and McKenna, "The Internet and Social Life."

42. Joinson, "Self-Disclosure."

43. Thomas Erickson, "From PIM to GIM: Personal Information Management in Group Contexts," *Communications of the ACM* 49 (January 2006): 74–75.

44. Jon Hemming, "British Spy Chief's Cover Blown on Facebook," *Reuters News Wire* (London), July 4, 2009, http://www.reuters.com/article/2009/07/05/us-britain-mi-idUSTRE56403820090705.

45. Eun-Ju Lee, "Effects of Visual Representation on Social Influence in Computer-Mediated Communication: Experimental Tests of the Social Identity Model of Deindividuation Effects," *Human Communication Research* 30, no. 2 (April 2004): 235.

46. Susannah R. Stern, "Expressions of Identity Online: Prominent Features and Gender Differences in Adolescents' World Wide Web Homepages," *Journal of Broadcasting and Electronic Media* 48, no. 2 (2004): 218–43.

47. Adam Crossley and Darren Langdridge, "Perceived Sources of Happiness: A Network Analysis," *Journal of Happiness Studies* 6, no. 2 (2005): 107–35.

48. Tom Postmes, Russell Spears, and Martin Lea, "The Formation of Group Norms in Computer-Mediated Communication," *Human Communication Research* 26, no. 3 (July 2000): 343.

49. Henry Markovits, Joyce Benenson, and Susan White, "Gender and Priming Differences in Speed of Processing of Information Relating to Social Structure," *Journal of Experimental Social Psychology* 42, no. 5 (September 2006): 663.

50. Joinson, "Self-Disclosure," 178.

51. Tidwell and Walther, "Computer-Mediated Communications," 320.

52. Nicole Ellison, Rebecca Heino and Jennifer Gibbs, "Managing Impressions Online: Self-Presentation Processes in the Online Dating Environment," *Journal of Computer-Mediated Communication* 11, no. 2 (January 2006): 415–41.

53. Joseph B. Walther and Ulla Bunz, "The Rules of Virtual Groups: Trust, Liking, and Performance in Computer-Mediated Communication," *Journal of Communication* 55, no. 4 (December 2005): 828–46.

54. Kristine L. Nowak, "Sex Categorization in Computer-Mediated Communication (CMC): Exploring the Utopian Promise," *Media Psychology* 5, no. 1 (2003): 83–103.

55. Artemio Ramirez Jr., Judee K. Burgoon, "The Effect of Interactivity on Initial Interactions: The Influence of Information Valence and Modality and Information Richness on Computer-Mediated Interaction," *Communication Monographs* 71, no. 4 (2004): 422–47.

56. Katelyn Y. A. McKenna, Amie S. Green, and Marci E. J. Gleason, "Relationship Formation on the Internet: What's the Big Attraction?" *Journal of Social Issues* 58, no. 1 (Spring 2002): 9–31.

57. Ellison, Steinfeld and Lampe, "Benefits of Facebook," 417.

58. Karen M. Douglas and Craig McGarty, "Identifiability and Self-Presentation: Computer-Mediated Communication and Intergroup Interaction," *British Journal of Social Psychology* 40, no. 3 (September 2001): 399–416.

59. Douglas and McGarty, "Identifiability and Self-Presentation," 401.

60. John A. Bargh, Katelyn Y. A. McKenna, and Grainne M. Fitzsimons, "Can You See the Real Me? Activation and Expression of the 'True Self' on the Internet," *Journal of Social Issues* 58, no. 1 (Spring 2002): 33–48.

61. Marjolijn Antheunis, Patti M. Valkenburg, and Jochen Peter, "Getting Acquainted Through Social Network Sites: Testing a Model of Online Uncertainty Reduction and Social Attraction," *Computers in Human Behavior* 26, no.

1 (January 2010): 100–109; Carly Brandenburg, "The Newest Way to Screen Job Applicants: A Social Networker's Nightmare," *Federal Communications Law Journal* 60, no. 3 (2008): 597–626; Kyle Stevens, "Checking Your Face and Space: When Companies Look Outside the Interview," *Campus News,* February 11, 2008, http://uwmpost.com/article/52/19/3039-Checking-your-face-and-space.

62. Mike Wehner, "Facebook Timeline Mandatory Rollout: You Have Seven Days to Scour Your Past," *Tecca,* January 24, 2012, http://news.yahoo.com/blogs/technology-blog/Facebook-timeline-mandatory-rollout-7-days-scour-past-185456598.html.

63. Punyanunt-Carter, "An Analysis of College Students"; Tidwell and Walther, "Computer-Mediated Communication"; Joinson, "Self-Disclosure."

64. Punyanunt-Carter, "An Analysis of College Students."

65. Punyanunt-Carter, "An Analysis of College Students."

66. Tidwell and Walther, "Computer-Mediated Communication."

67. Joinson, "Self-Disclosure."

68. Joinson, "Self-Disclosure."

69. Sabrina Saccoccio, "The Facebook Generation: Changing the Meaning of Privacy," *CBC News,* 2007, accessed June 18, 2012, http://www.cbc.ca/news/background/tech/Facebook-generation.html.

Part 2

Identity in Professional Contexts

Chapter 4

Compressed Crystals: A Metaphor for Mediated Identity Expression

Bree McEwan and Jennifer J. Mease

Compressed Crystals

During a recertification interview, Robert Collins, a Maryland correctional officer, was asked to supply his Facebook user name and password to qualify for recertification.[1] Collins initially submitted, revealing his personal information and social connections to the Maryland Department of Public Safety and Correctional Services. The case gained national attention when Collins filed a lawsuit with the American Civil Liberties Union of Maryland and successfully forced Maryland to suspend its policy.[2] However, this single case and the attention it gained reflect a broader social issue. Citizens are increasingly aware that present and future employers may be accessing information intended for social audiences and using that information in hiring and firing decisions.

Cases like these represent a growing trend in which online identities clash with organizational narratives about professional persona. Although there are multiple ways to have and maintain a personal online presence, the convergence of social network sites (SNS) and organizational control of identity construction is particularly pertinent as millions of people use SNS, such as Facebook, to virtually present themselves.[3]

Furthermore, the conceptions of privacy and identity guiding founders of these websites, in particular Mark Zuckerberg, are at odds with current scholarly research regarding the ethics of communication, organization, and identity.[4] We draw on existing communication scholarship addressing online and offline identity construction to emphasize the nuances of communication processes contributing to the convergence of multiple identities via the Internet and the implications of this convergence for organizational control. We present a theoretical argument regarding how individuals navigate organizational and societal pressures regarding their online performances. Missteps in this navigation may result in negative consequences for the individuals and may be presented in the greater societal narrative as warnings to others. Ultimately, we extend Tracy and Trethewey's crystallized self-metaphor which addresses the ethics of organizational control on individual selves and identities, in order to dissect the processes of mediated identity construction contributing to what we call the "compressed crystallization" of the self.

Performance of Self and Identities

The convergence of multiple identities via the Internet takes on particular significance when considering identities as socially constructed rather than essential, biological or distinct from social influence. Symbolic interactionists and performance scholars have been particularly influential in conceptualizing the self as a collaborative social accomplishment achieved through interactive performances, rather than a static internal construct.[5] Following Mead, symbolic interactionists have posited human beings produce an individual yet socially condoned self through processes of self-contemplation and self-manipulation. This process is guided by expectations communicated through social interactions rendering a social construction of self. According to Mead, the constitution of self is fundamentally social because individuals consider themselves from the imagined perspective of a "generalized other," an amalgamation of many perspectives individuals take on to construct appropriate self-presentations. Thus, symbolic interactionists have not only emphasized the self as fluid and continually adjusted and constructed through interaction, they have also emphasized the importance of an imagined audience integral to the production of self. When one's audience changes, perceived expectations change. As a result, the process and production of the self changes creating various performed facets of self.[6] One may shift between identities as wife, teacher, friend, and student based on the most salient audience in a given moment, presenting various facets of self at different moments in time.

Organized social networks—communities of people—often police identity in terms of appropriateness and consistency. Goffman argues individuals take up specific roles or identities within a social scene in order to maintain and sustain social continuity. One complies with such roles because failure to maintain and sustain social continuity could result in embarrassment for oneself or others. Furthermore, performance scholars emphasized individuals must satisfactorily perform according to social expectations in order to be recognized as having a particular identity.[7] Thus, one is only a "teacher" because one performs the social role of "teacher," a "friend" because one performs as a "friend," and so on. The pressure to take up particular identities at particular moments in time may be prompted by the need to maintain an acknowledged identity or to avoid social embarrassment.

To summarize our approach to identity and self thus far, we suggest individuals take up and perform identities in concert with and in response to the views of others, and it is precisely through this performance people constitute *selves* as socially recognized members of identity groups. Constitutive performances of self change depending on the most salient identities in a given moment. Bodies are significant to the extent they signal membership in identity groups, prompting expectations others have of a person and the consequent expectations the person has of oneself. Additionally, given selves are constituted through the manipulation of one's behaviors, limitations placed on the body's capacity to perform in particular ways effectively limit the identities available to a person. For example, the color of one's skin constrains the ways that one can perform race. The location of the body is also significant to the performance of identities as identity performances are regulated by who sees whom where.[8] For example, one might parent different when other adults are present or perform differently among co-workers if the boss is present.

Thus, constraints on the performance of self are a product of discursively constructed identities (the collaboratively negotiated the roles and expectations) *and* the way those identity constructs are applied to bodies by particular audiences and social relationships in particular social spaces. The latter point is important because, as we will argue, this relationship between bodies, space, and observation in the real world is altered by SNS. Of importance to our argument are three points. First, individuals take up different identities and construct different selves for different audiences. Second, the identities we take up are not a product of free choice. Discursively constructed identity categories, as well as material conditions such as relationships among bodies and spaces, regulate how people take up particular identities in particular moments. Finally, failure to take up a particular identity or to comply with the norms of a particular identity has consequences, including embarrassment, lack of acknowledgement, or exclusion. In short, the self is not a static entity, but rather it is fluid and based in social interaction and human beings regulate their constitutive performance of self according to which social pressures, identities, and audiences are most salient in a given situation.

While our argument focuses on how computer-mediated communication (CMC) influences the process of self-construction, we are especially concerned with ways computer-mediated identity construction intersects with organizational constructions of identity. Among critical organizational scholars, there is a long-standing concern with the "colonization" of everyday practice by discourses of work, including the discourses governing the constitution of selves.[9] Work not only becomes one of the most prominent identities, work can also circumscribe the very possibilities and expectations of "life" identities that individuals perform.[10] It is our argument that SNS such as Facebook have only strengthened the grip of organizational identities on social identities as a whole.

Computer-Mediated Performances of Self

82 percent of all American adults are online. While young people (age eighteen to twenty-nine) are the most saturated cohort in terms of internet use (97 percent of eighteen to twenty-nine year-olds use the Internet), large majorities of Gen Xers (91 percent) and Baby Boomers (77 percent) also use the Internet. On an average day, 48 percent of adult Internet users reported using online social network sites.[11] CMC has altered the possibilities for taking up identities and constructing a self albeit in two very different directions.

Early uses of the Internet pointed toward a release from the constraints of individual bodies on specific identities. Corporeally, bodies signal identities and serve as a point of surveillance regulating continued and consistent performances of self and identity among social audiences.

Early, text-based CMC offered the possibility of escape from the confinement of physically embodied attributes that signal identities and evoke discourses that lend meaning to and constrain identity performances. People could perform mediated identities that seemed separate from their physically embodied and socially constrained selves. Thus, a tension arose with increased social Internet use. People were intrigued by the ability to escape the constraints the body imposed on performances of self; the identity expectations or judgments imposed because of race, sex, or physical ability. However, this freedom also caused social concern that others could engage in socially inappropriate behaviors without the corporeal regulation and oversight of local communities.

Despite CMC's early allure of identity play, the role of the Internet in identity performance has changed. As the Internet moves from anonymous formats to SNS, it has evolved into a medium for maintaining social connections one knows on- *and* offline. The growing convergence between online and offline communities has brought forth a reassertion of the social forces regulating identity offline. Thus, while the Internet once held the promise and/or peril of freeing people from identity discourses and expectations evoked by their physical bodies, the emergence of SNS—where one's performance of various identities are captured, saved, and shared, has tightened the grip of particular identities on our multifaceted identities and productions of self.

Currently, the most popular SNS reporting over 900 million active users is Facebook.[12] Although Facebook was originally designed for a university community, more individuals from all age cohorts are using Facebook and users are aware Facebook is no longer a student only space.[13] Once users leave the college environment, Facebook users often find themselves managing connections from diverse social networks including social relationships, family, and colleagues.[14]

SNS represent a shift away from anonymous forays in online communication to maintaining online connections with people we already know offline.[15] To engage in CMC with people we also know from our offline lives we must perform in ways consistent with our "true" offline self because our social network can more easily identify falsified information. Thus, SNS differ from previous computer-mediated self-construction in that the extent to which individuals can engage in identity experimentation is limited. In addition to altering our understanding of online self and identity, this collapse of offline and SNS identities also demands theoretical attention to the ways everyday constructions of off-

line selves and identities are altered. In order to explore these issues we
will now return to issues of self and identity more broadly.

Crystallized Selves

Identity performances on SNS reach multiple audiences, creating
complications for individuals' ability to select and perform a particular
identity in a particular context. Extending from this, individual selves
may take on many different identities based on multiple situations. Early
identity theorists claimed a "healthy" self was one that thoroughly integrated all of these into one personal identity constituting one coherent
self.[16] In contrast, social and performative theories of self and identity
suggest a fragmented yet cohesive sense of self, based on multiple identities in multiple situations is actually necessary.[17]

Tracy and Trethewey's elaboration on the metaphor of a "crystallized self" offers a heuristic tool for conceptualizing this multifaceted
and fragmented self built from multiple identities. They chose this metaphor of the crystal because:

> Crystals may feel solid, stable, and fixed, but just as crystals have dif-
> fering forms depending on whether they grow rapidly or slowly, under
> constant or fluctuating conditions, or from high variable or remarkably
> uniform fluids or gasses, crystallized selves have different shapes de-
> pending on the various discourse through which they are constructed
> and constrained.[18]

From Tracy and Trethewey's perspective, each individual self has
multiple facets, reflecting different identities. As individuals move
through discursive communities they are able to develop and grow various facets of self. Furthermore, none of these facets of self should be
considered more or less real than others; there is no dichotomy between
real and fake selves. One's professional persona is "real" just as much as
one's home life, one's interactions with friends, etc. Although different
components of one's crystal may be developed or displayed depending
on the community one is interacting with, all facets are significant and
equally real parts of the self.

Compressed Crystals

While Tracy and Trethewey's crystal metaphor relied on separated discursive communities to allow various aspects of the self to flourish, Facebook and other mass-mediated self-presentations merge multiple identities into one presentation of self to multiple audiences. To extend the crystallization metaphor, we suggest the performance of self via social media results in compression. In the computer programming world, data compression is a process used to encode information using fewer bits. Data is compressed by systematically reducing redundancy, but compression also makes data less reliable.[19] We use the metaphor of compression to consider how crystallized identities might be performed, produced, and read online. Extending Tracy and Trethewey's argument that individual selves are ideally comprised of multiple facets reflecting different identities, we argue these multiple facets become compressed online as evidenced by three indicators identified in extant research: (a) the inability of the digital medium to handle complex nuanced expressions of crystallized selves, (b) the desire to perform socially approved selves to a masspersonal audience, and (c) the tendency for one audience to dominate.

Compression can occur in part due to the limitations of the medium to relate nuanced and complex contextually based identities. The designers of SNS make a tradeoff between usability and customizability. Facebook, for example, has a fairly user-friendly model. Users can post pictures, status updates, and messages on other people's walls. However, all of these forms of communication can be somewhat limited. Even before the emergence of SNS, Deetz argued society should remain concerned about the type of "cheap" data CMC substitutes for the richer data gathered in embodied social interaction. For example, Facebook users are more likely to make implicit rather than explicit identity claims.[20] Most identity claims were in the form of pictures. A picture may be worth a thousand words, but photos lack important contexts. In addition, people seem to be purposefully vague when creating the most explicit self-presentation, the "About Me" section.[21] Thus, the structure of the medium can lead to less nuanced, less informative performances of self.

Compression can also occur as individuals struggle to perform socially desirable identities to multiple audiences through one SNS platform. SNS are a type of *masspersonal communication* where individuals "generate mass communication and interpersonal communication simultaneously."[22] For example, individuals might post interpersonal messages on someone's Facebook wall which are then broadcast to the rest of the social network.[23] Social media's masspersonal nature challenges users to create messages to be received by audience members from a variety of social contexts.[24] Instead of worrying about self-presentation with a single other, or segment of similar others, individuals must perform their interpersonal messages and identity markers to multiple segments of their social network.

Zhao, Grasmuck, and Martin found evidence participants attempt to showcase a socially desirable identity on Facebook.[25] Users amplified group identification cues and compressed negative aspects of identity such as pessimistic messages. Of the number of students who identified with a particular religion in interviews, far fewer identified with that religion on Facebook. Similarly, some students who identified during interviews as bisexual or gay did not do so in their Facebook profile, whereas participants openly discussed heterosexual behavior. These findings provide evidence individuals may seek to perform only what they consider to be socially desirable identities. However, achieving a desirable identity may be difficult when messages sent through SNS reach multiple audiences with differing social norms. Thus, in addition to providing less nuanced expressions of self, evidence suggests fewer facets of self are being performed.

Individuals privilege one audience or identity over another. As people perform fewer and less nuanced facets of self on SNS, they do so by privileging particular audiences in their performative choices. Instead of encouraging the exploration of various facets of self via multiple identities, use of SNS leads individuals to make strategic choices regarding which identities they privilege in their performance. There are SNS designed for particular types of messages for segmented audiences, theoretically allowing for each SNS to build one facet of self. For example, LinkedIn or Academia.edu are focused on professional contacts. However, on the largest and most popular SNS, Facebook, people often add individuals from a variety of social contexts, including friends, family, co-workers, subordinates, supervisors, and co-community members.[26] By integrating one's social network into one undifferentiated audience, one collapses social contexts. boyd argued, "In networked publics, contexts often collide such that the performer is unaware of audiences from different contexts, magnifying the awkwardness and making adjustments impossible."[27] As SNS, and in particular Facebook, become increasing integrated into processes of self-constitution, people may not always be aware of how their social contexts have collapsed. Thus, the theoretical concerns of compressed crystals is not only the decreased number and nuance of identities and facets of self, but also what audience is becoming the increasingly dominant influence on processes of self-contemplation guiding the constitutive performance of the self online. While this could be different audiences for different people, we are particularly concerned with the confluence of compressed crystals with the corporate colonization of everyday life.

Becoming Organizationally Compressed Crystals

Existing research, social narratives, and recent cases in popular media, suggest organizations, in particular workplaces, are becoming one of, if not *the*, dominant force in the regulation of self-presentation online. College students are aware future employers may be viewing their Facebook profile.[28] As users enter the workforce they become even more concerned with self-representations employers may view negatively. DiMicco and Millen found the more work-related connections a Facebook user had in their friend list the less likely users were to provide personal information, join political, religious, or sexual orientation organizations and groups.[29] Individuals in their interview study spoke of needing to "clean" or "sanitize" their Facebook identity by removing information that might be viewed negatively by employers.

Using the language of compressed crystals to describe these findings, we argue although individuals might ideally experience the self in a multifaceted manner, online identity expressions are more likely to be compressions of one's crystallized identity. This compression likely occurs due to struggles to display socially desirable identities to multiple audiences. Due to the limitations of social media platforms, in particular the difficulty of editing identity performances for specific audiences, individuals may find themselves privileging one audience or another. Although, at times, the privileged audience may be the personal, social audience, over time individuals with "successful" identity expressions are those who meet the expectations of most conservative and powerful discourse communities, including employers, governments, and other identity constraining entities.

Recently there have been several highly publicized cases of individuals who faced organizational consequences as multiple facets of their crystallized self were presented and consequently compressed on Facebook. We offer four examples of compressed crystals. These examples function in two ways. For the purpose of our argument, they offer exemplars of the consequences of compressed crystals in everyday life. These stories are of course anecdotal and may not reflect generalizable social media experiences. However, these media examples are particularly potent because they function as an implicit threat. People comply with the expectations of an audience not just because they *are* being watched, but because they *might be* watched at any particular moment.[30] Thus, the media demonstrates that their Facebook messages *might be* watched, encouraging people to compress their crystallized identities even if there is little actual threat.

Compressed Crystal Exemplars

Gloria Gadsden, a professor at East Stroudsburg University posted some "vents" on her Facebook page including, "Does anyone know where I can find a very discrete hitman? Yes, it's that kind of day," and "had a good day today, DIDN'T want to kill even one student. :-) Now Friday was a different story."[31] Gadsen had intended these messages to be humorous exchanges with her friends. However, due to Facebook's changing privacy settings, they became available to everyone, including East Stroudsburg students. Students reported Gadsden's posts to university officials, which resulted in her suspension. Dr. Gadsden's performance of self as professor may have been an acceptable performance among an audience of other professors or friends. However, it was clearly not an acceptable performance of professor among a student audience.

In contrast to Gadsen's case, in which one identity was subject to scrutiny by multiple audiences, other examples demonstrate how multiple identities are compressed online. Ashley Payne, a former high school teacher for the Barrow County school district in North Georgia, had pictures posted on Facebook of her holding alcohol while on a European vacation, including one of her holding up a full glass of Guinness while visiting the Guinness brewery. Payne had made her status private and had not friended any students. However, she had friended other colleagues at Appalachee High School and the photos found their way to the principal's office. Payne was summarily dismissed even though her pictures were not even related to her teaching identity.[32] In a similar case, Washington State Patrol Cadet Math Blahut was forced to resign due to complaints about his Facebook page.[33] Blahut had displayed pictures in which he was dressed in uniform, posed with his police cruiser, as well as pictures in which he was drinking beer and partying. It is likely the parent of one of his Facebook friends reported Blahut to his superiors. In both of these cases, presenting an identity other than the sanctioned organizational identity outside of the organization resulted in dismissal from the workplace.

Our final example is Glen Busch, who was the director of the Chicago Chapter of Coats for Kids since 2005.[34] Busch was dismissed from the organization after commenting on Facebook about the shooting of Arizona Representative Gabrielle Giffords. Busch's remarks were made in a comment thread where Busch's Facebook friends debated possible motives of the shooter. In the comment thread Busch argued, "This was not a political thing, it was a psychotic thing. This kid was nuts! Now lets [sic] drop the ink wars and pray for the families. Maybe apologize in public just like your accusations as well? I'm just saying."

Paul Darby, president of the national chapter of Coats for Kids, fired Busch stating:

> As a public non-profit foundation, it is essential that we not become involved in public controversy, either in support or in opposition of an issue or cause. You have every right to make whatever comments that you wish as a citizen. We support that right as Americans. Unfortunately, your name is clearly associated with the Coats for Kids Foundation and the activities by the Foundation in Chicago.

We find this example particularly powerful, because it suggests the organization superficially supports the rights of an individual to speak as a citizen, but simultaneously denies Busch that identity and the rights associated with it. It seemingly endorses a crystallized self, in which citizen and organizational director are different facets, but denies the right of Busch to perform the identity of citizen online.

The nuances of each of these cases both illuminate and are illuminated by the theoretical metaphor of compressed crystallized selves in SNS identity expression. To begin, they show how these individuals' self-presentations are read without nuance or context. Multifaceted selves are compressed when a single piece of text or image became an indicator for the whole self, as each person's complete self was represented as being "disgruntled," "a drinker," "a partier," and "political." Second, the structure of the SNS made it difficult to ensure messages were received only by their intended audience, resulting in organizational consequences for presenting multiple facets of self online. This included both the presentation of multiple identities (teacher/drinker, cop/partier, citizen/organizational director) as well as the ideal or acceptable performance of a single identity (professor as judged by students/friend and peers). Once the unintended audiences of students, co-workers, bosses, and community members were made privy to the status updates and pictures posted by Gadsden, Payne, Blahut, and Busch, it became impossible for them to maintain a multifaceted crystallized self.

Without nuanced information and segmented audiences, both of which are lost in online compression, they could not be socially constituted as complicated multifaceted selves online. They could not be both a professor and a frustrated teacher and a vacation drinker, a police cadet and a man enjoying a night on the town, a charity worker and an individual with an opinion about a national news story. In the case of Gadsden, Payne, and Blahut the problem was while their visual and textual messages were intended for one audience for whom their performance of self may have been appropriate, the messages were deemed inappropriate for other segments of their social audience exposed to the messages. While one might simplify this to an individualized issue of managing audiences, the Glen Busch example emphasizes the broader implications of the demand to manage multiple audiences as it impacts the possibility of a crystallized self. In Busch's case we see how one particular audience, the workplace audience, regulates the potential identities individuals can take on. Rather than disciplining seemingly deviant behaviors, the national director acknowledges the behaviors are appropriate given a citizen identity, but denies Busch access to that identity. Busch may have intended his Facebook comments to be those of a private citizen, which the supervisor acknowledges would be appropriate, but because of his mere association with the organization, his claim to the identity of private citizen is denied.

Implicit Threats

Returning to the importance of these examples as public news stories, we must also take into consideration the broader social implication in which this disciplinary action serves as a warning to others. Although it might be ideal to constitute a crystallized self, these news stories show people who do not perform appropriately compressed selves online may be subjected to organizational and societal repercussions. The warning is clear: individuals who do not properly adjust to the compressed construction of self, by removing undesired identities and facets of self, face potential disciplinary actions in the workplace. When we consider that workplaces are crucial environments in which one's very livelihood rests upon meeting organizational standards the grip of this threat tightens. In the examples above it is quite likely that being a "professor," a "teacher," a "police officer," and a "charity director" were important identities to these individuals' selves. However, these workplace identities gain dominance over other identities due to the capacity of organizations to discipline and control desirable identity performances, consequently shaping individuals' self-contemplation and performative constitutions of self. As a result individuals may find themselves playing to the most salient, powerful, and threatening audience in their online performance of self. We do not mean to dismiss the possibility that other audiences such as family, volunteer groups, friends, may also provide various and significant constraints on what is an appropriate self. However, given the corporate colonization of identities and everyday lives reflected in these news stories, we find the enhanced control of workplaces on compressed crystallized identities particularly problematic. This concern is further exacerbated as the implications of compressed of crystallized identities bleed out into everyday embodied life.

Compression Bleed

As the previous stories indicate, online performances of self can significantly impact our physically embodied lives. We believe the real/offline-fake/online dichotomy collapses as compression of virtual selves bleeds into offline performances of selves. Online identities are no less real (or fake) than corporeal identity presentation. We attribute this collapse, in part, to problems of boundary coordination delineating who has ownership, as well as access to information that communicatively constructs identities. As we will explain, this impacts how online presentations of self can move to offline interactions, and how offline performances of self can find their way online.

Petronio argued when individuals share private information the receivers become co-owners of that information.[35] In order for information
to be appropriately managed, privacy boundaries must be coordinated.
Boundary turbulence occurs when people who co-own information do
not agree upon the appropriate release of said information.

In an SNS, boundary turbulence can occur in at least two ways. One,
individuals might not explicitly coordinate with each other about what
might be shared from their profile. Even if individuals do set high privacy settings, others who are privy to their information may share it with
unintended offline audiences, as we saw in the cases of Ashley Payne
and Math Blahut. Furthermore, these unintended audiences may lack the
appropriate context to interpret the leaked performances of self, which is
also not available due to compression. As boyd argues:

> Internet technologies follow a long line of other innovations in this ar-
> ea. What is captured and recorded are the bytes that are created and ex-
> changed across the network. Many systems make bits persistent by de-
> fault and, thus, the text that one produces become persistent. Yet, do
> people interpret the content in the same way as they did when it was
> first produced? This is quite unlikely. The text and multimedia may be
> persistent, but what sticks around may lose its essence when consumed
> outside of the context in which it was created.[36]

Thus, the persistence of online presentations of self further enhances the
stripping of nuance and context that marks the compression of online
identities, making it particularly problematic when information moves
from online presentations of self into embodied organizational contexts.

This brings us to a second boundary coordination issue: members of
an individual's social network can comment on another's wall, post information about, and tag them in photos. Consequently, a persistent Facebook self is created both by what the individual shares as well as what
others share about the individual.[37] Profile owners cannot fully control
the information others share about them but they are certainly judged by
these messages.[38] In fact, people may be more likely to believe Facebook
profile information posted by others than information posted by the profile owner.[39]

This second boundary coordination issue may be particularly problematic. In the case of the first boundary coordination issue, we have assumed the individual remains in control of information posted online.
However, in the case of the second boundary coordination issue, individ-

uals have little if any control over the messages constituting online selves. Thus, if one were dealing with only the first boundary issue, they could cope with the implications of a compressed crystallized identity by highly regulating which aspects of identity they post online. However, when faced with the second boundary issue, the only way to fully cope with implications of a compressed crystallized identity is live one's *entire life* with the understanding any performance of self could end up online. Otherwise stated, if one cannot control what others post about their private lives yet needs to maintain an online self catering to a particular narrative, then one might need to be more careful about the activities they engage in offline so that references and visual evidence of non-preferred activities do not appear online. Consequently, individuals may need to compress aspects of their crystallized selves in everyday lives in order to meet the identity criteria of the most dominant audience in their social networks.

The bleeding together of on- and offline selves should not be taken lightly. Online behaviors have a durability and transferability allowing them to be shared with offline audiences for whom they were not intended. This only furthers the compression fostered by computer-mediated identity construction, as even individuals who do their best to control their online audiences find their online behaviors have been shared beyond their intent. Furthermore, offline behaviors can be captured and shared online by others. This means that not only online behaviors, but all behaviors, are potentially subject to the dominance of workplace on compressed crystallized identities. No matter where a person is, or what they are doing, they must be mindful of all the potential audiences for whom they are potentially performing.

A Virtual Panopticon

Given the reach of societal scrutiny, we would be remiss to conclude without noting that in joining SNS, we have signed ourselves into a virtual panopticon.[40] Drawing on Jeremy Betham's work, Foucault describes a physical prison known as the panopticon wherein the goal was to "induce in the inmate a state of conscious and permanent visibility that assures the automatic functioning of power."[41] This physical prison was arranged in such a way prisoners could potentially be under surveillance at any time, yet prisoners would never know if they were under surveillance at any given moment. In this design, it is precisely the threat—the possibility they could be watched at any given time—that causes prisoners to internalize the watchful eyes of the warden inducing compliance and reducing the possibilities of resistance or rebellion. Foucault expands from this idea of a physical panopticon to describe what he calls a "disciplinary society" a society in which we move from space to space—schools, factories, hospital, organizations—constantly subjected to the norms and evaluations of various institutions.

SNS serve a similar function as this physical panopticon, but they extend the threat of visibility across time and space. Surveillance is no longer bound to particular institutions and spaces, it spans across them. This is particularly foreboding given the compressed crystallization of identities, in which one facet of self, one institution of surveillance and its corollary norms and expectations, takes precedence over others. Drawing on Althusser, it seems SNS are a contemporary tool of the ideological state apparatuses (ISA) the function of which is to guarantee a sufficient workforce.[42] According to Althusser, ISA function via repression and discipline to constitute individuals socialized to behave in a manner considered appropriate and useful according to the dominant ideology. As we have demonstrated, SNS can function as an ideological tool extending capitalist ideology, as manifested in the norms of the workplace or the corporation, into all aspects of our daily lives.

As online audiences collapse and the online offline dichotomy collapses as well, individuals have increasingly limited capacity to control, or even discern, the audience or audiences who may scrutinize their performance of self in the future. For Foucault, power of the panoptic gaze in a disciplinary society derives from the possibility anyone could potentially be the source of evaluative judgment:

> It does not matter who exercises power. Any individual, taken almost at random, can operate the machine: in absence of the director, his family, his friends, his visitors, even his servants. Similarly, it does not matter what motive animates him: the curiosity of the indiscreet, the malice of a child, the thirst for knowledge of a philosopher who wishes to visit the museum of human nature, or the perversity of those who take pleasure in spying and punishing. . . . The Panopticon is a marvelous machine which, whatever use one may wish to put it to, produces homogenous effects of power.[43]

The threat of any individual exercising the panoptic gaze presents a sizable threat only strengthened through the use of SNS, where the gaze of "friends, family, and visitors" can be appropriated by organizations without consideration of nuance or context. Furthermore, the media attention granted to such appropriations only further the threatening grip of organizations as the most powerful and dominant audience to which we must conform. When the ISA, in the form of workplaces, gain access to the opportune gaze enabled by computer-mediated identity representation, individuals must strive to perform a sanitized version of self acceptable to any viewer, that is, if we cannot compartmentalize our identity performances, we must compress.

Consequently, compression is enforced via the virtual panopticon. Individuals engage in compression as a strategy for coping with the constraining view of the multiple audiences of the virtual panopticon. However, this coping strategy also serves to further reinforce the narrative structure of the panopticon. The more individuals compress virtual identity performances the more it is seen as normative to do so. Deetz argued we should be particularly wary of the ways we adapt to new technologies may benefit the powerful.[44] In this case, SNS and other forms of online identity expression may provide ways ISA can confirm members are adhering to their ideological norms of appropriateness. Furthermore, the more we seek to compress identities by repressing performances of self that do not fit with societal, organizational, and ultimately ideological narratives, the more we reify the idea these selves are not conducive to society or organization. Unfortunately, as a society we seem to be complying with the mandates of the prison while rarely questioning the source of these mandates, and who exactly this virtual panopticon serves. As Deetz so poignantly stated almost twenty years ago: "Where is the forum for decisions of such public consequence?"[45]

Conclusion

In this chapter, we hope to have opened one such forum for the discussion of the costs and benefits of participating in SNS, especially those that conflate multiple audiences. As we have demonstrated, there is an existing understanding that Facebook is intended to be a *social* network of friends, but there is also a growing understanding one should take care the self one performs on SNS satisfies organizational and workplace expectations. As a result, we have demonstrated both theoretically and using examples from the media the pressure to hide or repress nonpreferred identities or aspects of self has leaked beyond the Internet and outside the work environment to influence even the most typical actions of everyday life. The reach of surveillance enabled by SNS is particularly problematic given a performative notion of self, in which the gaze of the Internet audience is internalized into self-constituting processes.

Although scholars such as Tracy and Trethewey argue for a transformative model of self that incorporates multiple identities, in which individuals are multifaceted, the underlying moral reflected in the examples we have analyzed is far closer to Zuckerberg's view of identity—that the time for having multiple selves in multiple places is over.[46] Although a charitable view may perceive that Zuckerberg considers this a social good, communication on a social network platfom exists within and is shaped by existing social pressures including corporate colonization.

Tracy and Trethewey's metaphor of the crystal arises from a particularly utopian view. One where individuals can discuss "doing home" and "nurturing" as legitimate choices. In sharp contrast, the metaphor of compression and compressions' function within a virtual panopticon is a dystopian view where individuals are under constant threat of surveillance and must, at the very least, give lip service to the dominant and corporate discourses if not actively strive to constrain identity performances to meet these narratives. The compression of identities makes the performance of a crystallized self problematic because it strips nuance, complexity, and context from our performance of self, it suppresses less than ideal characteristics of identities, and ensures that individuals perform according to expectations of the most dominant and powerful audience. Individuals respond by strategically leaving out information regarding various facets of their selves—compressing their crystallized identity—both online and potentially offline.

Notes

1. Aaron Davis, "Maryland Corrections Department Suspends Facebook Policy for Prospective Hires," *Washington Post,* February 2, 2011, accessed March 3, 2011, http://www.washingtonpost.com/wp-dyn/content/article/2011/02/22/AR2011022207486.html.

2. American Civil Liberties Union of Maryland, "Testimony for the Senate Finance Committee, SB 971 - Labor and Employment – User Name and Password Privacy Protection," 2011, accessed February 10, 2011, http://www.aclu-md.org/aLegislative/2011/SB971_social_media.pdf.

3. Zizi Papacharissi, "A Networked Self," in *A Networked Self: Identity, Community, and Culture on Social Network Sites,* ed. Zizi Papacharissi (New York: Routledge, 2011), 304–17.

4. Daniel Kirkpatrick, *The Facebook Effect: The Inside Story of the Company That Is Connecting the World* (New York: Simon & Schuster, 2010), 199; Sarah Jane Tracy and Angela Trethewey, "Fracturing the Real-Self-Fake-Self Dichotomy: Moving Toward Crystallized Organizational Identities." *Communication Theory* 15, no. 2 (May 2005): 168–95.

5. Herbert Blumer, *Symbolic Interactionism: Perspective and Method* (Englewood Cliffs, NJ: Prentice Hall, 1969); George Herbert Mead, *Mind, Self, and Society* (Chicago: University of Chicago, Press, 1934); Erving Goffman, *The Presentation of Self in Everyday Life* (New York: Doubleday, 1959); Judith Butler "Performative Acts and Gender Constitution: An Essay in Phenomenology and Feminist Theory," in *The Performance Studies Reader,* 2nd ed. Henry Bial (New York: Routledge, 2007), 187–99.

6. Tracy and Trethewey, "Crystallized Organizational Identities," 186.

7. Butler, "Performative Acts."

8. Michel Foucault, *Discipline and Punish: The Birth of a Prison* (New York: Random House, 1975), 195–230.

9. Stanley A. Deetz, *Democracy in an Age of Corporate Colonization: Developments in Communication and the Politics of Everyday Life* (Albany, NY: State University of New York Press, 1992).

10. Al Gini, *My Job, My Self: Work and the Creation of the Modern Individual* (New York: Routledge, 2000), 6.

11. Pew Internet and American Life Project, "Trend Data (Adults)," 2012, accessed June 27, 2012, http://www.pewInternet.org/Trend-Data-(Adults)/Online-Activities-Daily.aspx.

12. Facebook, "Key Facts," *Newsroom,* 2012, accessed June 27, 2012, http://newsroom.fb.com/content/default.aspx?NewsAreaId=22.

13. Kirkpatrick, *Facebook Effect,* 19–41; Cliff Lampe, Nicole B. Ellison, and Charles Steinfield, "Change in Use and Perception of Facebook" (paper presented at a meeting of the ACM conference on Computer Supported Cooperative Work, San Diego, CA, November 2008), 721–30; Lee Rainie, Kristen Purcell, and Aaron Smith, "The Social Side of the Internet," *Pew Internet and American Life Project,* 2011, accessed February 20, 2011, http://pewinternet.org/Reports/2011/The-Social-Side-of-the-Internet.aspx.

14. Joan Morris DiMicco and David R Millen, "Identity Management: Multiple Presentations of Self in Facebook." In *Proceedings of the 2007 Inter-*

national ACM Conference on Supporting Group Work (New York: ACM, 2007), 383–86.

15. Nicole B. Ellison, Charles Steinfield, and Cliff Lampe, "The Benefits of Facebook 'Friends': Social Capital and College Students' Use of Online Social Network Sites," *Journal of Computer-Mediated Communication* 12, no. 4 (July 2007): 1143–68; Adam N Joinson, "Looking At, Looking Up or Keeping Up with People?: Motives and Uses of Facebook." In *Proceedings of the SIGCHI Conferene on Human Factors in Computing Systems* (New York: ACM, 2008), 1027–36; Lampe, Ellison, and Steinfield, "Change in Use," 724–25.

16. Dorothy Holland, William Lachicotte Jr., Debra Skinner, and Carole Cain, *Identity and Agency in Cultural Worlds* (Cambridge, MA: Harvard University Press, 1998).

17. Tracy and Trethewey, "Crystallized Organizational Identities," 186–89.

18. Tracy and Trethewey, "Crystallized Organizational Identities," 186.

19. David Saloman, *A Concise Introduction to Data Compression* (London: Springer-Verlag, 2008), 5–6.

20. Deetz, *Democracy, Corporate Colonization*, 143; Shanyang Zhao, Sherri Grasmuck, and Jason Martin, "Identity Construction on Facebook: Digital Empowerment in Anchored Relationships," *Computers in Human Behavior* 24, no. 5 (September 2008): 1816–36.

21. Zhao, Grasmuck and Marin, "Identity Construction," 1824–26; Cliff Lampe, Nicole B. Ellison, and Charles Steinfield "A Familiar Face(book): Profile Elements as Signals in an Online Social Network." In *Proceedings of the 2007 ACM Conference on Human Factors in Computing* (New York: ACM, 2007), 435–44.

22. Patrick B. O'Sullivan, "Masspersonal Communication: Rethinking the Mass-Interpersonal Divide" (paper presented at a meeting of the International Communication Association, New York, May 2005), 2.

23. Joseph B. Walther, Caleb Carr, Sejung Choi, David DeAndrea, Stephanie Tom Tong, and Brandon Van Der Heide, "Interaction of Interpersonal, Peer, and Media Influence Sources Online: A Research Agenda for Technology Convergence," in *A Networked Self: Identity, Community, and Culture on Social Network Sites*, ed. Zizi Papacharissi (New York: Routledge, 2011), 17–38.

24. danah boyd, "Social Network Sites as Networked Publics," in *A Networked Self: Identity, Community, and Culture on Social Network Sites,* ed. Zizi Papacharissi (New York: Routledge, 2011), 17–38.

25. Zhao, Grasmuck and Martin, "Identity Construction," 1825.

26. boyd, "Social Network Sites," 50–51; DiMicco and Millen, "Identity Management," 383–86.

27. boyd, "Social Network Sites," 50.

28. Lampe, Ellison and Steinfield, "Change in Use," 725.

29. DiMicco and Millen, "Identity Management" 385.

30. Foucault, "Discipline and Punish," 201–2.

31. Jack Stripling, "Not So Private Professors," *Inside Higher Ed,* March 2, 2010, accessed October 3, 2010, http://www.insidehighered.com/ news/2010/03/02/facebook.

32. WSBTV.com, "Former Teacher Sues for Being Fired for Facebook Pics," 2009, accessed October 3, 2010, http://www.wsbtv.com/news/news/ former-teacher-sues-for-being-fired-for-facebook-p/nFCzs/.

33. Paula Horton "Two Washington Officers Fired over Facebook Indiscretions," *The Tri-City Herald*, 2009, accessed February 2, 2011, http://www.policeone.com/police-technology/articles/1776582-Two-Wash-officers-fired-over-Facebook-indiscretions/.

34. Amy Rutledge, "Charity Worker Fired over Facebook Comments," *WGN News*, 2011, accessed February 2, 2011, www.wgntv.com/news/wgntv-man-fired-over-facebook-jan12,0,7228739.story.

35. Sandra Petronio, *Boundaries of Privacy: Dialectics of Disclosure* (Albany: State University of New York Press, 2002), 28–35.

36. boyd, "Networked Publics," 47.

37. Emily Christofides, Amy Muise, and Serge Desmarais, "Information Disclosure and Control on Facebook: Are They Two Sides of the Same Coin or Two Different Processes?" *Cyberpsychology and Behavior* 12, no 3. (June 2009): 341–45.

38. Joseph B. Walther, Brandon Van Der Heide, Sang-Yeon Kim, David Westerman, and Stephanie Tom Tong, "The Role of Friends' Appearance and Behavior on Evaluations of Individuals on Facebook: Are We Known by the Company We Keep?" *Human Communication Research* 34, no 1. (January 2008): 28–49.

39. Joseph B. Walther, Brandon Van Der Heide, Lauren M. Hamel, and Hillary C. Shulman, "Self-Generated Versus Other-Generated Statements and Impressions in Computer-Mediated Communication: A Test of Warranting Theory Using Facebook," *Communication Resource* 36, no. 2 (April 2009): 229–53.

40. Foucault, "Discipline and Punish."

41. Foucault, "Discipline and Punish," 201.

42. Louis Althusser, "Ideology and Ideological State Apparatuses: Notes Towards an Investigation," in *Lenin and Philosophy and Other Essays: Louis Althusser,* trans. Ben Brewster (New York: Monthly Review Press, 1971), 85–126.

43. Foucault, "Discipline and Punish," 202.

44. Deetz, *Democracy, Corporate Colonization,* 143.

45. Deetz, *Democracy, Corporate Colonization,* 144.

46. Tracy and Trethewey, "Crystallized Organizational Identities," 186–89; Kirkpatrick, *The Facebook Effect,* 199.

Chapter 5

Branding as Social Discourse: Identity Construction Using Online Social and Professional Networking Sites

Corey Jay Liberman

If you have ever attempted to offer a definition of communication to any-one outside of academia, it is quite likely that doing so was difficult. On the one hand, it is a difficult feat because it encompasses so much. For example, communication can be studied and understood from a source-centered perspective, where such things as source credibility, knowledge, elocution, and social influence become important. Communication, how-ever, can also be studied and understood from a receiver-centered perspective, where such things as perception, interpretation, motivation, and capability become important. Communication can also be studied from a process-centered perspective, where such things as language, media, and nonverbal codes become important. On the other hand, it is a difficult feat because the study of communication transcends many other fields and disciplines. For example, Rogers claims that Wilbur Schramm, a journalist by training, was the founder and "father" of the formal study of communication.[1] Interestingly, however, Schramm's college degrees are in history, political science, American civilization, and English literature. As Rogers points out, other famous and foundational communication scholars were not much different; Harold Lasswell was a political scientist, Paul Lazarsfeld was a sociologist, Kurt Lewin was a psychologist, and Claude Shannon was a mathematician.[2] Perhaps Schramm said it best when he argued that ". . .the difficulty in summing up a field like human communication is that it has no land that is exclusively its own."[3] That is, communication is, at once, a field that examines the political, social, and psychological variables embedded in the interaction and dialogic processes.

The purpose of this chapter is to analyze an area of communication inquiry that transcends the political, social, and psychological worlds, and which has received much attention in these fields' literatures for at least the past six decades: the social construction of identity. Taking source-centered, receiver-centered, and process-centered perspectives into consideration, the construction of identity using two online social networking sites (Facebook and LinkedIn) will be examined, attempting to uncover the processes at work when social actors "become" themselves, and to uncover the individual branding that occurs while doing so. Gonzales and Hancock argue that ". . .instead of treating the Internet solely as an outlet for social interaction, the Internet also should be considered as an outlet for self-construction."[4] This chapter will highlight the social processes embedded in this social engagement.

The Study of Identity

There is perhaps no better place to start than using Goffman's text, *The Presentation of Self in Everyday Life*, as one receives a very powerful and significant discussion about the role of communication in the social construction of identity. According to Goffman, social actors have both agency and jurisdiction over the selves that they present in the face of others.[5] For example, dress and adornment are key variables that differentiate people based on profession, social status, and even religion. As another example, one's verbiage and vernacular at once define, and are defined by, a certain sense of self. That is, personal characteristics such as cordial, intelligent, and lackluster emerge based on the way that one communicatively presents, or constructs, herself. Both of these examples indicate that self is, at least partially, under one's control. Based on the opening paragraph of this chapter, this discussion emerges from a source-centered perspective.

According to Goffman, however, there is also a salient receiver-centered perspective that must not be avoided, nor devalued.[6] In his discussion about identity being analogous with dramatic performances, such as going to a theatrical event, Goffman argues that ". . .when an individual plays a part he implicitly requests his observers to take seriously the impression that is fostered before them."[7] In other words, those with whom one interacts must come to accept his sense of personhood. This is not unlike the suspension of disbelief about which Coleridge speaks, which argues that when stories are told, literary or otherwise, audience members must temporarily suspend notions of reality, such that the story being told comes to represent something other than fiction and imagination.[8] This social process requires that others allow us to become the selves that we desire, taking into consideration Eadie's notions of action (what we do to others) and interaction (what we do with others), both of which are embedded in discursive practices.[9] In the end, the study of identity is very much about the amalgamation of one's selves and the story that accompanies their social construction. Social actors put on different faces, at different times, with different audiences, telling different stories, using different language, resulting in (likely) different effects.

Not long after Goffman's text became a foundational reading for scholars and students of identity, Berger and Luckmann's *The Social Construction of Reality* was published.[10] Their thesis was very much aligned with Goffman's, insofar as they argued that realities do not exist outside of interaction. Rather, they are created through it. In one particular part of their book, Berger and Luckmann claim that "on the one hand, man is a body . . . [and] on the other hand, man has a body."[11] Although this can be interpreted in a multitude of different ways, the basic argument is that there is a semantic difference between what one *is* and what one *has*. Using the example of genetics, Berger and Luckmann explain that gender is something that one is, whereas gendered emotions are things that one has: has, here, being synonymous with Goffman's idea of the social construction of self. That is, although one might be a biological male, he has the ability to communicate alter-gendered emotions such as empathy, jealousy, and sympathy, validating Cerulo's concerns about the gender-sex link.[12] Thus, given this example, what one *is* can be conceived of as biologically determined, whereas what one *has* can be conceived of as a social construction.

It is clear that the social constructivist paradigm, from which Erving Goffman, Peter Berger, and Thomas Luckman emanate, is alive and well, explaining the relationship among human experience, social encounters, and the creation of identity. However, as we find ourselves situated in a social world that has few (if any) boundaries, and where the great majority of social encounters occur not through FtF dialogue, but through mediated forms, what becomes of the identities that are both created and shared? Are social actors becoming more narcissistic, as Bergman, Fearrington, Davenport, and Bergman contend, or have they just been afforded new technologies to manifest such narcissism?[13] Are social actors self-disclosing more about themselves, as Joinson argues, or have new technologies merely simplified such self-disclosure practices?[14] Have we reverted back to the romanticist view of the self, one that Gergen argues is perhaps an antiquity, or have we potentially moved beyond the postmodern view?[15] Before providing answers to these queries, it is first important to understand how the mass utilization of electronic communication media has reshaped how one thinks about identity construction and the effects of it.

The Social Construction of Identity in Online Environments

The social construction of online identities is certainly not new. For example, Turkle's pioneering text about the role of self in Multi User Dungeons has sparked nearly two decades of research on the link between computer-mediated communication environments and online personas.[16] As Turkle's results indicate, gamers in Multi User Dungeons found the ability to become whoever they wanted, regarding such things as name, gender, hobbies, interests, and personal characteristics, to be the predominant rationale for engaging in online role-playing activities. That is, it was not necessarily the game that intrigued online participants, but rather the forms of identity that were created and shared among gamers. The importance of the issues that were brought to the surface as a result of this work was highlighted by Cerulo when she claims that ". . .Turkle's work forces us to question any perspective that places virtual experience second to the concrete."[17] In other words, not only is the social construction of identity in online environments as important for communication scholarship as the social construction of identity in collocated, FtF environments, but that perhaps it is even more crucial and salient. Since Turkle's publication, identity scholarship focusing on other mediated forums has emerged, including Miller and Arnold's study of web pages, Whitty's study of online chat rooms, Segerstad and Ljungstrand's study of instant messenger, and Huffaker's study of online blogs, all of which have become springboards for the study of self in computer-mediated environments.[18]

Over the past five years, two social networking sites in particular have become so embedded in the everyday lives of individuals that their importance mustn't be overlooked, nor devalued. These two social networking sites, which rank, annually, in the top five regarding overall membership and monthly visits, are Facebook and LinkedIn. Created in 2004, Facebook is an online social networking tool that provides a unique outlet for relational construction and relational maintenance. Upon membership, individuals are afforded the opportunity to electronically network with others, oftentimes based on such independent variables as geographic location, special interests, education, and employment practices. LinkedIn, which was originally launched in 2003, is very similar to Facebook, though it is usually referred to as a professional, rather than social, networking platform. The major impetus for becoming a member of the LinkedIn community is to join a business network, rife with opportunities for sharing information about employment and staying connected to other business professionals. Although Facebook and LinkedIn were originally created for different reasons (the former for social relationships and the latter for professional relationships), and certainly have differences regarding membership, impetus for membership, and member privileges, both share one extremely important characteristic: the need for self-branding. The remainder of this chapter will focus on the branding processes embedded in both online networking sites, highlighting both the similarities and differences regarding the social construction of users' identities.

The Process of Branding

In its simplest form, the term branding, which emanates from the business world, refers to the process wherein a company constructs its own sense of self, communicating such an identity to existing and potential stakeholders (i.e., customers, investors, advertisers). As Juntunen, Saraniemi, Halttu, and Tahtinen explain, the branding process involves both defining and executing an organization's "corporate personality."[19] For example, McDonald's, a leading fast-food chain for the past five decades, has branded itself based on quickness, simplicity, affordability, menu options, and its family environment. By doing so, McDonald's has branded itself and has actively shaped its identity in the minds of the consumer public. In essence, organizational branding accomplishes two goals at once. First, as just mentioned, it allows a certain sense of self to emerge. If you enter a drug store with the purpose of purchasing an ibuprofen pill, you will likely be faced with many (depending, of course, on the size of the store) different options. You will notice that some are capsules and some are tablets; some are quick-acting and some are long-lasting; some will indicate a maximum dosage of six capsules/tablets in a twenty-four-hour period and some will indicate a maximum dosage of eight. What is each ibuprofen company doing? Each is branding itself, so as to construct its own identity. At the same time, however, it accomplishes a second, related goal: differentiation. Given the foregoing example, an ibuprofen company might differentiate itself based on price, quality, quantity, goals, chemical makeup, and dosage. The consumer wanting the least expensive product will likely purchase the ibuprofen that has differentiated itself based on low cost, whereas the consumer wanting the best product, regardless of cost or chemical makeup, will likely purchase the ibuprofen that has differentiated itself based on quality.

The question, however, is whether and to what extent branding occurs during the social, interactive processes in which individuals oftentimes find themselves embedded. In an intriguing article about brand commitment, Sung and Campbell provide informative answers to the aforementioned query.[20] Taken together, their results indicate that one's level of commitment to a given brand will be high when (a) the brand provides satisfaction, (b) there are few available brand alternatives, and (c) the size of the investments in the brand is large. This becomes easily relatable to the study of interpersonal relationships in that people will enjoy their relationships more if and when the relationship provides satisfaction, there exist few relational alternatives, and the investments in the relationship are extreme. Thus, Sung and Campbell provide evidentiary support that the branding processes embedded in organizational practices are quite similar to the processes involved in relational formation. Sung and Campbell solidify their arguments when they claim that ". . .brand relationship quality is an explicit analogue to concepts of relationship quality in the interpersonal field and implies that the relationship that consumers have with brands have qualities similar to those of human relationships."[21]

In a related article about branding practices, Mulyanegara, Tsarenko, and Anderson likened the idea of branding to the social construction of a brand personality.[22] When one thinks about an individual's personality, words such as friendly, outgoing, reserved, opportunistic, trustworthy, compassionate, sensitive, competitive, and energetic are likely to emerge. However, as Mulyanegara, Tsarenko, and Anderson claim, the same psychosocial processes emerge during the branding process, where "brand managers are interested in promoting a brand personality that attracts consumers' attention such that they may form a preference for a brand."[23] Based on this, as well as Sung and Campbell's discussion about brand commitment, one realizes that the branding process is, in many ways, analogous with the process of identity construction via online networking sites. Just like brand managers highlight and communicate the qualities of certain products to appeal to consumers and potential consumers, so, too, do Facebook and LinkedIn users highlight and communicate qualities about themselves to appeal to both existing and potential network members. Balmer captures the branding-identity link well when he claims that "brands are appropriated by individuals in order to convey to others a desired personal identity."[24] Such a desired personal identity is made possible by online networking sites such as Facebook and LinkedIn.

One question that has routinely surfaced in the literature about online networking sites is the extent to which the identities that users create mirror the identities that users communicate in public. In other words, and borrowing the language used by Higgins, and later Balmer, are online networkers communicating an actual or an ideal/desired identity?[25] Although there are certainly empirical, methodological, theoretical, and conceptual complications involved in providing answers to this question, results from a study conducted by Back et al. indicate that "people are not using their [profiles] to promote an idealized virtual identity . . .[but] instead [profiles] might be an efficient medium for expressing and communicating real personality."[26] Taking such results at face value, then, provides more certainty that there is an online-offline marriage regarding one's sense of self, in that both seem to be well-aligned. In other words, rather than online networking modalities allowing what Papacharissi calls identity reinvention, or what Turkle calls identity multiplicity, perhaps online identities are merely an extension of offline personas.[27] Although the question pertaining to actual versus desired identities using online networking forums extends well beyond the scope of this chapter, it is an important variable to consider when framing both the processes and effects of online identity construction.

From a methodological perspective, this chapter attempts to uncover the branding mechanisms available to, and used by, members of Facebook and LinkedIn. That is, what tools do users employ when socially constructing an online, computer-mediated identity? Perhaps not surprisingly, users construct profiles differently based on the online social networking site with which they are working, meaning that those using Facebook employ different branding strategies as compared to those using LinkedIn. For purposes of the current analysis, a total of fifty undergraduate students, ranging in age from nineteen to twenty-three, participated in unstructured interviews that attempted to tap into the social processes embedded in the identity construction process on the two aforementioned online networking sites. All students were enrolled in an upper-level course entitled *Communication and Social Networks*, wherein they began to understand, through empirical, theoretical, and practical lenses, their experiences in, motives for, expectations of, and difficulties associated with, social network membership. Based on basic course requirements, students were required to identify, interpret, and analyze the construction, maintenance, and dissolution of social networks, from sociological, anthropological, psychological, and, above all, communication, paradigms. Beginning with a discussion about the mass attention afforded to the study of social networks during the 1930s and 1940s, especially regarding the study of social influence, and ending with a discussion about how technologies have forced scholars to reconsider the antecedents, processes, and effects associated with social networks and the communication that accompanies them, students assessed and evaluated the empirical, theoretical, and practical issues related to the study of social networks.

Facebook Branding Practices

Based on the results from a series of unstructured interviews, three branding mechanisms surfaced regarding the use of Facebook. Again, it is important to keep in mind that Facebook, as opposed to LinkedIn, is a social networking site, where users join to create relationships that are social in nature. The most important branding mechanism for users of Facebook was the sheer quantity of Facebook friends. As Tong, Van Der Heide, Langwell, and Walther indicate, the "sum of the number of one's friends" is an easily identifiable marker of popularity and ultimately provides an immense amount of information about a network (or potential network) member.[28] This is very much aligned with Kleck, Reese, Behnken, and Sundar's claim that there exists a direct correlation between the quantity of one's friends on Facebook and subsequent positive characteristics associated with that particular user.[29] For example, those with more Facebook friends are also likely to be more popular, more outgoing, more socially energetic, and more personable. This is analogous with, and an extremely appropriate example of, the halo effect about which Thorndike spoke.[30] In fact, the halo effect is inextricably linked to the concept of branding. For example, consumers assume that a product that is expensive is also of higher quality and that a product that has high industry ratings must be the best. One student made particular mention of the quantity of Facebook friends and its link to branding and identity construction when she claimed that:

> I absolutely think that the number of friends that one has is an immediate indicator of such things as friendliness, outgoingness, and overall levels of relational interest. To be quite honest, when I friend someone, the first thing that I look at, even before I look at their profile, is the number of other people that they are connected to. I mean, come on . . . if the person has only 50 friends, this says something a lot different as compared to the person with 500 friends. Think, for a moment, about how one measured popularity before technology. It was based on the number of people that the person hung out with. The person who hung out with 10 people was much more popular and well-liked than the person who hung out with just three. It makes sense. Technology does not provide us with a different measure of popularity. It just makes the measure of popularity easier to determine.

Information about the sheer number of Facebook friends is not merely fabricated by individual users. Rather, it is factual data that is substantiated by others part of one's online network.[31] That is, others must accept a general "friend request" in order for one's quantitative measure of popularity to increase. As such, the quantity of one's Facebook friends is one social mechanism involved in the self-branding process. As another student indicated, adding Facebook friends can be likened to the process of an infomercial:

When you look at infomercials late at night that are attempting to sell a product, whether it be a new electronic device, a new knife that overcomes its competitors' weaknesses, or a set of religious audio recordings, you will notice that there is usually a counter, in the lower-left-hand corner of the screen, that notifies spectators of each and every new purchase. What is the purpose of such a business strategy? Well, I think that there is a power in numbers strategy going on. To the potential consumer, an increase in the number of orders likely translates into an increase in the probability of him/her purchasing. The same can be said of Facebook. Just like an infomercial product will likely have less buyers when the purchase count is low, Facebook (or potential Facebook) friends with few connections to others might be predictive of certain social and interpersonal issues. The number of Facebook friends that one has tells a very interesting story.

In essence, this branding strategy is no different than McDonald's informing the mass public about the number of people who eat at its fast food chain or Allstate informing the mass public about the number of people who have purchased its insurance policies or Tide informing the mass public about the number of people who are satisfied with its detergent products. In the world of corporate branding, numbers make a difference. Based on the current analysis, numbers matter for self-branding, too.

Although the number of Facebook friends was among the three branding mechanisms for online users, a second, more meaningful, mechanism is the number of Facebook groups to which members belong. Despite the fact that belonging to many groups might be construed as a narcissistic social activity, it is also informing of one's range and multitude of interests.[32] Take a moment to reflect on a first interpersonal encounter where you began to learn about someone new. In all likelihood, this social encounter was nothing more than a series of questions and answers, attempting to reduce interpersonal uncertainty and to socially penetrate one's outer core.[33] In one of his final standup routines, which publicly aired in 1998, Jerry Seinfeld likened a first date to a job interview. The only difference, according to Seinfeld, is that there is not much of a chance that a job interview will end with both parties being nude. Although comedic, Jerry Seinfeld explains the importance of uncovering information prior to relational engagement and/or development. In a FtF, interpersonal situation, one asks, and subsequently learns a lot, about a co-interactant, such as favorite books, favorite movies, favorite music genres, favorite quotations, favorite sports, favorite pastimes, and the like. The same social process endures on Facebook and users communicate the foregoing by joining certain Facebook groups. As one interview respondent explained, Facebook groups are great for communicating one's, and discovering others', interests:

> You want to find out who I am? Just go look at my groups. I belong to about 50 of them. Is this number a bit extreme? Well, compared to others, perhaps. But I don't think so. I belong to a number of different groups and for different reasons. For example, I have joined groups that deal with music (*There Is Nothing Like Classic Rock*), literature (*Malcolm Gladwell Rocks My Socks*), food (*A Vegetable A Day Keeps The Doctor Away*), sports (*I Love The Yankees And Whoever Is Playing The Mets*), and pop culture (*The Kardashians Make The Royal Family Look Normal*). They tell a lot about the person that I am. And this information tells a lot more than just the number of Facebook friends that I have. It starts to tell a story and interested people can begin to put the pieces of the puzzle together. By putting all of the pieces of the Facebook puzzle together, images of identity can be created. In fact, you would learn more about me by looking at my Facebook account than if we met for an hour to chat FtF.

Very much in line with the results from Christofides, Muise, and Desmarais' study, this participant claimed that she self discloses more about herself online than she would during interpersonal dialogue offline.[34] This increase in online self-disclosure might be due to ease, the potential lack of public identity commitment, a dearth of other self-disclosure methods, or perhaps a combination, thereof.[35] Regardless of the rationale undergirding one's decision to self disclose more about himself/herself using online technologies, one thing is certain: self-disclosure through membership in Facebook groups is another way that individuals brand themselves in a mediated environment. Again, if one frames branding as the process through which an organization or its product gains a certain sense of identity, then membership in Facebook groups, too, is an effective branding mechanism. As another respondent indicated, perhaps merely by looking at one's Facebook groups it is possible to learn everything there is to know:

> All of the options on Facebook are more about showcasing one's identity than hiding it. There are no games, there are no surprises, there is

nothing fabricated. By looking at my Facebook groups, you will learn what music I like, what books I dislike, my favorite vacation destinations, what I would do if I won a million dollars, who my perfect mate would be, what three things I would require if stranded on a deserted island, and what I would name my first pet. What is the point of not telling the truth? In FtF communication, there might be an inherent benefit of withholding the truth. But not online. There is nothing to lose by telling the truth and there is nothing to gain by lying. I remember one of my professors showing a comic strip where a dog is interacting with others in an online community and the caption of the cartoon read "On The Internet, Nobody Knows You're A Dog." But what is the purpose of altering your identity online? There is no point. It is honestly pointless. Join the groups that speak to your character and others will learn about the true you.

In an article published a decade ago, Papacharissi, whom was interested in the social construction of identity through the information presented on one's personal homepage, argued that "people choose to explore certain sides of their personalities . . . more extensively online, or even invent virtual-life personae different from their real personalities."[36] This, and similar, research about the construction of self through information provided on personal homepages, coupled with the research in the mid-1990s about the construction of self using Multi User Dungeons, indicates that online technologies provide a playground for the creation of identity, where fiction, not fact, becomes most important.[37] However, recent studies related to Facebook and the construction of identity have created a paradigm shift, as fact, not fiction, has become paramount. Contrary to basic assumption, predicated on much existing research, online environments provide a forum where social actors feel more able and willing to construct an identity that is based on accuracy, rather than deceit.[38]

A final branding mechanism and, based on the results of the current analysis, the predominant branding method, entails posting information about oneself and uploading photos and videos. Compared to a quantitative measure of one's friends and the groups to which one belongs, this branding mechanism involves a much more proactive approach to creating and shaping one's socially constructed identity. According to Walther and Parks, "the warranting value of [such] information . . . raises its value in making judgments about what a person encountered online is really like offline."[39] By posting information and uploading photos and videos, Facebook users are essentially taking their social experiences and sharing them with their network of friends. Just as organizations brand themselves in an effort to construct an attitude, feeling, reputation, and personality in the minds of current and potential consumers, Facebook users also engage in the branding process, by providing information about such variables as education, favorite books, current employment position, favorite television shows, gender, relationship status, languages known, and favorite movies. One student explained the role of the information that he provided in expediting the relational development process:

> I had met a girl at a party not too long ago and, at the end of the night, I told her to Facebook me. Later that evening, she posted on my wall that she, too, loved the Goo Goo Dolls, enjoyed eating spicy foods, hated high school algebra, was a big fan of the Bourne trilogy, and also saw a future career in the public relations or marketing industry. It could not have been better. She read my information and we bypassed those annoying questions that usually come along with a new relationship. I had successfully designed my page so that any visitor that I allow into my world can get an idea of the real me. Yes . . . that is totally an example of individual branding. I did. I branded myself.

When this participant met his new companion for the second time, there were, according to him, few, if any, surprises, providing further evidence for Gonzalez and Hancock's claim that "when people walk away from the keyboard they may take with them aspects of the online self-presentation."[40] A question that lingers is why technology users in the second decade of the twenty-first century are more willing to disclose accurate information about themselves online as compared to users in chatrooms and Multi User Dungeons in the early-to-mid 1990s? One plausible answer, as Valkenburg and Peter reveal, is that Facebook, as compared to chatrooms and Multi User Dungeons, entails communication (at least for the most part) with already existing friends, family members, and acquaintances, not strangers.[41] As such, and relating this idea back to the overarching thesis of this chapter, Facebook users are not branding themselves to new audiences, but rather to already existing networks. When communicating in chatrooms and Multi User Dungeons, where information, photos, and videos of online users were not technologically available, individuals were provided with much more flexibility for creating a fabricated self. After all, as Turkle explained, what is the impetus for constructing a real sense of self in a computer-mediated environment if users will never meet FtF?[42] One participant explained this well:

> The truth of the matter is that anyone who knows me knows to expect
> certain information about me. They know that I will post information
> about the newest book that I read. They know that I will post pictures
> of me with random people in random places. They know that I will post
> a video of my dog chasing his tail and doing his tricks. They come to
> expect this. I cannot hide from it. As I see it, Facebook has allowed us
> to share our lives with others who care. If you don't care about me,
> then don't read my information. Don't look at my photos. Don't view
> my videos. However, if you do know me and you do care about me,
> you will look at my information and be intrigued. You will look at my
> photos and be amused. You will look at my videos and wish you were
> there with me. I am not branding myself to people that I don't know. I
> am branding myself to the people that I do.

A second plausible answer relates to the private-public marriage created by Facebook, about which Papacharissi speaks.[43] The communication that transpired in chatrooms and Multi User Dungeons, which now
seem like technological antiquities, was private. That is, only users who
were technologically "present" had access to, and could attempt to make
sense of, the dialogues between and among individuals. Facebook provides a much different social environment, where the information, photos, and videos posted are available to all who are considered friends, or
what Grasmuck, Martin, and Zhao call a "nonymous community."[44] As
such, although users might be more proactive and tactical about constructing their identities, and subsequently marketing and branding themselves, such information is likely to be authentic. Given this social situation, it is much more difficult and, from a strategic communication
perspective, unwise to create a fabricated and unreal sense of self, as others will begin to put the puzzle pieces together and decode the falsely
constructed identity. One participant addressed this very issue:

> When Facebook users create and edit their profiles, they are not doing
> so to create a whole new persona. That is not the purpose of Facebook.
> The purpose of Facebook is to mirror your real self. Real personas,
> themselves, can be extremely fun. In all honesty, I think that the types
> of people who would need to create fictional identities are not the types
> of people suited for Facebook. They would be better off in an anony-
> mous chatroom where identity creation is the norm. In fact, it is proba-

bly encouraged. I think that the best way to explain is it that Facebook provides the opportunity to turn potentially private selves into public ones, without any fabrication or imagination at all.

In the end, it becomes clear that Facebook users do, in fact, market and brand themselves so as to present an enticing, although accurate, self depiction. Based on the quantity of Facebook friends, the quantity of Facebook groups, and the data presented in terms of information, photos, and videos, users certainly communicate a sense of social identity, which attracts others to them, in hopes of expanding their myriad of networks.

LinkedIn Branding Practices

The question that likely lingers is whether or not users of LinkedIn, a professional, rather than social, networking site, market and brand themselves and whether or not the marketing and branding mechanisms are similar to those used on Facebook. Based on the results of the unstructured interviews, students explained that the two methods for branding oneself using LinkedIn are creating one's online profile and using this networking site to connect to others in various, and potentially unrelated, fields. The profile option available on LinkedIn is not much different from the profile option available on Facebook, though the goal of the former deals with employment and the goal of the latter deals with sociality. As such, certain semantic differences do emerge. The profile is, for all intents and purposes, synonymous with a resume, wherein data about current employment position, past employment positions, level of education, and skills exist. In addition, there is also an electronic way of uploading an online recommendation for a friend or colleague. Since the overarching purpose of being an active LinkedIn user is to either find or announce employment opportunities, the profile acts as a siphoning device. That is, through the process of individual branding, potential employers can determine whether one's employment positions, education, skills, or recommendations seem to fit well with the job posting. One student claimed that creating his LinkedIn profile could likely have substituted outright for his job interview:

Last summer I was connected to someone who was connected to someone who was looking to hire an intern to conduct market research for a new product that the company was going to launch. I did not get the position. The woman said that they decided to go for someone with more field experience. However, every single question that she asked me during the interview could have been answered if she had looked at my LinkedIn profile. I even had the one sentence dealing with why I had an interest in the world of marketing and, more specifically, with market research. LinkedIn is great. I never would have heard about the job had I not been connected to Steven who was connected to this woman. Although I did not get the job, it makes one realize the power of the Internet for branding and marketing oneself. It is unbelievable.

The idea of branding oneself, illustrated in the previous example, is very much in line with Stern's idea of self-publication online.[45] Using websites as the major unit of analysis, Stern found that 94.4 percent of web homepage creators provided a descriptive biography so as to market and brand themselves as authentic and credible. Very similar to personal websites, LinkedIn users socially construct, and present, a sense of self, ultimately publicizing their identities. As Dominick explains, "self-presentation refers to the process by which individuals attempt to control the impressions others have of them."[46] Such self-presentation is perhaps the foremost function of LinkedIn. While partitioning five strategies of self-presentation and linking this to online social environments, Dominick claims that the ingratiation strategy is used to gain likeability from others, whereas the competence strategy is used to gain competence as a skilled and qualified practitioner.[47] Based on this, whereas Facebook users likely adhere to an ingratiation strategy of self-presentation, LinkedIn users likely adhere to a competence strategy. One student explained this quite well:

> Facebook and LinkedIn are two networking sites that are used for similar reasons. However, when it comes to the online profile, there is a major difference. Using Facebook, the purpose of the profile is to gain friends, while the purpose of the profile on LinkedIn is to gain employment and credibility. So, to answer your question, I do use both online networking devices and I have created profiles on both. The difference, however, is that on Facebook it is all about making friends and on LinkedIn it is all about substantiating one's qualifications.

In the end, therefore, although the profiles constructed by Facebook and LinkedIn users might be somewhat different in terms of rationale and goals, they are clearly very effective branding mechanisms for purposes of both social and professional networking.

The second branding mechanism, as uncovered throughout the unstructured interviews, involves the connections that one has to both similar and different others, as this becomes an indicator not only of the sheer amount of professionals to which one is connected, but also the heterogeneity embedded within one's network. Based on early studies of organizational psychology, Katz and Kahn discovered, among its general theory of systems, that employees are most effective and efficient to the extent that they can work collaboratively with dissimilar others.[48] That is, sales people must know how to work with marketers, and marketers must know how to work with employees in the finance department, and the employees in the finance department must know how to work with the engineers, and the engineers must know how to work with those in the purchasing department, and so on and so forth until the systems cycle reaches its final social permutation. The same systems thinking can be applied to the networks of people to which LinkedIn users are connected. Such connections provide a wealth of knowledge and certainly are, perhaps unbeknownst and inadvertently, important branding strategies. As Palmieri, Prestano, Gandley, Overton, and Zhang argue, " in the computer-mediated environment of social networking sites . . . it can be assumed that the initial information a person chooses to share will motivate others to either enter or not enter into a friendship."[49] Although these authors were addressing, more specifically, social networks, the same is true of LinkedIn: professionals are going to be less likely to form a social connection if the individual in question communicates a homogenous, rather than occupationally heterogeneous, network. This idea was highlighted well by one of the participants:

> It is funny to think that all of my Facebook friends are pretty much the same, but all of my LinkedIn friends are different. On LinkedIn, I am connected to an orthopedic surgeon, a trial attorney, a minor league baseball player, an actress, a restaurant owner, a college professor, a librarian, a pharmaceutical representative, an electronic technician, a certified nurse, a boutique owner, and a box office salesperson. If this does not prove that I am well-rounded and can get along with everyone, I am not sure what would.

Such information does not produce a narcissistic persona, as McKinney, Kelly, and Duran claim might occur in online formats.[50] Rather, it produces an image of a well-rounded, eclectic individual, who is able to work with dissimilar others, which, for a potential employer, speaks volumes. Just as Kay Jewelers brands itself with its "every kiss begins with Kay" slogan, communicating consumer necessity, LinkedIn users brand themselves by connecting to heterogeneous others, communicating adaptability. Such adaptability, although perhaps inadvertent to both employer and employee, is certainly among the prerequisites desired by organizations. Just like Facebook users might very well be blind to the branding mechanisms of both the quantity of friends and the quantity of groups, LinkedIn users might very well be blind to the branding mechanism of diverse professional networks. Nonetheless, such a branding mechanism is certainly at work and might ultimately be the difference between employment opportunities and lack thereof.

Conclusion

In the end, Facebook users and LinkedIn users, alike, are able to market themselves and, in essence, become what Mitchell calls brand ambassadors.[51] Such brand ambassadors are, at least partially, responsible for the social construction of their own image and are afforded the opportunity to create an identity rife with positive personal characteristics. It becomes clear, especially using the testimonies from this study's participants, that the construction of computer-mediated identities, although certainly different from the construction of FtF identities, is well aligned with Goffman's and Berger and Luckmann's social constructivist paradigm.[52] Through the creation of a profile, the quantity of friends, and the quantity of groups for Facebook users, and through the creation of a profile and the diversity of networks for LinkedIn users, individuals are able to become their own marketers, constructing an image of self that, based on scholarship, is much more aligned with one's true self than one might assume.[53] The problem, however, is that all five branding mechanisms might be inadvertently unknown to the users. As such, individuals might not be able to take advantage of all of the benefits that these two networking sites offer in terms of branding. The key, then, is to educate users about these mechanisms so that, rather than falling into the "self-idealization" trap about which Back et al. speak, they can engage in the "self-presentation" about which Papacharissi endorses.[54] If this occurs, and occurs with intention, Facebook and LinkedIn can become more than social and professional networking sites: they can become platforms for brand ambassadorship.

Notes

1. Everett Rogers, *A History of Communication Study: A Biographical Approach* (New York: The Free Press, 1994).

2. Rogers, *A History of Communication Study.*

3. Rogers, *A History of Communication Study,* 1.

4. Amy Gonzales and Jeffrey Hancock, "Identity Shift in Computer-Mediated Environments," *Media Psychology* 11 (2008): 167–85.

5. Erving Goffman, *The Presentation of Self in Everyday Life* (New York: Anchor Books, 1959).

6. Goffman, Erving. *The Presentation of Self.*

7. Goffman, Erving. *The Presentation of Self,* 17.

8. Samuel Coleridge, *Biographical Sketches of My Literary Life and Opinions* (New York: Fenner, 1817).

9. William Eadie, "Action, Interaction, and Transaction: Three Means of Viewing the Communication World," (paper presented at the annual meeting of the Speech Communication Association, New York, November 8–11, 1973).

10. Peter Berger and Thomas Luckmann, *The Social Construction of Reality: A Treatise in the Sociology of Knowledge* (New York: Anchor Books, 1967).

11. Berger and Luckmann, *The Social Construction of Reality,* 50.

12. Karen Cerulo, "Identity Construction: New Issues, New Directions," *Annual Review of Sociology* 23 (1997): 385–409.

13. Shaun Bergman, Matthew Fearrington, Shaun W. Davenport, and Jacqueline Bergman, "Millennials, Narcissism, and Social Networking: What Narcissists Do On Social Networking Sites and Why," *Personality and Individual Differences* 50 (2011): 706–11.

14. Adam Joinson, "Self-Disclosure in Computer-Mediated Communication: The Role of Self-Awareness and Visual Anonymity," *European Journal of Social Psychology* 31, no. (2001): 177–92.

15. Kenneth Gergen, *The Saturated Self: Dilemmas of Identity in Contemporary Life* (New York, Basic Books: 1991).

16. Sherry Turkle, *Life on the Screen: Identity in the Age of the Internet* (New York: Simon & Schuster, 1995).

17. Cerulo, "Identity Construction."

18. Hugh Miller and Jane Arnold, "Self in Web Home Pages: Gender, Identity, and Power in Cyberspace," in *Towards Cyberpsychology: Mind, Cognitions, and Society in the Internet Age,* eds. Giuseppe Riva and Carlo Galimberti (Fairfax, VA: IOS Press, 2001), 73–94; Monica Whitty, "Liar, Liar: An Examination of How Open, Supportive, and Honest People Are in Chat Rooms," *Computers in Human Behavior* 18, no. 4 (2002): 343–52; Ylva Segerstad and Peter Ljungstrand, "Instant Messaging with Web Who," *International Journal of Human-Computer Studies* 56, no. 1 (January 2002): 147–71; David Huffaker, "The Educated Blogger: Using Weblogs to Promote Literacy in the Classroom,"

Association for the Advancement of Computing in Education Journal 13, no. 2 (April 2005): 91–98.

19. Mari Juntunen, Saila Saraniemi, Milla Halttu, and Jaana Tahtinen, "Corporate Brand Building in Different Stages of Small Business Growth," *Brand Management* 18, no. 3 (2010): 115–33.

20. Yongjun Sung and Keith Campbell, "Brand Commitment in Consumer-Brand Relationships: An Investment Model Approach," *Brand Management* 17, no. 2 (April 2009): 97–113.

21. Sung and Campbell, "Brand Commitment," 98–99.

22. Riza Mulyanegara, Yelena Tsarenko, and Alastair Anderson, "The Big Five and Brand Personality: Investigating the Impact of Consumer Personality on Preferences Towards Particular Brand Personality," *Brand Management* 16, no. 4 (2009): 234–47.

23. Mulyanegara, Tsarenko, and Anderson, "The Big Five and Brand," 237.

24. John Balmer, "Explicating Corporate Brands and Their Management: Reflections and Directions from 1995," *Brand Management* 18, no. 3 (December 2010): 180–96.

25. Edward Higgins, "Self-Discrepancy: A Theory Relating Self and Affect," *Psychological Review* 94, no. 3 (July 1987): 319–40; Balmer, "Explicating Corporate Brands."

26. Mitja Back, Juliane Stopfer, Simine Vazire, Sam Gaddis, Stefan Schmukle, Boris Egloff, and Samuel Gosling, "Facebook Profiles Reflect Actual Personality, Not Self-Idealization," *Psychological Science* 21, no. 3 (March 2010): 372–74.

27. Zizi Papacharissi, "The Presentation of Self in Virtual Life: Characteristics of Personal Home Pages," *Journalism and Mass Communication Quarterly* 79, no. 3 (2002): 643–60; Turkle, *Life on the Screen.*

28. Stephanie T. Tong, Brandon Van Der Heide, Lindsey Langwell, and Joseph B. Walther, "Too Much of a Good Thing? The Relationship between Number of Friends and Interpersonal Impressions on Facebook," *Journal of Computer-Mediated Communication* 13, no. 3 (April 2008): 531–49.

29. Christine Kleck, Christen Reese, Dawn Behnken, and Shyam Sundar, "The Company You Keep and the Image You Project: Putting Your Best Face Forward in Online Social Networks" (paper presented at the annual meeting of the International Communication Association, San Francisco, CA, May 24–28, 2007).

30. Edward Thorndike, "A Constant Error in Psychological Ratings," *Journal of Applied Psychology* 4 (March 1920): 469–77.

31. Joseph Walther and Malcolm R. Parks, "Cues Filtered Out, Cues Filtered in: Computer-Mediated Communication and Relationships," In *Handbook of Interpersonal Communication* (3rd ed.), ed. Mark L. Knapp and John A. Daly (Thousand Oaks: CA: Sage, 2002).

32. Bruce McKinney, Lynne Kelly, and Robert Duran, "Narcissism or Openness? College Students' Use of Facebook and Twitter," *Communication Research Reports* 29, no. 2 (April 2012): 108–18.

33. Charles Berger and Richard Calabrese, "Some Explorations in Initial Interaction and Beyond: Toward a Developmental Theory of Interpersonal Communication," *Human Communication Research* 1, no. 2 (1975): 99–112; Irwin Altman and Dalmas Taylor, *Social Penetration: The Development of Interpersonal Relationships* (New York: Rinehart and Winston, 1973).

34. Emily Christofides, Amy Muise, and Serge Desmarais, "Information Disclosure and Control on Facebook: Are They Two Sides of the Same Coin or Two Different Processes?" *Cyberpsychology and Behavior* 12, no. 3 (2009): 341–45.

35. Joinson, "Self-Disclosure"; Anita Kelly and Robert Rodriguez, "Publicly Committing Oneself to an Identity," *Basic and Applied Social Psychology* 28, no. 2 (June 2006): 185–91; Cynthia Palmieri, Kristen Prestano, Rosalie Gandley, Emily Overton, and Qin Zhang, "The Facebook Phenomenon: Online Self-Disclosure and Uncertainty Reduction," *China Media Research* 8, no. 1 (January 2012): 48–53.

36. Papacharissi, "The Presentation of Self in Virtual Life," 645.

37. Turkle, *Life on the Screen*.

38. Simine Vazire and Samuel Gosling, "E-Perceptions: Personality Impressions Based on Personal Websites," *Journal of Personality and Social Psychology* 87, no. 1 (2004): 123–32.

39. Walther and Parks. "Cues Filtered Out," 545.

40. Gonzales and Hancock, "Identity Shift," 179.

41. Patti Valkenburg and Jochen Peter, "Social Consequences of the Internet for Adolescents: A Decade of Research," *Current Directions in Psychological Science* 18, no. 1 (February 2009): 1–5.

42. Turkle, *Life on the Screen*.

43. Zizi Papacharissi, "The Virtual Geogrpahies of Social Networks: A Comparative Analysis of Facebook, LinkedIn, and ASmallWorld," *New Media and Society* 11, nos. 1–2 (2009): 199–220.

44. Sherri Grasmuck, Jason Martin, and Shanyang Zhao, "Ethno-Racial Identity Displays on Facebook," *Journal of Computer-Mediated Communication* 15, no. 1 (October 2009): 158–88.

45. Susannah Stern, "Expressions of Identity Online: Prominent Features and Gender Differences in Adolescents' World Wide Web Home Pages," *Journal of Broadcasting and Electronic Media* 48, no. 2 (2004): 218–43.

46. Joseph Dominick, "Who Do You Think You Are? Personal Home Pages and Self-Presentation on the World Wide Web," *Journalism and Mass Communication Quarterly* 76, no. 4 (December 1999): 646–58.

47. Dominick, "Who Do You Think You Are?"

48. Daniel Katz and Robert Kahn, *The Social Psychology of Organizations* (New York: John Wiley and Sons, 1966).

49. Palmieri et al. "The Facebook Phenomenon," 49.

50. McKinney, Kelly, and Duran, "Narcissism or Openness?"

51. Colin Mitchell, "Selling the Brand Inside," *Harvard Business Review* 80 (2002): 5–11.

52. Goffman, *The Presentation of Self*; Berger and Luckmann, *The Social Construction of Reality.*

53. Back et al., "Facebook Profiles Reflect Actual Personality."

54. Back et al., "Facebook Profiles Reflect Actual Personality"; Papacharissi, "The Presentation of Self in Virtual Life.

Chapter 6

Like Us on Facebook and Follow Us on Twitter: Corporate Identity Management across Social Media Platforms

Binod Sundararajan and Malavika Sundararajan

Traditionally, individual identity, organizational identity, and corporate identity have been differentiated based on the lack of the latter two being related to the cognitive structures and internal processes of individuals but rather more related to external material manifestations of identity. More recently however, with the advent of social media platforms for communication, there is now value in and indeed a pressing need for interdisciplinary cross-fertilization when defining and studying organizational and corporate identity.[1] The manner in which, "identity of individuals may come to be anchored in some combination of gender, nationality, profession, social group, life-style, educational achievements or skills, so an organization's may be anchored in some specific combination of geographical place, nationality, strategy, founding, core business, technology, knowledge base, operating philosophy or organization design."[2] Cornelissen et al. further explain that similar to individual human beings expressing a sense of personal distinctness and autonomy, organizations are also viewed to equally have their own individuality and

uniqueness that they express in their dealings with others.[3] The greatest
need for interdisciplinary studies thus arises out of the similarity in the
way organizational and corporate identity like an individual's social
identity has the potential fluidity of identity and identification management through the judgment of self and others as well as context-based
negotiated identities that arise out of social media interactions with various stakeholders.[4] For ease of understanding and minimal confusion, we
therefore use the terms *corporation, organization,* and *company* interchangeably throughout this chapter.

The rise of social media platforms herein offers organizations a new
opportunity to engage with their customers and reaffirm their identities
online and offline. Social media tools, with their interactivity, constant
stream of data, and easy sharing, make two-way symmetrical communication between individuals and organizations technically possible thus
leaving the onus on the organizational representatives to utilize these
platforms to align their mission and values with the image and identity of
the organization in the market.[5]

With Web 2.0 gaining ground, social media sites like Facebook,
Twitter, Yelp, and a host of other such social networking sites allow for
direct social interaction, not only among individuals, but also among
groups and even populations. Much like teenagers and other older users
use social media sites to negotiate their social identities and statuses,
corporations too need to use these social media platforms to negotiate
their corporate identities and statuses directly with their consuming publics.[6] It then behooves organizations to actively seek out their most important stakeholders (users/consumers of their products or services) using
these social media sites and begin a process of proactively engaging with
this stakeholder group. Divol, Edelman, and Sarrazin state that while,
"executives can even claim to know what makes social media so potent,
i.e., its ability to amplify word-of-mouth effects, yet the vast majority of
executives have no idea how to harness social media's power."[7] They go
on to say that while companies regularly and "diligently establish Twitter
feeds and branded Facebook pages, few have a deep understanding of
exactly how social media interacts with consumers to expand product
and brand recognition, drive sales and profitability, and engender loyalty."[8] This echoes what Walther et al. say that the convergence of old
and new communication and media technologies demands new and uni-
fied perspectives on traditionally segregated processes, especially when
it comes to the interplay between interpersonal, mass media, and peer

All audiences external

communication.[9] When you throw corporate communication in this mix, especially with organizations seeking the attention of individuals, these perspectives require more than just a review, but a complete rethink on the part of organizations about their communication strategies and positioning of their corporate identities on these new media platforms.

Corporate identity is seen to relate to the general meaning of a corporate entity that resides in the values, beliefs, roles, and behavior of its members.[10] This is not very different from individuals creating social and professional identities and being ranked by their peers on their sociability or professional abilities, be it on Facebook or a professional networking site like LinkedIn. Gilpin says, "practitioners who construct their professional identity primarily through their 'public relating' are highly visible in search engine rankings and online professional social networks, but this visibility is not necessarily a reliable indicator of overall expertise."[11] Gilpin further notes that the manner in which individuals negotiate questions on self-presentation and personal branding and establish a constructed identity for themselves and the groups they belong to, is emerging as an important form of social interaction that is facilitated by digital media.[12] — *How do we decide what to post?*

Corporations then need to study these emergent behaviors as they seek to construct their own corporate identities on these new media platforms and keep in mind that visibility, reputation, and ranking alone are not sufficient to enhance their corporate images. Rather, they need to combine these indicators (rank, reputation, etc.) with direct engagement with their customers regarding issues that concern these customers (product related, ethical behavior, social responsibility, etc.) in order to benefit from the rankings and reputation.

Corporations are thus ranked every year in terms of their reputation and values or ethical behavior based on public and market perceptions. By assessing the relation between the top ranking firms on the most ethical company lists, and their social media platform use, we highlight the importance of retaining, reaffirming, and even regaining corporate identity through timely and appropriate engagement of a company's stakeholders using social media platforms. We begin with a brief review of literature related to corporate identity, key variables that impact corporate identity, the importance and need for social media platforms, and the impact of social media platforms on corporations' identities using recent examples from archival news data. Next, we assess the social media usage statistics of firms with the highest and repeated rankings on the most ethical companies' lists to describe the pattern and relation between the two in successfully managing the corporation's identity. Finally we conclude with the discussion and summary of our findings along with the implications of this study for the field of communication, marketing, and management.

Review of Literature

Corporate Identity

Corporate identity used to be primarily defined as the distinctive public image that a corporate entity communicates that structures people's engagement with it, but more recently it has been added that corporate identity also encompasses the shared meaning that a corporate entity is understood to have that arises from its members' (and others') awareness that they belong to it.[13] Specific to the context of social media platforms corporate identity is defined as the received image in the eyes of stakeholders such as employees and customers and consumers.[14]

Factors Impacting Corporate Identity

Corporate Reputation

While corporate identity is the way a company is perceived based on a certain message, at a certain point in time an individual's collective representation of past images of an organization (induced through either communication or past experiences) established over time constitute an organization's *corporate reputation*.[15]

An interesting finding in the corporate literature is that a firm can have numerous reputations, one for each attribute such as price, product quality, innovativeness, management quality or even an independent global reputation.[16] Corporate reputation can thus also be viewed as the "aggregation of a single stakeholder's perceptions of how well organizational responses are meeting the demands and expectations of many organizational stakeholders."[17]

Transparency and Credibility

Organizations are defined by their values and missions and consistency in the representation of these values form a large part in the perceived image of a corporation's identity by the market. Transparency is defined as "a state in which the internal identity of the firm reflects positively the expectations of key stakeholders and the beliefs of these stakeholders about the firm reflect accurately the internally held."[18] Thus, it becomes strategically critical for organizations to achieve alignment and transparency at multiple levels, specifically the alignment between organizational identity specified by senior managers and that experienced by employees, as well as, corporate identity and its alignment with corporate reputation.[19] The lack of this alignment is stated to result in employee disengagement, customer dissatisfaction, and general organizational atrophy.[20]

Importance and Need of Social Media Platforms for Corporations

Social media platforms include Facebook, Twitter, Foursquare, search engines, and LinkedIn among many others. Among these platforms Facebook and Twitter are rated to be the most effective in their reach and impact with consumers. Recent social media reports show that business brands that *post at least once every day on Facebook* are said to reach 22 percent of their fans in a given week.[21] Currently 44 percent of all small businesses use social media to ensure visibility, self-promotion, and to connect with their customers. Fifty percent of small business owners reported gaining new customers through social media—most notably through Facebook and LinkedIn. The primary reason being that nearly 51 percent of Facebook users and 64 percent of Twitter users are more likely to buy from the brands they follow.[22]

While it is clear that a firm's reputation may not be common among all the groups in the present day, where Twitter and Facebook have immediate and widespread effects, the social media related groups, become a key stakeholder group who can make or break the corporation's reputation and question the corporation's identity.[23]

Additional social media statistics for business obtained from the list created by Schoenfeld, indicate that while more companies have an active presence on social media sites, they still seem to see this as a vehicle for marketing and self-promotion.[24] Upon further observation of this list, we see that many of the leading companies like Pepsi, Best Buy, Comcast, Dell, and JetBlue have begun investing more and more marketing dollars on social media campaign. For example, Best Buy has over 2,500 employees helping customers on Twitter and has even purchased TV ads to raise awareness of their Twitter initiative. Further, 68 percent of small businesses plan to increase their social media marketing efforts and 56 percent of Twitter users say that they use the micro-blogging and communication service for business purposes.

From the side of nonbusiness users, over 40 percent of users have friended a brand on Facebook or MySpace, 46 percent of Facebook users say they would talk about or recommend a brand, 20 percent of tweets on Twitter are about products (queries and responses from peers about products), 44 percent of Twitter users have recommended a product and 58 percent of people said that if they had tweeted about a bad experience with a product or a company, they would like the company to respond to their comment. There is clear evidence of the growing influence of social media users who will discuss about products, recommend them, favor one brand over another, and expect to be listened to if they have a bad experience with a product. Thus, with an exponential increase in online social media usage, organizations that have not adapted to this environment will continue to struggle to maintain their corporate identities, much less enhance them.

It then becomes the function of an organization to constantly strive to maintain its reputation, image and identity, particularly among its stakeholders (internal and external), the public, and society. Organizations typically do this by employing specific corporate communication strategies and various public relations exercises. While perceptions about an organization's image, reputation, and identity among its various stakeholders will depend largely upon the organization's conduct, the products or services it offers, and the quality of service provided, how they engage with their various stakeholders on issues that affect the stakeholders with respect to the organization, will be a key component in maintaining a positive identity of the corporation in the views of these stakeholders.

Among the various stakeholders, internal and external, organizations have traditionally engaged well with members of the board, share/stock holders, most internal entities and most external vendors in the organizations' supply chains. However, when it comes to the clients/customers of the organizations, stakeholders that pay for and consume the goods/services provided by the organization, organizations have been found to be lacking in proactively engaging with this stakeholder group. And when they do engage with this particular stakeholder group (users/consumers) it has typically been a "spray and pray" or "withhold and uphold" approach, i.e., either too much or too little.[25]

Alternatively, organizations have engaged with these consumers when they want to find out their likes and dislikes and how they perceive the organization using customer polls, market research efforts, and focus groups. These have been conducted for the specific purpose of finding out ways to sell, upsell or cross-sell products and services to consumers, but not necessarily to really engage with them and find out what these consumers need, as opposed to what the corporation wants to sell to them. While it can be argued that reaching out to each and every customer of an organization would be a herculean, even an impossible, task, that argument no longer holds true due to the advent and proliferation of social media in the last few years.

Examples of Impact of Social Media Platforms on Corporations' Identity

Johnson & Johnson Case

Executives use tried and tested marketing, advertising, and PR techniques in an entirely new space, where "word-of-mouth" can make or break a brand, with little effect. Case in point, when Johnson & Johnson ran into a spot of trouble for marketing and selling their popular baby shampoo with a banned toxic chemical as one of the ingredients. That they sold the product with the banned chemical was less of an issue, than the fact that they sold one version of the product (without the banned chemical) elsewhere in the world, and the other version (with the banned ingredient) in the United States, Canada, and China. Messages from the Circle of Moms website, where concerned mothers communicated with one another regarding this particular issue, indicate an immediate intent to boycott all of Johnson and Johnson products.[26] We present a few of these next.

Writes Keli, (posted on 11/04/2011 on the Circle of Moms website):

> I use J&J Naturals, but I think I will try something else. The Live cLEAN line is pretty good too.

Lisa responds (posted on 11/04/2011 on the Circle of Moms website) by saying:

> We've never used Johnson & Johnson. We use chemical-free shampoo, soap and lotion. I don't wear makeup.

Stacey, who posted earlier (posted on 11/02/2011 on the Circle of Moms website), writes:

> I just posted an article on this on my local patch. I'm so outraged by this, it has me furious. I've trusted this company. So very frustrating as a parent. Read my article and let me know your thoughts.

These conversations among concerned mothers are just one example of how the users of products, goods, or services can mobilize and disseminate information and change minds of fellow consumers. Social media has given them not only an outlet to communicate and connect with likeminded people, but also an avenue to learn, help, guide, inform one another and most importantly give users and consumers a voice that can change attitudes and minds and often the intransigent behavior of groups or organizations. In this case it was one set of products of a giant, multinational corporation, Johnson & Johnson. For Johnson & Johnson, this was even more of an embarrassment because this alleged practice (of selling products with different ingredients in different parts of the world) went against their values, "The values that guide our behavior are spelled out in Our Credo, which puts the needs and well-being of the people we serve first."[27] They then had to proceed to actively engage with this particular consumer group (upset moms) on blogs, Facebook, Twitter, and the like, to convince them that this practice of selling same or similar products with different ingredients (especially banned ones) would change.

This is an illustration of one corporation's struggle with the effective use of social media networking sites while trying to manage their corporate identity, image, and reputation. Had they begun engaging with their consumers early on and in the spirit of trying to meet their consumers' needs and not to try and find ways to sell these consumers more products, then Johnson & Johnson would have been able to not only maintain their reputation, but enhance it.

Research in Motion Case

Another company which has struggled with responding directly to its consumers is Research in Motion (RIM). While they have had several other issues they have had to deal with recently (change of guard at the top, the Blackberry Playbook not faring well against the Apple iPad, Samsung Tablets, etc.), their biggest crisis of recent times was the Blackberry Blackout of 2011 that resulted in over 70 million Blackberry subscribers losing their connectivity and access to their telephones for four to five days.[28] It was only on Day 4 that Mike Lazaridis, Co-CEO of RIM came online and professed an apology directly to Blackberry users worldwide.[29] The apology, while sincere and genuine, was delivered much later than it should have been, to the great dismay of millions of Blackberry customers and puzzling to corporate communication researchers. How could a forward thinking, savvy, successful technology company, not respond quickly enough to this crisis? Some subscriber comments are quoted below.

Quattro017 writes:

blackberry user in Chicago- no emails in or out grrrrrr.

Rana Barua writes:

Blackberry India, I am very angry. hopeless service.

Copsonemlyn writes:

Yes, I've been affected by the Blackberry outage. I can't even sign onto Yahoo Messenger on my infernal device and to say I'm b liming annoyed is an understatement because I use it during the week to talk to my girlfriend in Makati in the Philippines, and I hate not being able to talk to her, I love her and I miss her chat so much on Wednesday!

While cell phone outages do happen, more often than people realize, the silence of RIM on this issue, specifically on blogs or social media sites was deafening. While they did provide updates on their own corporate service page, that was a pull strategy. Also, subscribers had to go to the RIM site to view the apology by Lazaridis. Eventually, the apology did make its way to the rest of the Internet, but as a whole, it was considered, too little, too late. The reputation of the company took a beating and users wondered why there was no conversation directly with them on any site, let alone social media sites.

Domino's Pizza Case

The RIM incident contrasts markedly with the way Domino's Pizza responded to a hoax video uploaded to YouTube by two of their employees.[30] The senior management at Domino's quickly found out that the video was a hoax, but used traditional media (TV, newspapers, etc.) to reach out to its customers to inform them. All the while, a majority of their customers, most of them online, were wondering why Domino's was not responding to them directly on the blogosphere or Facebook or Twitter, etc. However, the CEO quickly realized this and within forty-eight hours uploaded a video on the very same medium, YouTube, to speak directly to this key stakeholder group, assuring them that this was indeed a hoax, thanking them for their diligence (bloggers recognized the location of the restaurant where the hoax was filmed and informed Domino's) and pledged to improve not only Domino's communication efforts but also its products and services. Domino's delivered on its promise and within a few months consumers started seeing a substantial difference in the quality of the products served at Domino's restaurants.

Such agility is rarely witnessed by large corporations, mainly because they do not yet seem to comprehend the power of social media, but also because they are still driven by the profit motive and not the motivation to really listen to the needs of their customers and engage with them in their medium of choice. People have access to a platform that provides them with a voice and while a few voices may not ever get heard, millions of voices can change attitudes, corporate behavior, and even governments.

In the rest of the chapter, we will outline some statistics and trends on corporate social media usage, the online presence of some top ethical companies (as ranked by Ethisphere), on social media sites, specifically Facebook and Twitter and discuss some of the reasons for their apparent success in using these sites.[31]

Talking the Talk and Walking the Walk—Social Media Presence of Some Top Ethical Companies

Many companies start with the best of intentions and work very hard to produce and provide goods and services that really meet the needs of the people they serve, the communities they operate in and the environment that provides them with the raw material. Many such companies follow the concept of the "Triple Bottom Line" and embed social and ecological imperatives to their existing economic objectives of making a profit. For these organizations, corporate social responsibility is not just a buzz word, but an attitude that is ingrained it the organizational culture. And such companies make great efforts to continuously engage with all their stakeholders using an "underscore and explore" approach to communicating and engaging with their stakeholders.[32] In this approach, organizations work with each of their stakeholders (sometimes together, sometimes separately) in an open process of dialogue and conversation, using all available mediums and technologies, to identify and understand issues that concerns the stakeholders and find ways to solve or at the least alleviate some or all of these issues. Such companies often receive awards and mentions on lists like Ethisphere's, World's Most Ethical Companies rankings.

Presence and appearance on lists like these enhance a firm's reputation, speak to their transparency and credibility, and therefore reinforce a corporation's identity. Getting on such lists and staying on them, motivates companies to improve several aspects of their organizational cultures, like the way they do business (ethically) and how they impact and serve the communities they operate in. Since the Ethisphere list's inception, twenty-three companies have made the list all six years including: Aflac, American Express, Fluor, General Electric, Milliken & Company, Patagonia, Rabobank, and Starbucks, among others. These eight companies from the list of twenty-three WME companies were selected based on their representativeness of all industries on the list and we researched their respective social media presence, specifically on Facebook and Twitter.

Looking at the Facebook pages of Aflac, American Express, Fluor Corporation, and GE we observed the apparent lack of activity on the Facebook page of Fluor Corporation. While Fluor is one of the top ethical companies in the world, according to Ethisphere, they, like Milliken & Company (Table 6.1) are primarily a Business-to-Business (B2B) organization, dealing mainly with other businesses, i.e., the primary consumers of the goods and services of companies like Fluor and Milliken are other businesses or companies and not the average person. Companies like Coca Cola, Pepsi, Ford Motor Company, and many retail banking institutions sell their goods and services directly to the average end user and these companies are classified as Business-to-Consumer (B2C).Thus the levels of engagement in B2B companies would be different, than it would be with Business-to-Consumer (B2C) organizations like Aflac, American Express (both B2B & B2C), Starbucks, Patagonia, GE (B2B & B2C), and Rabobank (B2B & B2C). It is therefore not also a surprise that Fluor and Milliken do not have many "likes" or "people talking about them." However, with the B2C companies in this list of eight companies, almost all of them have very active users on their Facebook and Twitter pages, who post comments, talk to one another, and elicit and demand responses from the respective organizations. Such accountability is extremely good for the organizations to not just talk the talk, but forces them to walk the walk as well.

We note that while "number of likes" on Facebook or the "number of followers" on Twitter, may not be a definitive indicator of a company's popularity (often you have to like a company's profile to start posting—equivalent to friending them), the "number talking about the company" and the "number of tweets" by the company and other users, are definitely worth noting (Table 6.1). While not all will be talking positively or about positive experiences, it certainly points to user engagement and interest and at times the organization's level of engagement with this key stakeholder group. As people talk about a company and the company engages with its user group, the chances of improving the reputation of the company in the eyes this user group increases.

Discussion and Conclusion

We feel that there are only a few reasons why many corporations have not succeeded in effective management of their online or social media identities. Chief among them is that corporations still think social media is only a vehicle to market their products or services and not a platform to engage directly with their customers. We also feel if senior management would recognize this one fact, they will be better served in their approach to harness the power of social media. Second, corporations can

Table 6.1: Facebook and Twitter Page Activity for Top Ranked WME Corporations

Name of Organization	Date Joined Facebook	Number of Likes on Facebook	Number Talking About the Company on Facebook	Number of Tweets on Twitter	Number of Followers on Twitter
Aflac	2009	17,112	176	3,199	14,866
American Express	n/a	2,449,043	12,743	12,898	435,186
Fluor	n/a	6,607	55	No Account	n/a
General Electric	n/a	285,157	4,320	10,997	58,700
Milliken & Company	n/a	721	3	No Account	n/a
Patagonia	n/a	168,848	3,458	2,815	55,784
Rabobank	n/a	30,766	1,822	9,299	23,337
Starbucks	n/a	29,912,775	257,794	10,279	2,433,718

Source: Facebook and Twitter pages of the above companies (accessed May 4, 2012).

no longer hide behind their logos, brands, or past glories. They are answerable to their clients and these clients know how to use their voices on such social media platforms and these voices can become a collective roar, especially when they perceive or sense that the organization is either lying to them or conducting business unethically. Corporations need to know that their actions can be challenged and they are now not only answerable to their boards of directors or stockholders, but the public that consumes the corporations' products or services. If 58 percent of people would like the company to respond to a comment (tweet) about a bad experience with that company's product, the number is large enough and one that a firm cannot ignore.

When competitive advantage is measured in marginal improvements in product or service quality, the quality of communications employed corporations to directly engage with its customer base becomes the differentiator and ineffectual communication can lead to brand switching, loss of revenue, and a negative view of the corporation. The costs of not actively engaging with the customer base far outweigh any costs of employing personnel specifically to engage with customers on Facebook, Twitter, etc. We thus feel that corporate rankings should include the corporation's record on direct customer engagement on all platforms (not just the social media platforms) in addition to their reputation, values, and ethical behavior.

Companies can no longer get away with the pull strategy and take the, "if we build it, they will come" (*Field of Dreams*) approach. They can also no longer use any of the communication strategies that allow the organization to maintain a perception of low levels of responsibility for its actions (nonexistence, distance, association and bridging strategies).[33] Especially in times of crises, they must accept a high level of responsibility and adopt either an acceptance strategy (full apology, remediation, and repentance) or a rectification approach in order to better manage their corporate identities. Since this approach is crucial in leadership and change communication, senior leaders of organizations must combine the "underscore and explore" approach with an "equal participation strategy" build consensus where possible and seek out opportunities to keep a dialogue going with the customer base. Online social media and social networking sites provide organizations and its customers a platform for equal participation and it would be prudent for organizations to grab this opportunity to better understand their customers' needs and wants and cater to as many of them as possible. The reputation of the organization will grow, the corporate identity will be maintained or enhanced and leave a positive image of the corporation in the minds of the customers and the general public.

As Leitch and Davenport indicate, that corporate identity can be both an enabler and a constraint for the organization's pursuit of its objectives, we aver that mismanaging corporate identity on social media platforms will definitely constrain the organization in its pursuit of its objectives, while managing their presence on these social media sites well, will actually align not only with the organizational objectives, but the organization's core values as well.[34] Further, Nguyen and Leblanc, while studying the nature of the relationship between corporate reputation and corporate image and their effect on the customers' retention decisions, found that the degree of customer loyalty has a tendency to be higher when perceptions of both corporate reputation and corporate image are strongly favorable.[35] Moreover, they found that the addition of the interaction between both constructs contributes to better explain customer loyalty. While this study did not include corporate presence on social media sites (Facebook and Twitter and the likes were not even on the landscape then), the results from this study alone should alert managers and senior executives in corporations to rethink their corporate branding and communication strategies in the new social media landscape.

Harquail stresses that strategies for making the organization socially present online put the ultimate goal of authentic communication within reach of organizations.[36] Harquail continues to state that, in order to take advantage of these opportunities, organizations and reputation management practitioners will need to reconsider the roles of distinct, distributed interactions and individual stakeholders on creating reputation. What this means is that organizations have been given a great opportunity to interact directly with consumers of their products or services on these social media platforms and to not take advantage of this to engage with their consumers would seriously deter the organization from maintaining its reputation and corporate identity, not just on these platforms, but outside of them as well. Gilpin, while examining the role of different online and social media channels in constructing organizational image, suggests that the structural and social characteristics of these social media channels give them varying roles in the image construction process, creating new challenges for the public relations function in coordinating image management among various new media.[37]

The most important contribution of this chapter is its cross-disciplinary implications to the fields of communication, marketing, and management. The chapter reinforces the importance of open communication and continuous engagement through social media platforms (communication), but also brings forth the issue of use of social media by firms only for self-promotion and visibility (marketing), which can have an adverse negative impact on a firm's corporate identity. If the corporation's intention is found to be insincere, stakeholders can question the transparency, credibility, reputation, and hence the corporate identity, becoming a core issue for management. Griffin - Relational studies

This chapter is an exploratory attempt to highlight patterns and behaviors of firms engaged in social media use and its impact on the firm's reputation and corporate identity. The research however is limited in that it is preliminary, requires the development of sound theory based hypotheses, identification of key variables and extensive empirical data to help us understand the various relational pathways that will provide substantive insights into corporate identity and reputation management on social media platforms. As boyd and Ellison suggest, "vast, uncharted waters still remain to be explored while studying social media and social networking sites (SNS)."[38] They state that, methodologically, SNS researchers' ability to make causal claims is limited by a lack of experimental or longitudinal studies and recommend that large-scale quantitative and qualitative research combined with richer, ethnographic research on populations more difficult to access (including nonusers) would further aid scholars' ability to understand the long-term implications of these tools. Thus, future work will involve a series of case studies that look at how large and small organizations have responded to and adopted social media sites to engage with their key stakeholders. Researchers can combine these case studies with an empirical study to determine causal relations between corporate social media presence, management of corporate social media identities and customer perceptions of the organization's image, identity, and reputation.

Notes

1. Tom J. Brown, Peter A. Dacin, Michael G. Pratt, and David A. Whetten, "Identity, Intended Image, Construed Image, and Reputation: An Interdisciplinary Framework and Suggested Methodology," *Journal of the Academy of Marketing Science* 34, no. 2 (Spring 2006): 99–106.

2. Joep P. Cornelissen, S. Alexander Haslam, and John M. T. Balmer, "Social Identity, Organizational Identity, and Corporate Identity: Towards an Integrated Understanding of Processes, Patternings, and Products," *British Journal of Management* 18, s1 (March 2007): 1–16.

3. Cornelissen, Haslam, and Balmer, "Social Identity."

4. Cornelissen, Haslam, and Balmer, "Social Identity."

5. Celia V. Harquail, "Re-creating Reputation through Authentic Interaction: Using Social Media to Connect with Individual Stakeholders," in *Corporate Reputation: Managing Opportunities and Threats*, ed. Ronald J. Burke, Cary L. Cooper, Graeme Martin (UK: Gower Publishing Ltd., 2011), 245–66.

6. danah boyd and Nicole Ellison, "Social Network Sites: Definition, History, and Scholarship," *Journal of Computer-Mediated Communication*, 13, no. 11 (October 2007): 210–30.

7. Roxanne Divol, David Edelman, and Hugo Sarrazin, "Demystifying Social Media 2012," *McKinsey Quarterly,* Friday, April 20, 2012, http://www.mckinseyquarterly.com.

8. Divol, Edelman, and Sarrazin, "Demystifying Social Media."

9. Joseph B. Walther, Caleb Carr, Sejung Choi, David C. DeAndrea, Stephanie Tong, and Brandon Van Der Heide, "Interaction of Interpersonal, Peer, and Media Influence Sources Online: A Research Agenda for Technology Convergence," in *A Networked Self: Identity, Community and Culture on Social Network Sites,* ed. Zizi Papacharissi (New York: Routledge, 2011), 17–38.

10. Jonathan E. Schroeder and Miriam Salzer-Morling, eds., *Brand Culture* (London: Routledge, 2006).

11. Dawn R. Gilpin, "Organizational Image Construction in a Fragmented Online Media Environment," *Journal of Public Relations Research* 22, no. 3 (July 2010): 265–87.

12. Gilpin, "Organizational Image Construction."

13. Brown et al., "Identity, Intended Image."

14. Cláudia Simões, Sally Dibb, and Raymond P. Fisk, "Managing Corporate Identity: An Internal Perspective," *Journal of the Academy of Marketing Science* 33, no. 2 (April 2005): 153–68; C. B. Bhattacharya and Sankar Sen, "Consumer-Company Identification: A Framework for Understanding Consumers' Relationships with Companies," *Journal of Marketing* 67, no. 2 (2003): 76–88.

15. Brown et al., "Identity, Intended Image."

16. Nha Nguyen and Gaston Leblanc, "Corporate Image and Corporate Reputation in Customers' Retention Decisions in Services," *Journal of Retailing and Consumer Services* 8, no. 4 (July 2001): 227–36.

17. Steven L. Wartick, "The Relationship between Intense Media Exposure and Change in Corporate Reputation," *Business and Society* 31, no. 1 (Spring 1992): 33–49.

18. Charles Fombrun and Violina Rindova, "The Road to Transparency: Reputation Management at Royal Dutch/Shell," in *The Expressive Organization,* ed. Majken H. Schultz, Mary Jo Hatch, and Mogens M. Larsen (Oxford: Oxford University Press, 2000), 78–96.

19. Brown et al, "Identity, Intended Image."

20. Brown et al, "Identity, Intended Image."

21. Comscore, "It's a Social World: Top 10 Need-to-Knows About Social Networking and Where It's Headed," December 21, 2011, accessed August 8, 2012, http://www.comscore.com/Press_Events/Presentations_Whitepapers/2011/it_is_a_social_world_top_10_need-to-knows_about_social_networking.

22. Phil Mershon, "26 Promising Social Media Stats for Small Businesses," November 8, 2011, accessed August 8, 2012, http://www.socialmediaexaminer.com/26-promising-social-media-stats-for-small-businesses/

23. Fombrun and Rindova, "The Road to Transparency."

24. Adam Schoenfeld, "Social Media for Business: 31 Stats and Anecdotes," accessed May 4, 2012, http://www.slideshare.net/schoeny/social-media-for-business-31-stats-and-anecdotes.

25. Phillip G. Clampitt, Robert J. DeKoch and Thomas Cashman, "A Strategy for Communicating about Uncertainty," *Academy of Management Executive* 14, no. 4 (November 2000): 41–57.

26. The source of this information is from the Circle of Moms website, http://www.circleofmoms.com/parenting-debates-hot-topics/toxins-in-baby-shampoo-671679?

27. Johnson and Johnson, "About Us," last modified April 27, 2012, accessed August 8, 2012, http://www.jnjcanada.com/our-values.aspx.

28. Christopher Williams, "BlackBerry Blackout Enters Day Three," Telegraph, accessed May 4, 2012, http://www.telegraph.co.uk/technology/blackberry/8821912/BlackBerry-blackout-enters-day-three.html.

29. "BlackBerry Service Update," accessed May 4, 2012, http://wwdsfew.rim.com/newsroom/service-update.shtml.

30. Shari R.Veil, Timothy L. Sellnow, and Elizabeth R. Petrun, "Hoaxes and the Paradoxical Challenges of Restoring Legitimacy,"*Management Communication Quarterly* 26, no. 2 (2012): 322–45.

31. Ethisphere, 2012, accessed August 8, 2012, http://ethisphere.com/wme/.

32. Brown et al, "Identity, Intended Image"; Nguyen and Leblanc, "Corporate Image."

33. "Ethisphere"

34. Shirley Leitch and Sally Davenport, "Corporate Identity as an Enabler and Constraint on the Pursuit of Corporate Objectives," *European Journal of Marketing* 45, no. 9–10 (2011): 1501–20.

35. Nguyen and Leblanc, "Corporate Image."

36. Harquail, "Re-creating Reputation."

37. Gilpin, "Organizational Image Construction."

38. Boyd and Ellison, "Social Network Sites."

Part 3

Managing Intersectionality

Chapter 7

Virtual Closets: Strategic Identity Construction and Social Media

Bruce E. Drushel

"After all, you can call yourself anything you want on a social network."[1] The recent scandal involving New York Republican Congressman Christopher Lee, who concealed both his marital status and elected office in a Craig's List personal ad seeking women to date, highlights the potential use of online social networking sites for the creation of multiple, agenda-driven virtual identities. For example, Facebook, which long has permitted distinct professional and personal pages, now also facilitates the discreet creation of multiple personal pages by allowing users to segregate "friends" into mutually exclusive "networks" with privacy settings that hide them from its search functions. Thus, by deception or strategic omission or both, a user may for instance construct a sanitized virtual identity for consumption by family or professional contacts and another more candid one for friends and casual relations. Particularly for lesbian, gay, bi-sexual, transgender, and queer (LGBTQ) individuals, this ability facilitates the resurrection of "the closet," which long allowed sexual minorities to dodge the disapprobation of conservative elements of mainstream culture by allowing the individuals to exist simultaneously in that culture and the demimonde. This chapter will revisit Sedgwick's work on "the closet" as metaphor for the concealment and revealing of identity, Goffman's observations regarding individuals' identity management, and other pioneering works in its interrogation of this practice and its implications.

A Background Anecdote

Some time ago, the author was tracking down college friends on the online social network Facebook and sent a "friend" invitation to one who also had briefly been a subordinate back when the two were journalists. The friend's profile indicated he had moved to the southern United States, was working in public relations, now self-identified as a gay man, and had a partner as well as a sizable network of friends. Months went by without a reply to the "friend" request. Then, one day, the author received a "friend" request from the same individual. Upon confirming the request, the author discovered a very different Facebook profile: one which mentioned his location, profession, and educational background but was devoid of partner and friends other than a single elderly woman whose surname suggested she was a relative. The author, puzzled, sent a message to his friend, thanking him for the invitation as well as briefly updating him on the author's life since they last were in contact and asking for an update from the friend. The friend sent a reply apologizing for the delay in connecting on Facebook, explaining that he found some of the procedures confusing. His own update provided few details beyond the sparse information in his profile. The author decided to up the ante: in a return message, he mentioned his own status as a gay man and his recent teaching and writing in queer theory and the media. Abruptly, he was removed from his friend's sparse profile page and his original "friend" request–to the more complete and candid profile—was accepted.

The incident demonstrated that the closet, that time-worn line demarcating the boundary between the known lives of lesbians and gay men that have been cleansed of any signs or symbols that would prove troublesome in their interactions with mainstream culture and their secret lives as members of a still-marginalized subculture, which many assumed to be, if not less oppressive in a post-Stonewall/post-Ellen/post-*Modern Family* context, then at least less in evidence, was alive and well and alternately bursting open and slamming shut in cyberspace. Such was the observation of Sedgwick who, noting that remarkably few of even the most open lesbians and gays aren't in the closet to someone per-

sonally, economically, or institutionally important to them, put it suc-
cinctly:

> To the fine antennae of public attention the freshness of every drama of
> (especially involuntary) gay uncovering seems if anything heightened
> in surprise and delectability, rather than staled, by the increasingly in-
> tense atmosphere of public articulations of and about the love that is
> famous for daring not speak its name. So resilient and productive a
> structure of narrative will not readily surrender its hold on important
> forms of social meaning.[2]

In this case, the meaning was not entirely plain, since it had been
nearly three decades since the author and his friend had been in contact.
The bond between them, though multidimensional, never was particularly a close one and the friend clearly had established personal and professional lives not dependent on the author's approval. In fact, the temporal
lapse and geographic and relational distance between them might have
provided a ripe opportunity for self-disclosure. Certainly the downside
cost of disclosure—alienation of a long-ago acquaintance—would seem
so slight as to have made it worth the risk. And, the fact that a fair
amount of the friend's life previously had been made available in such an
undiscriminating manner prior to the friend request suggests that the way
lesbians and gay construct their identities may be strategic but also as
much driven by instinctive reaction as critical thought.

A Brief History of Gay Identity

In fact, a review of the scholarship related to identity construction reveals
that it typically is conceptualized as a conscious act. People perform
what Barbara Ponse refers to as "identity work" when they actively inte-
grate their thoughts and experiences into a consistent biography that le-
gitimizes their place in the world.[3] Identity has been defined as the part
of the self by which we are known to others.[4] It entered the social science
literature as a serious subject of study only in the 1950s and quickly
found application in several streams of sociology, including role theory,
reference group theory, and symbolic interactionism.[5] This early work
included publication of Daniel Webster Cory's pioneering *The Homo-*

sexual in America, the first major work in which lesbians and gays were examined as a distinct subculture.[6] Though Evelyn Hooker was considered progressive for her advocacy of homosexuality as a deviation within the range of normalcy and not pathological, her work retained an emphasis on distinctions that were behavioral and not cultural, while Cory and Gordon Westwood believe the prevalence and social acceptance of antigay prejudice made the same framework used to study minority races and ethnicities more appropriate.[7] Though some (e.g., Barry Dank) at the time rejected the analogy to minority status, largely because of the differing modes of socialization into the community, the notion of LGBT people as comprising a subculture (or perhaps *subcultures* as Nikki Sullivan would have it) eventually would provide the foundation for the development of Queer Theory.[8]

As for the relationship of lesbians and gay to mainstream society, Mary McIntosh argues many of them embraced the construction of homosexuality as a health condition, since doing so tended to legitimize its continuation without requiring their rejections of contemporary behavioral norms.[9] McIntosh was a proponent of Role Theory, in which homosexuality was viewed, not as a series of behaviors, but rather as a "role" in which there would be social expectations for certain sexual and gender behaviors, including pedophilia and predation. The popularity of Role Theory as a social scientific framework for lesbian and gay identity persisted into the 1980s, bolstered by the belief that it explained the absence from the historical record of LGBT identities until the comparatively recent past.[10]

While Role Theory did perpetuate the criminality of lesbians and gays, it did represent a departure from essentialist thinking and toward queerness as a social construction. Steven Epstein alluded to the possibilities for lesbians and gays to take an active part in that construction, rather than acquiescing to one that was externally imposed. Such a process would be both conscious and unconscious and would consider the individual, their relationships with significant others, and comparisons with existing typologies.[11]

Given that the concept, if not the historical reality, of the homosexual individual is comparatively recent, dating only to the late-nineteenth century, and that more expansively defined "gays" and "lesbians" are constructions of the twentieth century, arriving at comprehensive definitions of the terms is harder than that it first might seem. Vivienne Cass notes that five themes have permeated the scholarly literature with respect to these identities, including:

(1) defining oneself as gay
(2) a sense of self as gay
(3) image of self as homosexual
(4) the way a homosexual person *is*, and
(5) consistent behavior in relation to homosexual-related activity.[12]

It is ironic that Cass would not include the liminality of gays among her themes, particularly since her best known work arguably is her refinement of the stepped model for self-disclosure by sexual minorities. Maurice Lenznoff and William Westley by contrast were occupied with the closet in their studies of homosexuality, arguing that the distinction between what they referred to as "overt" and "secret" homosexuals frequently amounted to whether their sexual identity would be tolerated in the workplace.[13] The formation of lesbian and gay subcultures and the proto-queer communities of the early to mid-twetiethth century owed largely to gays' fear of detection, which compelled them to seek affiliation with others for collective support, social acceptance, and to relieve the anxiety associated with detection. To Laud Humphreys, the liminality of lesbians and gays would be represented in those who self-identified as a sexual minority but who would strategically control information about themselves with the goal of concealing that part of themselves from straight family, friends, and coworkers.[14] Tactically this would come to be known as "passing" and would be employed particularly by recently self-identified gays as a stigma-avoidance technique. Richard Troiden sees "passing" as the simultaneous inhabiting of distinct gay and straight spheres by those whose hope was that the two never would collide.[15]

Echoes of Humphreys's and Troiden's practices of control over identity information would later be found in Epstein's observation that power inheres in the ability to name (or to identify) and that what individuals call themselves has implications for political practice.[16] Taken together, this suggests that those who situationally straddle the line between "closeted" and "out" are not acquiescing but instead exercising their power over their identity more strategically.

The power to identify or to self-identify ultimately raises the question of to whom one's identity belongs. If the power to name essentially can be thought of as a defensive act—preempting external forces who would name by naming oneself—it could also be an aggressive one in that it shifts the balance of power from external to internal. As Sedgwick says,

> In many, if not most, relationships, coming out is a matter of crystallizing intuitions or convictions that had been in the air for a while already and had already established their own power-circuits of silent contempt, silent blackmail, silent glamorization, silent complicity. After all, the position of those who think they know something about one that one may not know oneself is an exited and empowered one—whether what they think one doesn't know is that one somehow is homosexual, or merely that one's supposed secret is known to them.[17]

The increased visibility of LGBT persons both in the media and in multiple domains of an individual's lived experience may tend to create the impression that lesbians and gays self-identify at a young age and self-disclose broadly. But Cass reminds us that the coming out process remains a gradual if now more accelerated one and that one may remain closeted in some life domains long after self-disclosure in others.[18] The management of the dual or perhaps multiple identities that result is a burdensome process if only because it often requires attention to details about what one has disclosed to whom. The ability to construct profile pages on social networking sites (SNS) websites such as Facebook seems to facilitate the process though, not surprisingly, it is accompanied by more fundamental questions about identity and its ownership.

Identities in Virtual Space

When an individual presents himself/herself to others, he/she tries to maintain control over that persona and to minimize the appearance of characteristics that run contrary to one's idealized identity.[19] In FtF interactions, the physical presence of the individual prevents the construction of an identity inconsistent with the visible portions of that individual's physical characteristics. In addition, shared knowledge of the individual's social background makes it difficult for him/her to pretend to be something he/she is not.

In their "The Social Context Cues Theory" Lee Sproull and Sara Kiesler have proposed that online and FtF communication differ in the amount of social information available.[20] In online environments such as SNS, neither social cues, such as nonverbal behaviors, nor the physical environment are available. The absence of such cues, they argue, can lead to more uninhibited behavior, such as verbal aggression, blunt disclosure, and nonconforming behavior. According to Sherry Turkle, it also facilitates out-and-out lying.[21] Shanyang Zhao, Sherri Grasmuck, and Jason Martin find this tendency to "act out" or to assume a role with a personality contrary to the user's physical world persona to be related to the degree of anonymity afforded in a particularly online environment. Sites offering more anonymity seemed to foster assumption of these roles; those with more "nonymity" (the opposite of anonymity) did not.[22]

Typically, as Monica Whitty observe, in virtual environments the boundary between public and private spaces is a blurry one at best.[23] At the very least, the simultaneously public and private nature of social media complicates traditional conceptions of shared communication, including the construction of public identity. danah boyd and Jeffrey Heer observe, when people converse in physical space, they actively read contextual cues, including an assessment of their audience, to determine the social appropriateness of their communication. In virtual environments like SNS, context is not produced structurally but rather through performative interaction and that critical piece of the context, the audience, is nearly impossible to gauge, particularly if the physical space relationship between user and audience lies outside of the present.[24] boyd and Alice Marwick term this "context collapse," wherein users can no longer assume a distinct set of contextual cues by which to shape their exchanges.[25]

This tends to create new and uncertain terrain for the formation and maintenance of relationships, since, according to Monica Whitty and J. Gavin, the ideals that are important in traditional relationships, such as trust, honesty, and commitment, are equally important online, but the cues that signify these ideals are much different.[26] For users of SNS, their profiles represent a tradeoff between the potential social gain associated with opportunities to establish ties and the social pain of relinquishing some control of presentation of self.[27]

Nevertheless, human beings are remarkably adaptive in their communication practices. Early research into online relationships indicates that the perceived differences between relationships online and offline dissipate over time.[28] Despite the finding that the absence online of stigmatizing physical features enabled some users to bypass obstacles to social interactions that normally would be present in the physical world, Nicole Ellison and her colleagues found virtual identities in online dating websites were remarkably similar to users' "authentic selves" other than some "truth-stretching" regarding their physical appearance.[29]

A Brief Note on the Art of Lying

The lack of contextual cues in cyberspace that are a routine part of the physical environment creates possibilities for profiles that are fictitious, either as a whole or in part. Similar to more authentic profiles, the fictions can be explicit (e.g., pseudonymous names) or implicit (e.g., the absence of photographs and friend lists.) At its extreme, this relatively boundless ability to manipulate identity means there is no way of knowing if a Facebook account was created by the person it purportedly represents.[30]

And in fact, SNS have a history of nonauthentic profiles. At the early SNS Friendster, fictitious identities were so common that users coined names for distinct categories, including "Fakesters" (nonbiographical profiles for playful purposes), Fraudsters (deliberately fraudulent duplicates of authentic profiles for malicious intent), and Pretendsters (realistic-appearing profiles constructed from random online photos). Though much of the motivation for the creation of these faux profiles was the amusement of users, their friends, and the community as a whole, boyd and Heer argue that entertainment was co-extensive with the more serious goal of reminding the Friendster community that "none of this is real."[31] Moreover, the early proliferation of these false, purpose-built identities demonstrates not only that the tradition of deception in online identity management virtually was co-emergent with SNS, but also that knowledge of the capacity for users to construct multiple online identities was broadly dispersed, both among their creators and their audiences.

Identities on Facebook

A key distinction, then, between traditional notions of identity and identity on SNS (and Facebook in particular) is that while the former, though self-constructed, is singular, the latter is neither individual nor innate but rather a social product that is the outcome of a given social environment subject to varying contexts.[32] As early as 2007, a scant three

years after the creation of Facebook and just a year after Facebook profiles were made available to those without university email accounts,
some users fresh from the transition from university student to corporate
employee already reported managing their identities for different audiences, a practice that had been common among those with personal web
pages and weblogs for several years.[33]

At their most basic, Facebook profiles amount to a series of identity
statements, both explicit and implicit. The former are affirmative disclo-
sures of such descriptors as age, location, education, employment, and
relationship status. The latter may be made through selective listing of
friends as well as favorite entertainment media, groups, activities, photographs, videos, and hobbies.[34] Successive refinements to user privacy
options on Facebook have facilitated strategic identity management by
allowing users to group friends according to the parts of their profiles to
which they are willing to permit access. Originally, users were limited to
"taming" their profile data, but sometimes found commonalities in the
data available on less discreet friends' pages to be incriminating.[35]

Friend lists associated with Facebook profiles frequently are as varied as they are lengthy, often including not just family, friends, and
coworkers the user encounters on a regular basis in the physical world,
but also those they are unlikely to meet up with in person in the future,
including more distant relatives; friends from primary school, secondary
school, and college; coworkers from past workplaces; more casual acquaintances; and even some they never have encountered outside of virtual spaces. Since Facebook allows for the mixing of people users know
to varying degrees and in varied domains, and since Facebook allows for
the strategic and targeted performance of identity, one would expect Facebook users to tailor profiles to particular audiences. And, indeed, people in nonymous online environments are more likely to present themselves in ways that place them more in line with normative expectations
and that Facebook profiles, particularly, tended to reflect highly socially
desirable identities—sometimes even identities that at least in part reflected aspirations that had yet to be realized.[36] Even so, such presentations may not alter the basic constituents of personality: one recent study
found that at least in terms of five major personality traits—openness,
conscientiousness, extroversion, agreeableness, and neuroticism—there
was evidence to suggest that online personalities were similar to the
those revealed psychological inventories.[37]

When those normative expectations differ among those a user has "friended" or when specifications for socially desirable identities are in dispute, Facebook currently offers at least two possible solutions: grouping of "friends" into a near-limitless number of categories, each with its own level of accessibility to content in the user's (or the user's other "friends") profiles or the creation of multiple distinct profiles (and therefore identities), all hidden to casual browsing but made visible to those the user wants to see them. The former requires continued attention to the appropriateness of new content to the categories and occasionally to the most appropriate category for a "friend" in cases where the nature of the relationship with that "friend" is not static. The latter allows for less vigilance but for a geometric increase in work to maintain relationships with those one "friends" in each profile.

For lesbian and gay users whose sexuality has been self-disclosed to those in close proximity, both in terms of physical geography and frequency and depth of contact, and therefore for whom the closet was either a quaint anachronism or a gratefully abandoned part of their distant past, this capability raises the specter of a voluntary return to an oppressive symbol and an acknowledgment of a failure to live up to the expectations, real or imagined, of important others. It also is a reminder that in a period offering so much evidence of its post-queerness—with marriage and Ellen and military service and lesbian and gay legislators—people collectively have progressed more than individual persons have and there is validation of Sedgwick's insightful prediction of the resilience of the very embodiment of secrecy, enforced distance, convenience, and perhaps even shame.[38]

Who Owns Identity?

Potentially more significant questions are raised by the conception of identity as something subject to ready manipulation and multiplication. The varied spaces in which an identity may be made manifest—face-to-face, mediated, and virtual—are perhaps what led Altheide to the simple but eloquent definition of identity as the part of the self by which we are known to others.[39] Gregory Stone's definition anticipated greater complexity but also more operational accuracy. It is more of a subject for negotiation, in which the construction of identity embraces both the identity announcement made by the individual and the identity placement made by others endorsing it. Identity, then, to Stone is not established until the placement and announcement coincide.[40] If, to use Altheide's approach, the part of the self known to the self is constant but the part of the self by which we are known to others must vary, then to whom does identity truly belong?[41]

There also is the matter of what might be called "identity primacy," or which among multiple and perhaps conflicting identities may be assumed to be the most accurate and the most comprehensive. As has been noted, Facebook enables users to create hoped-for possible selves that are not possible in the offline world. For Facebook "friends" who will not encounter the user again in physical space, the profile *is* the user; none other is imaginable or recognizable or relevant. Thus, these digital selves not only enhance the user's self-image and identity announcement, but also are, as Zhao, Grasmuck, and Martin have argued, clearly real in the sense that they have real consequences for the lives of those who constructed them.[42] They are not fictionalizations or exaggerations or inferior copies of the offline identities. There is no single, authentic identity—no identity primacy—particularly when identities acquire value only in their usefulness as a currency for social exchange with others and, like most goods, can be reproduced and customized at will.

This is not to say identities in the age of SNS have no value; indeed, they are invaluable because of the exchanges they facilitate—exchanges no longer proscribed merely by the geographical location of the parties. Perhaps one's identity cannot belong even to a single other. In what is certainly a telling statement, one Facebook user confided to researchers that he considered his identity, along with those of the other Facebook users he knew, to be tied up in their Facebook pages.[43]

Looking Forward

There are significant theoretical implications for what has been gleaned from the findings of those who study SNS and from the self-reports of their users. Among the most significant, the author would argue, is that online identity provides a space for rethinking the immutable roles in social exchange of production and reception.

In their recent article on multiple online identities, Alice Marwick and danah boyd speculate SNS have created a third type of audience— not the writer's audience, which is specific to the intent of the author, nor the broadcast audience, whose diverse and undefined nature restricts producers to content with mass appeal—but a networked audience, whose members are connected to the author/producer but also to each other.[44] This takes note of the phenomenon of "context collapse" which occurs when a user can no longer be certain of a common set of impressions and expectations from those with whom she/he is connected. It also suggests a more engaged audience that may construct an identity for the user not just based upon their own exchanges with the user, but also based upon exchanges with others in their networks, with those in other networks, and through observation of exchanges between the user and others.

Identities can be thought of as the principal currency of SNS. Even when exchanges on Facebook aren't about a user—when, for instance, a user offers a viewpoint, re-posts a story, or invites "friends" to play a game or to join a group—the significance of the exchange lies more in the "who" than in the "what." If, as the author has suggested in the preceding section, identities cannot be individually owned because of their multiplicity and subjective authenticity (or lack of primacy), it follows that the functions surrounding that currency lose the meaning they once had. Marwick and boyd's networked audience implies a networked producer as well. The cultural studies bulwark of identity as a product of negotiation between producer and audience may no longer be valid if a multiplicity of negotiations (not all of them involving the ostensible producer) take place, though meaning (in this case, identity) still resides in those in the exchange.

If this is the case, then multiple pathways for further inquiry seem plain. First, what role do a user's "friends" (or the networked audience, as Marwick and boyd would describe them) play in constructing their version of the user's identity and do the connections among the "friends" result in each constructing a single, composite identity for the user, or are they able to construct and maintain simultaneous identities for the user? What are the possibilities and risks involved in a user's efforts to modify her/his identity, particularly if those efforts are selectively aimed at certain "friend" networks and those networks are connected to other "friend" networks? And, if no one truly "owns" her/his (or another's) identity, given the seeming trend in social media of users' being compelled to surrender their privacy to obtain goods of perceived value (e.g., exclusive access to products and services, discounts on purchases, or SNS applications) what is the potential for the manipulation of identity by parties other than one's friends, though association with products, services, causes, and so on?

For the LGBT user, the irony is that the same SNS—Facebook, Twitter, LinkedIn, and their competitors—that seemingly facilitate creation of multiple identities (and closets) may make them more difficult to maintain if the others in their networks—"friends," followers, and "circle" members—are involved in the construction and maintenance of those identities and also are aware of each other. Assuming SNS are at least as ubiquitous in the future as they are at present, which seems likely with the emergence of their social media and social marketing progeny, exchanges among the others that users perceive to be part of discrete domains of their lives almost certainly will be more common and identity less under their ownership or even influence.

A further irony is that, while Sedgwick's closets may be more difficult to maintain in such a future and therefore exist only for individuals with friends and family unconnected, directly and indirectly, to SNS, but also that the excited and empowered legions of "those who think they know something about one that one may not know oneself" will be greatly swelled in number.[45]

Notes

1. Jocelyn Noveck, "Gay Users Applaud Facebook Options," *Cincinnati Enquirer*, February 19, 2011, A15.

2. Eve K. Sedgwick, "Epistemology of the Closet," in *The Lesbian and Gay Studies Reader*, ed. Henry Abelove, Michèle A. Barale, and David M. Halperin (New York: Routledge, 1993), 45.

3. Barbara Ponse, *Identities in the Lesbian World: The Social Construction of Self* (Westport, CT: Greenwood Press, 1978).

4. David L. Altheide, "Identity and the Definition of the Situation in a Mass-Mediated Context," *Symbolic Interaction* 23, no. 1 (May 2000): 1–27.

5. Philip Gleason, "Identifying Identity: A Semantic History," *Journal of American History* 69, no. 4 (March 1983): 910–31.

6. Daniel Webster Cory, *The Homosexual in America* (New York: Greenberg, 1951).

7. Evelyn Hooker, "Male Homosexuality in the Rorschach," *Journal of Projective Techniques* 22 (1958): 33–54; Cory, *The Homosexual*; Gordon Westwood, *A Minority: A Report on the Life of the Male Homosexual in Great Britain* (London: Longmans, 1960).

8. Barry Dank, "Coming Out in the Gay World," *Psychiatry 34* (1971): 180–97; Sedgwick, "Epistemology." Sedgwick would respond that lesbians and gays do differ from even less immutable signs of marginality (such as Jewishness) by the latter's clear ancestral linearity and answerability in the roots of cultural identification through family. That there is no such provision for ritualized transmission of culture does not mean there is no culture to transmit. Instead, it places added burden on the newly self-identified lesbian or gay person to seek out these cultural roots through affiliation with a chosen family. The closet as metaphor for identity thus is all the more oppressive for gays; Nikki Sullivan, *A Critical Introduction to Queer Theory* (New York: New York University Press, 2003).

9. Mary McIntosh, "The Homosexual Role," *Social Problems* 16 (1968): 182–92.

10. Kenneth Plummer, "Homosexual Categories: Some Research Problems in the Labeling Perspective of Homosexuality," in *The Making of the Modern Homosexual*, ed. Kenneth Plummer (London: Hutchinson, 1981), 53–75.

11. Steven Epstein, "Gay Politics, Ethnic Identity: The Limits of Social Constructionism," *Socialist Review* 93/94 (1987): 9–54.

12. Vivienne C. Cass, "Homosexual Identity: A Concept in Need of a Definition," *Journal of Homosexuality* 9 (1983/1984): 108.

13. Maurice Lenznoff and William A. Westley, "The Homosexual Community," *Social Problems 3* (1956): 257–63.

14. Laud Humphreys, *Out of the Closets: The Sociology of Homosexual Liberation* (Englewood Cliffs, NJ: Prentice-Hall, 1972).

15. Richard Troiden, *Gay and Lesbian Identity: A Sociological Analysis* (New York: General Hall, 1988).

16. Epstein, "Gay Politics."

17. Sedgwick, "Epistemology," 53.

18. Cass, "Homosexual Identity."

19. Erving Goffman, *The Presentation of Self in Everyday Life* (New York: Anchor), 1959.

20. Lee Sproull and Sara Kiesler, "Reducing Social Context Cues: Electronic Mail in Organizational Communication," *Management Science* 32, no. 11 (November 1996): 1492–1512.

21. Sherry Turkle, *Life on the Screen: Identity in the Age of the Internet* (London: Weidenfeld & Nicolson, 1996).

22. Shanyang Zhao, Sherri Grasmuck, and Jason Martin, "Identity Construction on Facebook: Digital Empowerment in Anchored Relationships," *Computers in Human Behavior* 24, no. 5 (March 2008): 1816–36.

23. Monica Whitty, "Peering into Online Bedroom Windows: Considering the Ethical Implications," In *Readings in Virtual Research Ethics: Issues and Controversies*, ed. Elizabeth A. Buchanan (Hershey PA: Information Science Publishing, 2004), 203–19.

24. danah boyd and Jeffrey Heer, "Profiles as Conversation: Networked Identity Performance on Friendster," *Proceedings of the Hawaii International Conference on System Sciences*, Kauai HI (January 2006).

25. Alice E. Marwick and danah boyd, "I Tweet Honestly, I Tweet Passionately: Twitter Users, Context Collapse, and the Imagined Audience," *New Media & Society* 13, no. 1 (2012): 122.

26. Monica Whitty and Jeff Gavin, "Age/Sex/Location: Uncovering the Social Cues in the Development of Online Relationships," *Cyberpsychology and Behavior* 4, no. 5 (October 2001): 623–30.

27. Anne Hewitt and Andrea Forte, "Crossing Boundaries: Identity Management and Student/Faculty Relationships on the Facebook," *Proceedings of the ACM Conference on Computer-Supported Cooperative Work* (New York: ACM, 2006).

28. Martin Lea and Russell Spears, "Love at First Byte? Building Personal Relationships over Computer Networks," in *Understudied Relationships: Off the Beaten Track*, ed. Julia T. Wood and Steven W. Duck (Newbury Park, CA: Sage, 1995), 197–233; Joseph B. Walther, "Computer-Mediated Communication: Impersonal, Interpersonal and Hyperpersonal Interaction," *Communication Research* 23, no. 1 (February 1996): 3–43; Malcolm R. Parks and Kory Floyd, "Making Friends in Cyberspace," *Journal of Communication* 46, no. 1 (Winter 1996): 80–97.

29. Kristen Y. A. McKenna, Amie S. Green, and Marci E. Gleason, "Relationship Formation on the Internet: What's the Big Attraction?" *Journal of Social Issues* 58, no. 1 (Spring 2002): 9–31; Nicole Ellison, Rebecca Heino, and Jennifer Gibbs, "Managing Impressions Online: Self-Presentation Processes in the Online Dating Environment," *Journal of Computer-Mediated Communication* 11, no. 2 (January 2006): 415–41.

30. Hewitt and Forte, "Crossing Boundaries."

31. boyd and Heer, "Profiles as Conversation."

32. Zhao, Grasmuck, and Martin, "Identity Construction."

33. Joan Morris DiMicco and David R. Millen, "Identity Management: Multiple Presentations of Self in Facebook," In *Proceedings of the 2007 International ACM Conference on Supporting Group Work* (New York: ACM, 2007), 383–86.

34. Zhao, Grasmuck, and Martin, "Identity Construction."

35. boyd and Heer, "Profiles as Conversation."

36. Zhao, Grasmuck, and Martin, "Identity Construction."

37. Megan Garber, "Who You Are on Facebook Is Probably Pretty Much Who You Are," *The Atlantic*, January/February 2012, accessed January 13, 2012, http://www.theatlantic.com/technology/archive/2012/01/who-you-are-on-facebook-is-probably-pretty-much-who-you-are/251318/.

38. Sedgwick, "Epistemology."

39. Altheide, "Identity and the Definition."

40. Gregory P. Stone, "Appearance and the Self: A Slightly Revised Version," in *Social Psychology through Symbolic Interaction*, 2nd ed., ed. Gregory P. Stone and Harvey A. Farberman (New York: Wiley, 1981), 187–202.

41. Altheide, "Identity and the Definition."

42. Zhao, Grasmuck, and Martin, "Identity Construction."

43. Noveck, "Gay Users Applaud," A15.

44. Marwick and boyd, "I Tweet Honestly."

Chapter 8

The Performative and Performance Possibilities of Social Media: Antoine Dodson and *The Bed Intruder*

Amber Johnson

Social media's asynchronous, yet ubiquitous and inviting, structure yields wide-open spaces for people to insert their bodies, performances, and narratives into the virtual realm. This means more stories, more often, in more forums, and less single story dangers.[1] New media theorists Janet Murray confirms the capacity for digital media to generate new narrative forms that move beyond the individual story.[2] Within these digital stories are rich research sites for exploring (1) identity shifts within audiences; (2) the ways in which individuals strategically exploit social media for impression management; (3) the ways in which bodies become discursively inscribed as social media users insert their selves into cyberspace; and (4) the immediate, political, public, and easily disseminated dialogic spaces social media affords.[3] Social media exploration brings new complexity and possibility to what Erving Goffman coins the presentation of self in everyday life.[4] As scholars researching the nuances of identity performance in mediated networks, danah boyd and Nicole Ellison highlight the significance of social network sites as topics of research because not only do social networks mirror, support, and challenge everyday practices, participation in social networks leaves a trail, thereby creating unprecedented possibilities for research.[5]

One of the possibilities of social media is the space for the performance, and subsequent investigation of intersectional identity. In her groundbreaking article, Kimberle Crenshaw delineated the qualitative differences between women's experiences with sexual assault and domestic abuse across intersections of race, class, and gender.[6] The distinctions in experience were staggering, suggesting that intragroup variances are just as important as broader categories of difference like race or gender. Ange-Marie Hancock broadens Crenshaw's definition and defines intersectionality as "both the normative theoretical argument and an approach to conducting empirical research . . . that considers the interaction of race, gender, class, and other organizing structures of society a key component influencing political access, equality and the potential for any form of justice."[7] Several scholars have called for utilizing intersectionality in communication research.[8] The goal of intersectional research is to recognize (1) the significance of multiple categories' explanatory power and (2) the vast intragroup differences instead of singling out aspects of identity as if they are discrete, neat concepts we can separate.[9]

Within social media contexts, social networks create space to study the ways in which people insert their intersectional identities into the virtual world. While some users hide behind anonymity, others are bolder in their insertion of intersectional identities, weaving together elaborate and digitized narratives. At the crux of insertion is the possibility of virality, or the incessant clicking and sharing, which results in cyber-fame, a spotlight on the self, and potential for exploitation. Because our identities fluctuate in a milieu of negotiation, conceptual change, and mediated representations, it is important to look at the ways in which social media challenges the way we perform, authenticate, appropriate, and exploit intersectional identities. In this essay, I look at social media as a space to explore intersectionality through the case of Antoine Dodson.

On July 28, 2010, North Alabama's NBC affiliate WAFF-48 reported an attempted rape in the Lincoln County Projects. News anchor Elizabeth Gentle arrived on the scene and met Kelley Dodson, a young black woman who claimed a rapist climbed into her window and attempted to rape her. When her older brother, Antoine Dodson, an openly gay, black man, heard her scream, he went into the room and struggled with the intruder who got away by climbing out of the kitchen window. The story aired on the morning news on July 28. Later that same day, YouTube user CrazyLaughAction uploaded the video.[10] On July 29, the video went viral with over 5 million views. On July 31, the Gregory brothers, known for spoofing news anchors with autotuned version of their news reports, uploaded an autotuned version of Antoine Dodson's interview and dubbed it *The Bed Intruder Song*.[11] *The Bed Intruder Song* video went viral again. Within the first 2.5 weeks, the song sold over sixty thousand copies on iTunes and had over 25 million views. To date, it has more than 103 million views. In addition to these two main videos, people have reposted and added their own twists or remakes to the song, artwork, opinions, etc. As of March 2012, a search for Antoine Dodson on YouTube results in over twelve thousand videos, and over 203 million views on the first page of videos alone. There are post interviews with the news station, interviews of Dodson traveling to New York and Los Angeles for meetings, shows, and interviews, as well as a video of Antoine Dodson performing at the BET Hip Hop Awards, signifying an appropriation of his fame and celebrity. There is even a college marching band performing *The Bed Intruder Song*. On August 11, YouTube user SpeechlessQue uploaded a video of the North Caroline A&T marching band practicing *The Bed Intruder Song*.[12] On August 28, the band performed it at the Sprite Battle of the Bands. Together, the videos have over 1 million views. Antoine Dodson is a household name, and even common within intellectual circles, because of one video gone viral on YouTube.

YouTube started as a name on a garage wall on Valentine's Day 2005. Seven years later, it is home to billions of viewers who upload more than 100 million videos per day. The ability to "broadcast yourself" opened space for new digital communities where people create and share videos, comment on videos via text, and create response and spin-off videos. YouTube changed the game from overnight success to thirty-second success. What Lev Grossman calls viral videos, YouTube clips grow like viruses.[13] Once unleashed, the owner cannot get it back. The video spreads from server to server, tower to tower, monitor to monitor, phone to phone in seconds. Users witness an anonymous person growing to unforeseen celebrity in a matter of the few seconds it takes to click and share. With friendly social network sites like Facebook and Twitter linking directly to YouTube, YouTube videos have unparalleled marketing capabilities, resulting in a vast network of over 1.5 billion users worldwide as of March 2012.

With such large user numbers, people can become celebrities for various reasons. While Dodson's message started on the local news to inform people about a potential rapist attack to try and find the perpetrator, the video quickly became an object of obsession. Social commentary ceased asking about the rapist and regarded the incident with nonchalance. YouTube users wanted to know about Antoine, who he is, what he is doing, whether or not he is getting paid, and what's next. So far, there is an iTunes song selling over one hundred thousand copies legally, numerous T-shirts, an Antoine Dodson website, antoinedodson.net, a Halloween Costume, and Dodson landed a nationally digitized commercial for an iPhone App, *The Sex Offender Tracker App*.[14] Antoine made enough money to purchase a home for his family away from the projects and start a foundation for Juvenile Diabetes, which affected his sister and mother. On the surface, it appears Antoine Dodson has made it. He has money, fame, and celebrity status. But the issue is much deeper than whether Dodson's fame is deserved, or if he is wrong for *acting like that* on television. While it is inarguable that he has made it to a certain degree, his fame begs the question, "at what cost and to whom?" In this analysis, I argue that because of the viral video's potential, YouTube and other social media stars are unable to regulate the exploitation of their identity, nor are they able to frame their own stardom; it is entirely up to the mass audience that pushes for the video's viral status. However, unlike traditional media outlets, social media stars do not have to relinquish all control of their identity, reputation, and future opportunity potential. Social media houses limitless space for individuals to insert their bodies and stories alongside viral videos to create a more complex view of the self. Antoine Dodson managed to ride the back of his viral videos and create an inspiring intersectional narrative that disrupts binary notions of identity.

Antoine Dodson is both a celebrity and target for exploitation because of the specific ways his identities intersect. His black, gay, lower class, seemingly unintelligent identities create space for media to exploit him as a stereotype that frames black, homosexual masculinity negatively, and appropriates a stereotype that denies its authenticity by reducing it to coonery.[15] However, if we see Dodson through a critical lens, his story complicates notions of class, education, access, and masculinity. His business savvy marketing moves and self-promotion challenge stereotypical notions of poor, undereducated people. His feminine performance coupled with his ability to care for his family physically, emotionally, and financially complicate gender roles. From an intersectional perspective, I analyze the viral social media that beget the caricature Antoine Dodson, and locate the ways in which Dodson inserts his own narrative to create and manage a fuller story of self and identity.[16]

Performative Identities

Categorizing and classifying what it means to be black and gendered is dangerous work because blackness and gender are both performative identities. In her discussion of gender reality, Judith Butler argues:

> If a word might be said to do a thing, then it appears that the word not only signifies a thing, but that this signification will also be an enactment of the thing. It seems here that the meaning of a performative act is to be found in this apparent coincidence of signifying and enacting.[17]

Butler says that constructions like gender are performative, meaning gender only exists to the extent that it is performed. Performative identities, then, are those that are embodied by actors and performed through speech acts, gesticulation, clothing, and other subtle nuances. Without the performer, the actual construction would not exist.

With this distinction, we can separate socially constructed identities that are performative from interactions that take place where other types of constructions are purposefully performed in similar manners. Richard Schechner refers to performance as an act that can be rehearsed and recreated.[18] Anthony Kubiak offers a similar distinction between performance and performativity as well:[19]

> Performance as a more or less consciously elucidated act or series of acts can never be performative, in Butler's terms, because performance is to *apriori*, too conscious of itself and its biases and internal social forces. Performance is more a showing than a becoming. The forces at work in performativity are more insidious, hidden, concealed, and self-concealing.[20]

In this sense, performance is a conscious effort to influence during interaction or create an impression. Performativity is the subconscious performance of a societal role or norm through language and enactment.

Race, then, is performative.[21] By naming a subject as a racial being, the discourse is calling into being that which it names.[22] The actual act of naming an individual as raced is what makes the subject a racial person. Louis Miron and Jonathan Inda concur that regardless of race appearing to have an inner essence, it is only accepted as a norm in society because it is reiterated and enacted to such an extent that it appears to be static.[23] Race is constituted through the mandatory repetition of racialized norms.[24] It is performative and exists because we allow it to exist socially. Performativity, then, "rests upon a constitutive theory of language [and] . . . presupposes the idea that words are active as well as descriptive . . . and have the capacity to do things, whether provoking an estrangement between meaning and performance or creating new meaning."[25]

Distinguishing between performance and performativity charters a starting point for investigating the possibilities inherent in social media. However, I agree with E. Patrick Johnson in that performativity fails to articulate a deeper politic of resistance.[26] Bryant Alexander and John Warren remind us that skin is political; it participates in the meaning created in culture, which social actors carry with them.[27] Antoine Dodson is no exception. His raced skin carries implications in terms of sexuality, gender, and class, among other markers of identity. The way his body performs in social media illuminates not only what is brought into being (performativity), but also "what it *does* once it *is* constituted [in performance] and the relationship between it and the other bodies around it."[28] Like E. Patrick Johnson, I also desire a response to performativity that allows subjectivity, agency, and change, thus bringing forth "interpretative frames whose relationship is more dialogical and dialectical."[29] Antoine Dodson and *The Bed Intruder* meme present opportunities to study the tensions between identity performance and performativity via social media, and the implications of those tensions on black masculinity.

Appropriating Black Masculinity

Feminization of the black male body is germane to understanding the links between femininity and homosexuality. In patriarchal society, we undervalue feminine characteristics and associate femininity with inferiority. Because effeminate is read as a sign of homosexuality, it follows that effeminate homosexual men are considered inferior and undervalued.[30] Thus, heterosexual masculinity is superior and authentic, whereas homosexuality is inferior and inauthentic. To reiterate, Hutchinson contends:

> From the cradle to the grave, much of America drilled into black men the thought that they are less than men. This made many black men believe and accept the gender propaganda that the only real men in American society where white men. In a vain attempt to recapture their denied masculinity, many black men mirrored America's traditional fear and hatred of homosexuality. They swallowed whole the phony and perverse John Wayne definition of manhood, that real men talked and acted tough, shed no tears, and never showed their emotion. These were the prized strengths of manhood. When men broke the prescribed male code of conduct and showed their feelings, they were harangued as weaklings and their manhood was questioned.[31]

This poses a problem for black men who perform more normatively feminine roles. Society instructs them to hide those feelings and behaviors, and go so far as to poke fun of men who exhibit those behaviors, giving rise to homophobia. According to Johnson, homophobia is a byproduct of proving masculinity.[32] A man cannot be black, masculine, and gay simultaneously. He is either black and masculine, or he is gay. To appropriate gayness is to forgo blackness because, like oil and water, they do not mix. To reduce a man to his sexual identity, and deny him a space to perform intersectional identities produces what Riggs calls negro faggotry.[33] Negro faggotry refers to the diminution of complex identities into comedic performance of sexuality and race that results in black gay male stereotypes in movies, television, music, and more recently, social media. It is a type of comedy that fully illustrates the act of shunning everything gay in attempt to prove how masculine a man is, or just how gay he is or is not.[34] As Riggs posits, because of his sexuality, he cannot be black. "A strong, proud, 'Afrocentric' black man is resolutely heterosexual, not even bisexual."[35] Thus, he says that he is a negro, and his sexual preference is a "testament to weakness, passivity, [and] the absence of real gut—balls . . . [He] remains a sissy, punk, faggot."[36] Riggs suggests that for black, gay men, their identity was reduced to negro faggot, denying blackness and hegemonic, heterosexual masculinity. With the title of negro faggot comes the susceptibility for "play, to be used, joked about, put down, beaten, slapped and bashed, not just by illiterate homophobic thugs in the night, but by many black American culture's best and brightest."[37] Dwight McBride further complicates this notion of homophobia stating:

> What appears to be homophobia on the part of Black rap and hip hop artists is really engaged in a complicated form of cultural signifying that needs to be read not as homophobia, but the context of a history of derisive assaults on black manhood.[38]

What was once reductive and limited to negro faggotry in popular cultural performance has evolved. The same flamboyant characteristics that once danced across our television screens are now visible in everyday life, complicating strict gender binaries. In the new millennium, we see a surge of fashion, attitude, vocal characteristics, and unpredictable feminine and masculine performances among men across varying races, sexualities, classes, ethnicities, and cultures. Televised representations that do not reduce black gay identity to negro faggotry, but show complexities emerged in *Noah's Arc, The Wire*, and *True Blood*.[39] Dodson's performance is no exception. From the elaborate weaves, girl jeans, flashy sunglasses, and flamboyantly feminine behaviors to protecting his family, supporting his family financially, and setting up a foundation for juvenile diabetes, Antoine Dodson cannot be reduced to a negro faggot. Antoine Dodson doesn't try to fit into normative gender roles, but instead embraces his gender and sexuality and performs what it means to him to be homosexual, black, a man, a provider, a student, and many other aspects of his identity. He complicates strict notions of identity, and can push viewers to question stereotypes. To approach Antoine Dodson's identity from an intersectional perspective is to see the nuances that challenge binaries, thereby creating broader awareness of gay identities and gay masculinities that have traditionally been completely invisible. As Dwight McBride asserts, "in mediated images and public discussion of the Black community, of Black intimacy, of Black class issues, and of race relations, once again, the Black gay man and the Black lesbian were completely invisible."[40] Dodson disrupts this tradition, rendering black gay male bodies visible with a magnificent 190 million views. Even though some YouTubers exploited Dodson at the intersections of race, class, gender, and sexuality, he uses the space afforded by his social media celebrity status to manage his identity and paint a fuller picture.

Race, Class, and Sexuality:
Mediated Portrayals of Ghetto
Fabulous Homosexuality

Race and class characterized the American ghetto since its inception. Historians, sociologists, and filmmakers immortalized descriptions and images of the ghetto as a geographical location within a city where one ethnic or class group is forced to live in oppressed financial, environmental, and educational surroundings.[41] In recent times ghetto markers have moved from fixed economic and social stratifications to celebrated, fostered, and emulated identity markers. The ghetto identity is now one often boxed and sold through new media genres of ghetto lit, ghetto fabulous films, and television series. Rather than seek to become middle class (read black bourgeois), there is a distinct celebration of the ghetto vernacular in hip-hop bling attainments. In his article "Border Patrolling," Watts best demonstrated the liminal discourse of the ghetto fabulous bling lifestyle. Marked by limited interests in lasting wealth, the ghetto identity is specifically one that is interested in the attainment of cash money for the here and now.[42]There is no interest or value in the long-term accumulation of wealth. In his discussion of the film *8 Mile,* Watts demonstrates the ways in which ghetto vernacular and discourse use the markers of class to limit the options for wealth management.[43] Living becomes a matter of spending and consumption versus saving and upward mobility, even though the dangers of these celebrations of the ghetto are many.

The media portrays Dodson as ghetto fabulous. He was a resident of Lincoln Park, a low-income housing project in Hunstville, Alabama, that NBC affiliate WAFF-48 associates with high crime, minimal educational opportunities, and minority residents. Dodson's use of vernacular English coupled with his geographic location marked him as ghetto. He used statements like "Hide yo kids, hide yo wife, and hide yo husbands cuz they rapin errybody up in here," and "Run tell dat homeboy." In post interviews where Dodson is calm, he relies on some African American vernacular English tropes and slang, for instance, "You know what I'm saying?" "Let the police handle they business," "What had happened."[44] However, Dodson's command of the English language seems on par for the average American regardless of race. Lucy Ferriss proves that his language use in the original footage diagrams perfectly.[45] Antoine also shows his ability to codeswitch. When angered, Antoine Dodson relied on codes and tropes to better articulate his sentiments. The ability to speak standard English and code-switch complicates Dodson's perceived ghetto fabulousness.

Dodson's clothing and fashion sense on the surface mark his body as gay and ghetto fabulous. He wears name-brand women's clothing, sporting big names like Ed Hardy, designer jeans, and name-brand pricey sneakers. He also appropriates the queen through his tone, gestures, and mannerisms. However, Dodson's behavior cannot be reduced to gay and ghetto fabulous. As aforementioned, the ghetto fabulous marker is one that encourages spending on material items, but not long-term savings or upward mobility. After Dodson made money, he started a foundation for juvenile diabetes (long-term investment), and moved his family out of the housing projects (upward mobility). Dodson might sport long weaves, bright blond and brown cornrows, press and curls, ponytails, and the infamous doo-rag over an unkempt afro, all of which caused Dodson's body to be labeled a fabulous ghetto queen.[46] While Dodson's performance creates a space for the queen, his identities are more than that. Unfortunately, the Gregory Brothers capitalized on exploiting his identities as reductive ones with little room for critical questioning. Within the two-minute and eight-second video, Dodson is unable to insert his complex identities through performativity. Instead, the Gregory Brothers edit the video in a way that exaggerates his race, class, and sexuality. His performance was literally concocted for entertainment. After so many click and shares, that performance authenticates stereotypes. Antoine's body fits criteria for exploitation as a racial and sexual minority with lower class standing. If he spoke in standard English, wasn't flamboyant, and didn't fulfill any stereotypes associated with blackness, the original newscast video wouldn't have been fodder for the Gregory brothers, and it wouldn't have gone viral. What audiences expect and accept are stereotyped, watered down versions of complex identities. There's a reason Flavor Flav was cast as the first black reality television bachelor, with Real, Chance, and Ray J following in his footsteps. However, in the next section I discuss the ways in which Dodson flipped the script. Using his own YouTube channel, website, twitter feed, and other social media sites, Dodson was able to insert his own body into the storyline, creating a fuller story, and exploiting media in the same ways media exploited him.

Exploiting Media and Appropriating Stereotypes

Exaggerated performances of class, race, sexuality, and gender abound on social media platforms. Nicki Minaj, the notorious Real Housewives of Atlanta, or the catty young talents of Making the Band perform exaggerated caricatures formulated for entertainment and profit. Mainstreaming those performance, much like the Gregory Brothers did for Antoine Dodson, creates a level of authenticity and visibility for those caricatures. When Bryant Keith Alexander asks, "who gets to tell the story—why, how, and with what consequences," the costs rests in the intersection where exploiter and exploited meet, even if in the same body.[47] There is a risk associated with authenticated caricatures; but there is much to gain when creating a space within that brand of authenticity to insert multiple stories of the body and generate a more complex narrative of self. Social media provides that space. There are no gatekeepers or people specifically hired to silence others. While some sites employ rules in terms of what can and cannot be shared based on age restrictions, graphic sexual content, or hate, for every site that has restrictions, there are sites with far less restrictions that welcome graphic sexual content, hate, and other types of information that are generally censored in more heavily monitored media like television. Sites like YouTube, Facebook, Twitter, Tumblr, Wordpress, and many more provide unlimited space to upload, share, retweet, follow, and comment on content. These performative gestures speak to who we are every time we perform them, albeit authentic representations or not, because they exist within already embedded power structures. Antoine Dodson took advantage of the micro-level worldmaking, Henry Jenkins articulates.[48] He was able to use social networking sites and new media to create a fuller story of self. His official website contains personal stories, videos, and fan comments that he controls. His YouTube site has various personal videos that do not directly relate the Bed Intruder incident, but work with the memes toward creating a believable story. As DeAndrea and Walther contend, Dodson participates in strategically exploiting social media as a form impression management where he has more control over his portrayals of identity versus an invisible, hegemonic puppeteer.[49]

Dodson is exploiting the media in the same way that the media exploits him. We can be critical of representations of race, class, sexuality, and gender, but in the end, Dodson used social media to create a niche for himself, protect his family, and better his lifestyle. He went so far as to ask for donations to move his family out of the projects and into a nicer home, and to raise money for juvenile diabetes research. What started as a public service announcement turned into a brilliant self-marketing campaign.

An example of Dodson exploiting his performative identity is evidenced in his commercial *The Sex Offender Tracker App*. Dodson's agent contacted him about doing the commercial. In every video of Dodson post-incident, he is quiet, humble, and shy. He dresses in what he considers to be fashionable clothing. We don't see tank tops, doo-rags, or bad hair days. However, in the commercial, which aired on October 20, 2010, we see Dodson in his original form, replete with black tank top and red doo-rag covering blow-dried hair. He borrows key phrases from the original newscast and delivers his message in similar ways.

This video, much like the first few, caught the viral wave. By October 25, the video had over ninety thousand views. By the twenty-seventh, the video had over seven hundred thousand views between several reposts. With these numbers, it is clear that social media users like to click and share the boisterous, flamboyant, stereotypical, Dodson. His performance, albeit authentic or not, is a caricature of himself that he is willing to perform to make money.[50] In appropriating his caricature, he further authenticates stereotypes that limit the publics' viewing of his complex character to a reductive portrayal of race, sexuality, class, and gender. It is no coincidence that the producers chose to further capitalize on the viral wave of the original news cast hoping that viewers will find the video humorous and click and share it, resulting in free viral advertising for their product. However, Dodson found ways to balance the caricatured performance through the performative possibilities of social media.

Performative/Performance Possibilities of Social Media

Appropriation is not always a negative phenomenon. We appropriate behaviors, attitudes, style, and language use through our everyday ways of being. E. Patrick Johnson interrogated the way blackness is appropriated by both black and whites, and how, through that appropriation, we create political turmoil centered on performing blackness in restricted ways.[51] Mediated spaces like television and film, which are dominated by gatekeepers, appropriate blackness in limiting ways.[52] However, social media doesn't have the same type of gatekeepers, or limited space and hours (think primetime television versus late night infomercials). Social media has the power to reproduce any type of image, albeit oversimplified representations of identity through clicking and sharing videos, or more complex and intersectional narratives through personal blogging, websites, or twitter feeds. Social media, then, affords a space to challenge representation. Social media users can participate in worldmaking at a micro-level by inserting detailed stories alongside the viral videos and memes to allow a fuller story to emerge where each story feels like it fits with the others.[53]

While social media creates a space for fuller depictions of identities, I would be remiss to claim social networks are utopian ideals. Everyday users choose what to watch, what to share, and what is viral worthy. Not surprisingly, social media users generate the same "nonthreatening images" portrayed in media controlled by large corporations and gatekeepers. While social media is embedded in existing power structures, social networks are not closed systems dominated by gatekeepers or large corporations like more traditional media outlets. Individuals can insert their own stories into the asynchronous timeline of events, creating more complex and fluid representations. Once a person rises to social media fame, people seek out those stories and participate in world-making.[54] Antoine Dodson does this through his many interviews and music videos on YouTube, his personal website replete with definitions, a bio, and updates, as well as through his twitter feed and comments on other peoples posts. Social media is free, virtual, limitless, and not bound by time restrictions. As of June 2012, people were still commenting on his website, tweets, and YouTube videos. Antoine Dodson's case illuminates the ability to insert one's own body and complicates the relationship between the exploiter/exploited, as well as performance/performativity. When social media users chose to exploit Antoine Dodson's identities, he had every right to capitalize off that exploitation as well. Dodson admits to his intention of capitalizing off his "cyber spotlight," stating "I took it an I was running with it, and I'm still running with it."[55] Dodson exercised agency, was active, and smart in the situation. He seized the opportunity for upward mobility, and it worked. Dodson was able to move his sister and himself to Los Angeles, he negotiated with the Gregory Brothers to make 50 percent of the profits from Youtube sales, and he continues to pursue his dream of owning a beauty salon and getting his degree in business. Some social media users mocked Antoine Dodson as a coonery minstrel show of black homosexuality alongside ghetto fabulousness by posting videos that demonized his black body as wrong, bad, unintelligent, and emasculated, he inserted himself into the mix.[56] However, he told his story in a way that complicated identity and invited others into his intersections of race, class, sexuality, and gender. He brought his body into being through performativity, but also used his body in performance to resist sexual violence, resist exploitation as a victim, and enact agency in order to create change.

By exploiting the possibility of social media, Antoine Dodson told his own version of the story. In his own rendition, we see Dodson's body doing things through performance. He embodied heroic attributes by protecting his family, financially taking care of his family, thwarting off rapists, utilizing his voice, and exercising agency in the media to talk about rape and the dangers of sexual predators. Dodson is also doing things to better himself like going to school to get his degree, making smart business decisions, and using media's exploitation of him as a means to make money to take care of his family. All admirable stories readily available on his YouTube channel, website, and other media outlets he created for himself. Dodson's accomplishments alongside his effeminate performance creates a space for multiple and complex performances of identity that bend rigid binaries like masculine and feminine. Beyond limited and reductive classifications exists a much more complex character, not caricature, that denies binaries.

Dodson's success shows that gendered and racialized boundaries are changing, and, for Dodson, that is largely in part due to the possibility of new media. Dodson's ability to insert his own narratives into social media made possible the rendering of more complex displays of identity. Dodson created a space to be the Queen, exerted his masculinity when it has been continually denied to him because if his sexuality and race, capitalized on his ability to fight back, utilized his voice, and exercised agency.

As we embrace Dodson, we embrace people previously denied on the basis of sexuality, class, and a lack of formal education in the form of a college degree among other things. In addition, the acceptance of Dodson on the basis of his intersectional performance allows room for more complex identities and narratives. As Adiche reminds us, it is not that stereotypes aren't true, it's that they aren't all there is.[57] Social media creates space for people to perform their complex identities, authenticate those identities, and sometimes be exploited on the basis of those identities. As Johnson notes, "Blackness, too, is fragile when subsumed by rules of inclusion; yet, like gender and sexual performativity, its mobility is never forestalled once it is set into motion in/through performance, no matter who is in the driver's seat."[58] Because of the lack of gatekeepers, limitless space, and asynchronous nature, social media allows for less inhibited constructions of sexuality, gender, class, and race.

Using an intersectional approach, the goals of this research were to: (1) to unpack the different intersections of Antoine Dodson's identity in a way that authenticates his performance of a complex self versus reducing him to a stereotype; and (2) investigate the performative and performance possibilities of social media. I hope to have made apparent that while reductive identities are easy to exploit via media, social media allows for individuals to redefine their identities in more complex ways, insert their bodies into the social networking landscapes, and exploit social media as a form of impression management and individual change. Dodson did just that by telling his story across multiple sites like Facebook, Twitter, and Youtube, generating income, and creating a level of mobility for himself and his family that otherwise might not have been possible without exploiting the opportunities present via social media. In terms of my second goal, I hope I illuminated the ways in which social networks (1) create space to insert the body without time restrictions or gatekeepers, thereby rendering elaborate, digitized narratives; and (2) leave a trail for scholars to study the ways in which people insert their intersectional identities into the virtual world.

The same facets that create possibilities also generate challenges. The politics of representation shift as individuals have more control over self-presentation. Also, the amount of stimuli can be overwhelming. There are countless spoofs of *The Bed Intruder* song that I didn't have the chance to analyze because there were just too many. Social media spaces can be difficult to contain, access entirely, and control. Future research should continue to address the performative and performance possibilities of social media and the fluidity of identity within intersections. Future research should also explore what types of videos go viral and what those themes (if any) of virality suggest in terms of existing power structures.

Notes

1. Chimamanda Adiche, "The Dangers of a Single Story," TED video, 18:49, filmed October 2009, http://www.ted.com/talks/chimamanda_adichie_ the_ danger_of_a_single_story.html.

2. Janet Murray, *Hamlet on the Holodeck: The Future of Narrative in Cyberspace* (Cambridge, MA: MIT Press, 1999).

3. Joseph B. Walther, Yuhua Liang, David C. DeAndrea, Stephanie Tong, Caleb Carr, Erin L. Spottswood, and Yair Amaichai-Hamburger, "The Effect of Feedback on Identity Shift in Computer-Mediated Communication," *Media Psychology* 14, no. 1 (January 2011): 1–26; David C. DeAndrea, and Jospeh B. Walther, "Attributions for Inconsistencies between Online and Offline Self-Presentations," *Communication Research* 38, no. 6 (January 2011): 805–25; Alex Campbell, "The Search for Authenticity: An Exploration of an Online Skinhead Newsgroup," *New Media and Society* 8, no. 2 (April 2006): 269–94; W. Benjamin Myers and Desireé Rowe, "The Critical Lede: New Media and Ecological Balance," *Text and Performance Quarterly* 32, no. 1 (January 2012): 73.

4. Erving Goffman, *The Presentation of Self in Everyday Life* (Garden City, NY: Doubleday, 1959).

5. danah boyd and Nicole B. Ellison, "Social Network Sites: Definition, History, and Scholarship," *Journal of Computer-Mediated Communication* 13, no. 1 (October 2007): 210–30.

6. Kimberle Crenshaw, "Mapping the Margins: Intersectionality, Identity Politics, and Violence against Women of Color," *Stanford Law Review* 43, no. 6 (July 1991): 1241–99.

7. Ange-Marie Hancock, "When Multiplication Doesn't Equal Quick Addition: Examining Intersectionality as a Research Paradigm," *Perspectives on Politics* 5, no. 1 (2007):75.

8. Elizabeth R. Cole and Abigail J. Stewart, "Invidious Comparisons: Imagining a Psychology of Race and Gender Beyond Differences," *Political Psychology* 22, no. 2 (June 2001): 293–308. Mary Hawkesworth, "Congressional Enactments of Race-Gender: Toward a Theory of Race-Gendered Institutions," *American Political Science Review* 97, no. 4 (November 2003): 529–50; Leslie McCall, "The Complexity of Intersectionality," *Signs: Journal of Women in Culture and Society* 30, no. 3 (Summer 2005): 1771–1800; Stephanie A. Shields, "Gender: An Intersectionality Perspective," *Sex Roles* 59, nos. 5–6 (September 2008): 301–11; Lisa Bowleg, "When Black Plus Lesbian Plus Woman Does Not Equal Black Lesbian Woman: The Methodological Challenges of Qualitative and Quantitative Intersectionality Research," *Sex Roles* 59, nos. 5–6 (September 2008): 312–25; Carolyn Nielsen, "Moving Mass Communication Scholarship beyond Binaries: A Call for Intersectionality," *Media Report to Women* 39, no. 1 (Winter 2011): 6–11.

9. Hancock, "When Multiplication Doesn't Equal Quick Addition," 63–79.

10. "Antoine Dodson Warns PERP on LIVE TV! (Original)," YouTube video, 2:09, posted by "CrazyLaughAction," April 11, 2012, http://www.youtube.com/ watch?v=EzNhaLUT520.

11. "The Bed Intruder Song!!! (now on iTunes)," YouTube video, 2:08, posted by "schmoyoho," July 31, 2010, http://www.youtube.com/ watch?v=hMtZfW2z9dw.

12. "The Original A&T Bed Intruder Song 8.11.2010," YouTube video, 3:26, posted by "SpeechlessQue," August 12, 2010, http://www.youtube.com/ watch?v=Q3UsvLyu3N0.

13. Lev Grossman, "How to Become Famous in 30 Seconds," *Time Magazine,* April 24, 2006, accessed October 22, 2010,http://www.time.com/ time/magazine/article/0,9171,1184060,00.html.

14. "Antoine Dodson's Commercial for the Sex Offender Tracker App," YouTube video, 1:13, posted by "Hoodtmz5's," October 28, 2010, http://www.youtube.com/watch?v=L2uJyCPCy5w.

15. Coonery is a new term that is widely used in the streets to refer to the act of cooning. A person can be labeled a coon, or they can participate in coonery.

16. Akleman, Palmer and Logan define a caricature as a portrait or literary description using exaggeration of some characteristics and oversimplification of others. A caricature refers to real life people's depictions. Character refers to a person presented in a story or the aggregate features and traits that form an individual nature of some person or thing. A character is a well-rounded depiction. A caricature is more of an exaggeration of a particular character trait. See Ergun Aklemen, James Palmer and Ryan Logan, "Making Extreme Caricatures with a New Interactive 2dDeformation Technique with Simplicial Complexes," in *Visual 2000 Proceedings* (2000), 100–105.

17. Judith Butler, *Bodies That Matter* (New York: Rutledge, 1993), 198.

18. Richard Schechner, *Between Theatre and Anthropology* (Philadelphia: University of Pennsylvania Press, 1985).

19. Anthony Kubiak, "Splitting the Difference: Performance and Its Double in American Culture," *The Drama Review* 42, no. 4 (Winter 1998): 91–114.

20. Kubiak, "Splitting the Difference," 91.

21. Nadine Ehlers, "Passing Phantasms/Sanctioning Performatives: (Re) Reading White Masculinity In Rhinelander V. Rhinelander," *Studies in Law, Politics, and Society* 27, no. 1 (2003): 63–91.

22. Nadine Ehlers, "Hidden in Plain Sight: Defying Juridical Racialization in *Rhinelander* v. *Rhinelander*," *Communication and Critical/Cultural Studies* 1, no. 4 (December 2004): 313–34.

23. Ehlers, "Hidden in Plain Sight."

24. Louis F. Miron, and Johnathan Xavier Inda, "Race as a Kind of Speech Act," *Cultural Studies: A Research Annual* 5, no. 1 (2000): 85–107.

25. E. Warwick Slinn, "Poetry and Culture: Performativity and Critique," *New Literary History* 30, no. 1 (Winter 1999): 64.

26. E. Patrick Johnson, "'Quare' Studies, or (Almost) Everything I Know about Queer Studies I Learned from My Grandmother," In *Black Queer Studies: A Critical Anthology*, eds. E. Patrick Johnson and Mae G. Henderson (Durham, NC: Duke University Press, 2005), 136.

27. Bryant Keith Alexander and John T. Warren, "The Materiality of Bodies: Critical Reflections on Pedagogy, Politics, and Positionality," *Communication Quarterly* 50 (2002): 340.

28. Johnson, "'Quare' Studies," 136.

29. Johnson, "'Quare' Studies," 137.

30. E. Patrick Johnson, *Appropriating Blackness: Performance and the Politics of Authenticity* (Durham, NC: Duke University Press, 2003).

31. Earl Ofari Hutchinson, "My Gay Problem, Your Black Problem," in *The Greatest Taboo: Homosexuality in Black Communities*, ed. D. Constantine-Simms (Los Angeles: Alyson Books, 2000), 3.

32. Johnson, *Appropriating Blackness*.

33. Marlon Riggs, "Black Macho Revisted: Reflections of a Snap! Queen," in *Out in Culture: Gay, Lesbian and Queer Essays on Popular Culture*, eds. Cory K. Creeknur and Alexander Doty (Durham, NC: Duke University Press, 1995).

34. Johnson, *Appropriating Blackness*.

35. Riggs, "Black Macho Revisited," 390.

36. Riggs, "Black Macho Revisited," 390.

37. Riggs, "Black Macho Revisited," 390.

38. Dwight McBride, *Why I Hate Abercrombie and Fitch: Essays on Race and Sexuality* (New York: New York University Press, 2005), 208.

39. *Noah's Arc*, Directed by Patrik-Ian Polk (2005, Santa Monica, CA: MTV Studios), DVD; *True Blood*, Directed by Alan Ball (2008, Studio City, CA: HBO Studios, 2009), DVD; *The Wire*, Directed by Alex Zakrzewski (2002, Studio City, CA: HBO Studios, 2009), DVD.

40. McBride, *Why I Hate*, 18.

41. Joseph A. Sarfoh, "The West African Zongo and the American Ghetto," *Journal of Black Studies* 17, no. 1 (September 1986): 71–84.

42. Eric King Watts, "Border Patrolling and 'Passing' in Eminem's *8 Mile*," *Critical Studies in Media Communication* 22, no. 3 (2005): 187–206.

43. Watts, "Border Patrolling."

44. "CBS Interview with Shira Lizar," YouTube video, 9:59, posted by "antoniedodson24," August 18, 2010, http://www.youtube.com/watch?v=Jb-ewYxdLJ4.

45. Lucy Ferris, "Antoine Saves My Class," *The Chronicle of Higher Education*, September 7, 2011, Accessed March 14, 2012 http://chronicle.com/blogs/linguafranca/2011/09/07/antoine-dodson-saves-my-class/.

46. Jam Donaldson, "Antoine Dodson: Why He Makes Us Laugh and Uncomfortable," *Black Voices,* August 4, 2010, accessed October 22, 2010, http://www.bvBlackspin.com/2010/08/04/antoine-dodson/.

47. Bryant Keith Alexander, *Performing Black Masculinities: Race, Culture, and Queer Identity* (Lanham, MD: AltaMira Press, 2006), xiv.

48. Henry Jenkins, *Convergence Culture: Where Old and New Media Collide* (New York: New York University Press, 2006).

49. DeAndrea and Walther, "Attribution for Inconsistencies."

50. In his interview with Shira Lizar, Dodson acknowledges the stereotypical representation of his first appearance, claiming that neither he nor his family is angry or loud. He said he didn't realize he was "acting like that on camera." I do not want to dismiss Dodson's self-critique, but I do think he had every right to be upset, perform his reaction on camera, and reenact those sentiments for the commercial, which is still about sexual predators and the reason for the original story.

51. Johnson, *Appropriating Blackness.*

52. Johnson, *Appropriating Blackness*; Stuart Hall, *Representation: Cultural Representations and Signifying Practices* (Thousand Oaks, CA: Sage, 2000).

53. Jenkins, *Convergence Culture.*

54. Jenkins, *Convergence Culture.*

55. NPR Staff, "Antoine Dodson: Riding YouTube out of the 'Hood,'" *National Public Radio,* August 23, 2010, accessed March 2, 2012, http://www.npr.org/templates/story/story.php?storyId=129381037.

56. See the following videos for spoofs and commentaries that make fun of Antoine Dodson for being black, poor, gay, and undereducated and/or outright call him a coon. "Woman Wakes Up to Find Intruder in Her bed (SPOOF)." YouTube video, 0:45, posted by "AfricanoBoiShow," August 2, 2010, http://www.youtube.com/watch?v=tLgF_ZjFD9I; "Black Man ANGRY at Antoine Dodson." YouTube video, posted by "dcigs," 8:13, December 11, 2010 http://www.youtube.com/watch?v=YJQRX6gg3pA; "Hideja Kids, Its Antoine Dodson." YouTube video, 4:49, posted by "Fdeez," October 27, 2010, http://www.youtube.com/watch?v=yxTPKQ_sv98; "Antoine Dodson's Chimney Intruder' Song." YouTube video, 5:46, posted by "Lovelyti2002," December 23, 2010, http://www.youtube.com/watch?v=xCHvDML0IYU; "Antoine Dodson – Woman Wakes Up to Find an Intruder in her Bed (Parody)." YouTube video, 0:45, posted by "ShortFunnyAsian," August 4, 2010 http://www.youtube.com/watch?v=VP38qBAXpAk.

57. Adiche, "The Dangers of a Single Story."

58. Johnson, *Appropriating Blackness.*

Chapter 9

Developing a Transgender Identity in a Virtual Community

Sara Green-Hamann and John C. Sherblom

Social identities are negotiated and developed through the communication processes that occur within a person's social network and community.[1] The community's values confirm, corroborate, or contradict that person's identity.[2] As the boundaries between physical lives and social media become increasingly fluid and inseparable, an individual's online identity and community participation interact with and affect the physical one.[3]

Transgender Identity and Social Media

Transgender describes the identity of a person whose gender expression or behavior is different from that stereotypically associated with their assigned sex at birth.[4] People having a transgender identity have many influences on their self-presentation in community and multiple motives for participating in social media. Transgender individuals often receive less social support from their families than do their non-transgender siblings and less support from friends than either heterosexual women or homosexual men.[5]Male to female transgender individuals, in particular, often become estranged from their birth families and childhood friends.[6] In addition, transgender individuals experience discrimination in employment; limited housing opportunities; victimization from hate crimes; and prejudice from religious, military, education, and healthcare institutions.[7]

Even when transgender individuals do maintain close relationships with their birth families they may feel uncomfortable talking with them about being transgendered. They may be secretive and less forthcoming with family and childhood friends due to the social stigma attached to being transgendered.[8] Many report experiencing ridicule, social isolation, and alienation.[9]

Composing only 1 percent of the population transgender individuals rarely find others similar to themselves in their physical communities.[10] Young transgender people especially feel isolated and rarely have access to others like themselves. Yet, those who do have transgender friends and relatives report experiencing less depression than those with fewer transgender friends and relatives.[11]

Social media provide platforms upon which people can build social networks and virtual communities. Blogs, podcasts, wikis, and sites such as Facebook, Pinterest, Second Life, Twitter, and YouTube each provide a medium within which people can share ideas, opinions, insights, experiences, and perspectives; pursue relationships; and engage in social networking with a community of like-minded friends.[12] Socially stigmatized minorities like transgender individuals often turn to social media to find a network of friends and confidants.[13] The anonymity of participation and access to others who have similar experiences and values make involvement in social media attractive.[14] Participation in a virtual community can be particularly influential on a person's self concept. Involvement in a virtual community can alter, even transform, an individual's real-life behaviors and identity.[15]

Virtual Communities and Social Capital

Community denotes feelings of commonality and belonging that connect participants within a social network. Community members matter to each other.[16] Individuals identify as part of the community and that identity entails a sense of responsibility and reciprocal obligation.[17] Virtual communities offer an opportunity to interact with others outside of one's physical location. These communities reflect one's personal interests rather than happenstance of birth.[18] Participants share experiences, develop identities, and participate within the community's social network and norms.[19]

Participation in a virtual community provides a number of positive outcomes.[20] Pediatric transplant recipients experience an increased sense of normalcy, enhanced self-worth, and enlarged social network by participating in a virtual community.[21] Individuals living with a physical disability develop a more positive sense of well-being.[22] In general, participation in a virtual community contributes to personal growth, recognition, and social capital.[23]

The term social capital takes on various meanings in the literature. However, it can be defined broadly as the resources an individual secures by participating in a social network. Network theory portrays social capital as embedded in the assets and resources of the social network itself.[24] It develops through the ongoing, cyclical processes of social relationship that occur within a community. Social capital creates positive outcomes for both the individual and the community.[25] It generates trust among community members and commitment to the community as a whole.[26]

People purposefully invest in social relationships with the expectation of personal benefit and communities thrive by facilitating bridging and bonding social capital.[27] A community's social network provides a valuable resource to the individual in the form of information, relationships, and personal recognition. Positive affective bonds form within these relationships that provide emotional support and encouragement to the individual.[28] These, in turn, build and sustain the community.

Bridging social capital occurs in more diffuse social networks. These networks include individuals with a broad range of backgrounds who may form only tentative relationships with each other. These weak-tie bridging networks offer relatively loose connections among a wide range of people, but provide access to a broader set of information. Relationships formed within these networks bridge social horizons and open up new opportunities. Weak-tie social networks tend to be more tolerant of diverse perspectives on an issue, provide access to more diverse types of information, and offer personal examples that can inspire and motivate an individual.[29] The social capital generated provides an opportunity for personal identity growth and community development.

Bonding social capital forms in tightly knit, strong-tie networks of close friends and relatives.[30] Norms of reciprocity and trustworthiness arise and these networks offer emotional support and understanding.[31] The emotional support of strong-tie bonding networks creates higher participant involvement, interdependence, well-being, self-esteem, and satisfaction with life.[32]

Social media can facilitate and enhance the generation of bridging and bonding social capital in ways that produce a variety of positive outcomes for participants.[33] The ease of access to others similar to oneself and the relative anonymity afforded by social media lower the barriers to interaction and encourage self disclosure.[34] Fuller discussions of social capital and its role in social media and virtual communities abound in the literature.[35]

The Transgender Resource Center in Second Life

A virtual community provides one type of social medium for interacting in a social network. The Transgender Resource Center in Second Life is a virtual community meeting place for individuals who identify as transgender. It provides a safe place for individuals to interact with other transgender people from around the world and to get together for regularly scheduled group meetings.

Second Life is a three-dimensional virtual world that has the visual dimensions of physical space and the social characteristics of a virtual community.[36] More than 15 million registered users participate in this virtual world. Participants create symbolic visual representations of themselves called avatars and interact with other participants through a nearly synchronous form of communication. Second Life avatars take on a virtual physicality, interact socially, and participate in communication processes that are symbolically similar to those that occur in FtF group meetings.[37] Communicating through avatars maintains participant anonymity while facilitating the immediacy, interactivity, social presence, trust, and socioemotional communication.

Participants communicate with each other in real time in an environment that does not require them to leave their physical homes to attend group meetings. They remain personally anonymous to each other, identified only by their avatar name and image, but over time develop an online reputation and identity within the group. Group meetings occur at a predetermined time and virtual location, and take on a social routine and structure. Participants get to know each other as they interact, negotiate meanings, and construct social knowledge in ways that influence both their social media reputations and real-life identities.[38]

Disclosing a socially stigmatized identity to close friends and family in real life runs the risk of disapproval and the potential of a high social cost. The anonymity of Second Life enables a freer expression of self than is usually available in real-life relationships. The potential for sanction from violating social expectations is greatly reduced. Hence, the social medium of Second Life provides an opportunity for individuals to explore transformations in personal identity that may not yet be communicated openly or fully to real-life family and friends. Disclosing this identity in the Transgender Resource Center group meetings can create relationships of understanding and bonds of empathy among community participants.[39]

Method

Procedures

This chapter analyzes the personal identity and social capital processes that occur in discussions among male-to-female transitioning transgender individuals attending meetings at the Transgender Resource Center in Second Life. Members of this community identify as transgender and are in various phases of transitioning their gender identity, from cross dressing to undergoing sexual reassignment surgery. The lead researcher received permission from the group leader, and then in turn from group members, to attend ten of the regularly scheduled weekly group meetings. These meetings occurred for approximately one hour each. An average of nine members attended each meeting with the largest meeting having sixteen participants. Each meeting was recorded using Second Life software. To assure anonymity avatar names were removed from the transcripts before the analysis began.

A Constant Comparative Analysis

Participant conversational turns were analyzed using a grounded theory constant comparison method. The goal of this constant comparison analysis is to generate a set of concepts that describe patterns in the data holistically rather than as isolated themes. To achieve this goal data analysis proceeds as an iterative process that starts with the text and gradually refines it into a set of inter-related themes. The researcher becomes immersed in the text and develops an understanding by reading and rereading it; reviewing the context; moving back and forth between text and context; examining relationships among the expressed meanings as represented by the text; developing a broader understanding of the underlying dimensions of meaning, themes, subthemes, and inter-relationships; reflecting upon them; and constantly revising interpretations.[40] Through this iterative process the researcher strives to develop a more cogent understanding of the patterns in the text and interpretation of the purposeful communication action underlying those patterns.[41] Constant comparison analysis provides a good method for exploring the multiple perspectives and meanings of being transgendered, and the social capital dynamics underlying these discussions that occur during the Transgender Resource Center meetings.

Results

Three general themes emerge from the present analysis of these conversations. The first theme recognizes the sharing of language and identity among participants. The second identifies a theme of reciprocity in the subthemes of sharing information and personal acknowledgment. The third theme articulates a bonding among group members in the subthemes of sharing personal perspectives and feeling understood.

Sharing Language and Identity

The sharing of language and identity develops as individuals within the transgender group discuss being transgendered in their own words and from their own personal experiences. "Just so you know, the absence was due to my having had SRS [sexual reassignment surgery] a month ago." "Not everyone wants or needs GRS [gender reassignment surgery] or FFS [facial feminization surgery]." "I have been feminizing for the last few years although I only began taking HRT [hormone replacement therapy] 1 am on Friday." "Does the NHS [national health service] require the one year RLE [real life experience] before hormones?" "Blending is about a lot more than appearance." "I think my asexuality is normal at eighteen months into HRT." "I expect that about two years into HRT my sexual interest will return with a vengeance." "In Georgia you have to have GRS to have your gender marker changed." Group membership and identity are recognized through an understanding and use of these linguistic abbreviations.

Reciprocity

Sharing Information

By sharing information with the group individuals provide a knowledge and understanding of how to navigate the process of being transgendered. One participant notes: "Not usually that expensive for the hormones themselves, but visits and blood tests would be." Others ask questions such as: "Anyone know any good SRS [sexual reassignment surgery] places in the UK [United Kingdom]?" "Is being a TS [transsexual] a preexisting condition?" "I had pretty good evidence that my own bouts with depression were related to testosterone surges." "I've calmed down a lot since I started estradiol." "Self medication can be dangerous, estrogen can cause high blood pressure." "Laws differ from state to state about name change, sex change, all of that." "UK: name changes are trivially easy and don't even require a legal professional."

Personal Acknowledgment

In addition, participants acknowledge each other, offer assistance, show support, and join in celebrations. "Cindy, you should feel special, you see things through a broader view than the status quo." "How can we help, Susie?" "Rosie, though hormones are wonderful, you are being yourself living as a woman." "Even though it's stressful, you holding on ok?" "Congrats, Amy." "Have a good week, sisters." "You've got support online anyway." "Lyn, I'm more on that wavelength myself."

Bonding

Sharing Personal Perspectives

In sharing personal perspectives participants demonstrate an underlying assumption that others in the group have had similar experiences and can understand the perspective beneath what they are saying. Others respond with tolerance and support rather than arguing or challenging the specifics of these diverse perspectives. "In fact, not even trans any more. Had that fixed. ;-)." "Transsexualism is a birth defect in my view." "I do feel 'special' in that both aspects are within me." "I prefer to celebrate being trans because I can't do much to be anything but trans." "I had to try and learn how to be male, being female is natural. Being male felt like faking." "The worst part of the hormones is acting masculine, and then feeling feminine." "I've had a lifetime hormone deficiency (pituitary gland) . . . and I'm pretty sure it's related to that."

Feeling Understood

With these expressions of sharing and acceptance participants increasingly feel understood, become more willing to share their own personal feelings, and become more open to offering personal support and empathy to the expressions of others. "There's a sense I have of an incomplete self, both when I am presenting as male and as female." "For myself, I consider it a defect, because I needed to get it fixed." "It is helpful to know that some of the confusion that plagues my brain I'm not alone in." "It's the testosterone, dear, so much of our behavior is hormonal." "Jill you've always been whole, never feel that you're not." "You're not alone, but it's good to talk to people who have gone through the same thing." "My brother at first said, "wouldn't it be easier to be gay" and I said . . . 'well yeah!'" "Someday you'll fall in love and it's going to be with a man, woman, or otherwise."

Discussion

Sharing Language and Identity

Many of the complex issues involved in maintaining a transgender identity are evident in the participant communication in this transgender community. Within the group there is an ease of communication, in part because of the shared language. As with other marginalized groups, transgender individuals create an in-group language that describes their mutual experience. Much of that shared language revolves around medical terms such as sexual reassignment surgery (SRS), hormone replacement therapy (HRT), and gender reassignment surgery (GRS). Medical procedures play a large part in the transgender experience; however the shared language extends beyond the medical to experiences of individuals prior to surgery and resulting from those procedures in their real-life experiences (RLE) with blending and feminizing. This language helps an individual through the multiple simultaneous processes of developing a transgender identity and builds social ties within the group. The shared language emphasizes group member similarities while positioning non transgender individuals as other. With shared language comes shared understanding and perspective.

Reciprocity

Sharing Information

A transgender individual is unlikely to have met or talked with many other transgender people in his daily life. In addition, there is little information about transgender issues available in the media. This transgender community provides participants access to information they may be unable to find elsewhere. Individuals share personal experiences, ask questions, and learn from others who have experienced similar things. The diversity of group members in geographic location and background gives participants access to a broad range of information and expertise.

Personal Acknowledgment

Marginalized individuals often feel alone. Access to a group that acknowledges a person by name and recognizes one as a valued participant can lessen the feeling of marginalization and loneliness. Members show an interest in each other, support each other, share their personal experiences with the transitioning process, and celebrate the successes of their everyday lives. Participants recognize when others are experiencing difficult times and offer emotional support. They offer support and encouragement to members who are just beginning to experience the turbulence of the transitioning process, and they celebrate transition milestones. Vicariously experiencing the transitions of others can help a participant better prepare for, understand, and deal with any difficulties they face in the future.

Bonding

Sharing Personal Perspectives

They identify with each other's experiences, confusion, frustration, and joy. Participants often share frustrations with the medical and social aspects of being transgender, and with family members who may not understand why individuals can't just be the sex and gender they were born. Through sharing these personal experiences they develop strong relationships.

Feeling Understood

Sharing these experiences with others who have had similar experiences leads group members to feeling understood. The complexities of gender identity may not be understood fully by family and friends, but other members of this group can understand the experience and its emotional implications. Community members understand the difference between their gender and their sex, know the emotional turmoil a person can experience when acting in their assigned biological role, and understand the medical and emotional aspects that come with being transgender. Group members can offer advice and emotional support in the transition from one's original biological sex, and can share stories of their own experiences, helping participants further along the way.

Bridging and Bonding Social Capital

These themes identify bridging and bonding relational communication processes. Membership in the transgender community changes as individuals transition through their personal sex-change processes. This creates a constant opportunity and need for bridging social capital. When an individual enters the group initially they form weak-tie social network connections with the existing group members. Participants speak with others who have had similar experiences and gain access to the larger extended social network of information, knowledge, experience, and expertise. These weak-tie relationships provide comfort to an individual who may not have access to people with similar experiences in their daily lives. Throughout the transitioning process individuals continue to develop relationships with others in the group and begin to foster feelings of connectedness and bonding.

Weak-Tie Bridging Social Capital

Social media have been recognized by past research as fostering the opportunity for participants to build weak-tie bridging social capital.[42] Joining a large, weak-tie social network provides access to people who are similar in experience and perspective but who come from diverse backgrounds and understandings. This weak-tie network provides bridging social capital in access to the thoughts and knowledge of others, and can help an individual develop a feeling less of isolation, more ease in disclosing personal information, and greater self-confidence. The development of bridging social capital can have a positive effect on personal health and reduce individual tendencies toward risky behavior, as the community imbues the individual with hope, trust, a set of social norms, and access to needed resources in information and moral support.[43] The Transgender Resource Center promotes weak-tie social networks. Participants in the group initially develop weak-tie, bridging relationships with others who form the virtual community and who inform and inspire them.[44]

Strong-Tie Bonding Social Capital

Over time these weak-tie bridging relationships can transition into strong-tie bonding social capital. Strong-tie bonding relationships develop as members share language, identity, information, personal acknowledgment, personal perspectives, and feeling understood in ways that they have not experienced in the broader society. A sense of personal connection, interdependence, and emotional reciprocity develops among community members that creates greater reciprocity in emotional support and encouragement.[45]

Developing this bonding social capital is especially important to individuals who participate in a transgender community. As socially marginalized individuals they are often not able to express their transgender identity fully in their daily lives or experience the same level of understanding and support in their other social networks. Family and friends are unlikely to understand the biological, emotional, and physical complexities of being transgender. The Transgender Resource Center community provides specialized knowledge and expertise for dealing with personal physical, psychological, and social challenges. The emotional understanding and support facilitate a greater expression of self and sense of community. Sharing language, identity, information, acknowledgment, perspective, and understanding creates reciprocal relational bridging and bonding social capital.

Sharing language provides a conceptual point of integration and access into the thinking of the community. Individuals familiar with the terms and the complexity of their meanings develop a mutual understanding. As members interact they share information and acknowledge others as individuals and as valued members of the community. Relationships develop as participants reciprocally share information and offer expert advice based on their personal perspectives. Participants bond over their shared experiences and support each other's being understood. The relational bridging and bonding social capital together help participants form a cohesive transgender identity as individuals and as a community. Through the support provided by these bridging and bonding community social network ties, individuals can express their transgender identity more fully, with a relational comfort that supports expressing it in their physical world identities as well.

Conclusions

Developing a transgender identity requires more than changing one's biology by having a sex-change operation. There are concomitant hormonal, emotional, psychological, and social identity issues to be worked through in the transition process. For individuals who have been socially marginalized and often stigmatized in their real-life communities a virtual community like the Transgender Resource Center can provide a personally affirming social medium in which to develop that identity. The social network of this virtual community offers participants access to supportive bridging and bonding social capital. Participation in a community of others who are similar in biological, psychological, and social identity, yet diverse in personal background and experience, provides bridging social capital as expressed in sharing language, identity, information, and personal acknowledgment. Bonding social capital builds upon this reciprocal sharing in the expression of personal perspectives and feeling understood.

Both bridging and bonding social capital are important to the vibrant development of this virtual community and of the individual participants within it. Bridging social capital opens up new individual opportunities through access to diverse perspectives and sources of information, greater tolerance for the expression of a variety of opinions, and exposure to personal examples that inspire and motivate. Bonding social capital provides emotional support, feelings of being understood, higher self-esteem, and a satisfaction with life that are particularly important during times of identity transition.

Together bridging and bonding social capital encourage individuals to explore their transgender identities. As an ongoing, cyclical process social capital creates positive outcomes. Without this community of fellow experts the transgender transition experience is liable to be a lonelier and more difficult one for the individual. The weak-tie bridging information and strong-tie emotional bonding support of the community reduce some of the uncertainty and potential anxiety about the biological, hormonal, psychological, and social changes involved in that transition. The bridging and bonding social capital apparent in the community are important to the individuals going through these identity transitions.

Notes

1. Bernadett Koles and Peter Nagy, "Who Is Portrayed in Second Life: Dr. Jekyll or Mr. Hyde? The Extent of Congruence between Real Life and Virtual Identity," *Journal of Virtual Worlds Research*, 2012, accessed June 24, 2012, www.journals.tdl.org/jvwr/issue/view/254; John Monberg, "Trajectories of Computer-Mediated Communication Research," *Southern Communication Journal* 70, no. 3 (Spring 2005): 181–86.

2. Narciso Pizarro, "Structural Identity and Equivalence of Individuals in Social Networks," *International Sociology* 22, no. 6 (November 2007): 767–92; Silvio Waisbord, "When the Cart of Media Is Before the Horse of Identity: A Critique of Technology-Centered Views on Globalization," *Communication Research* 25, no. 4 (August 1998): 377–98.

3. John C. Sherblom, Lesley A. Withers, and Lynnette G. Leonard, "Communication Challenges and Opportunities for Educators Using Second Life," in *Higher Education in Virtual Worlds: Teaching and Learning in Second Life,* ed. Charles Wankel and Jan Kingsley (Bingley, UK: Emerald, 2009), 29–46; Sabine Trepte, Leonard Reinecke, and Keno Juechems, "The Social Side of Gaming: How Playing Online Computer Games Creates Online and Offline Social Support," *Computers in Human Behavior* 28, no. 3 (May 2012): 832–39.

4. Emilia L. Lombardi, "Integration Within a Transgender Social Network and Its Effect Upon Members' Social and Political Activity," *Journal of Homosexuality* 37, no. 1 (1999): 109–26; National Center for Transgender Equality, "Transgender Terminology," 2009, accessed March 30, 2012, www.transequality.org/Resources/NCTE_TransTerminology.pdf; Susan Stryker, *Transgender History* (Berkeley, CA: Seal Press, 2008), 2–30.

5. Rhonda J. Factor and Esther D. Rothblum, "A Study of Transgender Adults and Their Non-Transgender Siblings on Demographic Characteristics, Social Support, and Experience of Violence," *Journal of LGBT Health Research* 3, no. 3 (2008): 11–30; Jessica M. Xavier, "The Washington Transgender Needs Assessment Survey," accessed June 22, 2012, www.gender.org/vaults/wtnas. html.

6. Patricia Gagné and Richard Tewksbury, "Conformity Pressures and Gender Resistance among Transgendered Individuals," *Social Problems* 45, no. 1 (February 1998): 81–101.

7. Jae M. Sevelius, Adam Carrico, and Mallory O. Johnson, "Antiretroviral Therapy Adherence among Transgender Women Living with HIV," *Journal of the Association of Nurses in AIDS Care* 21, no. 3 (May–June 2010): 256–64; Catherine Williamson, "Providing Care to Transgender Persons: A Clinical Approach to Primary Care, Hormones and HIV Management," *Journal of the Association of Nurses in AIDS Care* 21, no. 3 (May–June 2010): 221–29.

8. Kathryn P. Davison and James W. Pennebaker, "Who Talks? The Social Psychology of Illness Support Groups," *American Psychologist* 55, no. 2 (February 2000): 205–17; Factor and Rothblum, "A Study of Transgender," 11–15.

9. Sevelius, Carrico, and Johnson, "Antiretroviral Therapy," 256; Williamson, "Providing Care," 221.

10. Davison and Pennebaker, "Who Talks?" 205; Kate O'Riordan and David Phillips, *Queer Online: Media, Technology and Sexuality* (New York: Peter Lang Publishing, 2007), 5–10; National Center for Transgender Equality, "Transgender Terminology," 2009.

11. Lombardi, "Integration Within," 110; O'Riordan and Phillips, *Queer Online,* 10.

12. Dennis H. Wilcox, Glen T. Cameron, Bryan H. Reber, and Jae-Hwa Shin, *THINK Public Relations* (Boston: Allyn & Bacon, 2011), 232–33.

13. John A. Bargh and Katelyn Y. A. McKenna, "The Internet and Social Life," *Annual Review of Psychology* 55, no. 1 (January 2004): 573–90.

14. Nan Lin, "Building a Network Theory of Social Capital," *Connections* 22, no. 1: (1999): 28–51; Trepte, Reinecke, and Juechems, "The Social Side" 832–39.

15. Bargh and McKenna, "The Internet," 574–75.

16. David W. McMillan and David M. Chavis, "Sense of Community: A Definition and Theory," *Journal of Community Psychology* 14, no. 1 (January 1986): 6–23.

17. Michele A. Willson, *Technically Together: Rethinking Community within Technosociety* (New York: Peter Lang, 2006), 119–29.

18. Willson, *Technically Together*, 124–29.

19. Shani Orgad, *Storytelling Online: Talking Breast Cancer on the Internet* (New York: Peter Lang, 2005), 28–34; Felicia Wu Song, *Virtual Communities: Bowling Alone, Online Together* (New York: Peter Lang, 2009), 1–9.

20. Alexander Hars and Shaosong Ou, "Working for Free? Motivations of Participating in Open Source Projects," *International Journal of Electronic Commerce* 6, no. 3 (April 2002): 25–39.

21. Marina U. Bers, Laura M. Beals, Clement Chau, Keiko Satoh, Elizabeth D. Blume, David Ray DeMaso, and Joseph Gonzalez-Heydrich, "Use of a Virtual Community as a Psychosocial Support System in Pediatric Transplantation," *Pediatric Transplantation* 14, no. 2, (March 2010): 261–67.

22. Patricia Obst and Jana Stafurik, "Online We Are All Able-Bodied: Online Psychological Sense of Community and Social Support Found through Membership of Disability-Specific Website Promotes Well-Being for People Living with a Physical Disability," *Journal of Community and Applied Social Psychology* 20, no. 6 (November/December 2010): 525–31.

23. Barry Wellman, Anabel Quan Haase, James Witte, and Keith Hampton, "Does the Internet Increase, Decrease, or Supplement Social Capital? Social Networks, Participation, and Community Commitment," *American Behavioral Scientist* 45, no. 3 (November 2001): 436–55; Constance A. Steinkuehler and Dmitri Williams, "Where Everybody Knows Your (Screen) Name: Online Games as 'Third Places,'" *Journal of Computer-Mediated Communication* 11, no. 4 (August 2006): 885–909.

24. Nan Lin, "Building a Network Theory of Social Capital," *Connections* 22, no. 1: (1999): 28–51.

25. Andrea L . Kavanaugh, John M. Carroll, Mary Beth Rosson, Than Than Zin, and Debbie Denise Reese, "Community Networks: Where Offline Communities Meet Online," *Journal of Computer-Mediated Communication* 10, no. 4 (2005), accessed June 24, 2012, jcmc.indiana.edu/vol10/issue4/kavanaugh.html.

26. Nicole B. Ellison, Charles Steinfield, and Cliff Lampe, "The Benefits of Facebook 'Friends': Social Capital and College Students' Use of Online Social Network Sites," *Journal of Computer-Mediated Communication* 12, no. 4 (July 2007): 1143–68.

27. Ellison, Steinfield, and Lampe, "Benefits of Facebook,"1145–46.

28. Dmitri Williams, "On and Off the 'Net: Scales for Social Capital in an Online Era," *Journal of Computer-Mediated Communication* 11, no. 2 (2006), accessed June 22, 2012, jcmc.indiana.edu/vol11/issue2/williams.html.

29. Ellison, Steinfield, and Lampe, "Benefits of Facebook," 1146; Williams, "On and Off the 'Net."

30. Lin, "Building a Network Theory," 28–30; Trepte, Reinecke, and Juechems, "The Social Side," 832–36.

31. Kavanaugh et al., "Community Networks."

32. Bargh and McKenna, "The Internet," 573–90; Andrea L. Kavanaugh, and Scott J. Patterson, "The Impact of Community Computer Networks on Social Capital and Community Involvement," *American Behavioral Scientist* 45, no. 3 (November 2001): 496–509.

33. Ellison, Steinfield, and Lampe, "Benefits of Facebook," 1148; Wellman et al., "Does the Internet Increase," 440–50.

34. John A. Bargh, Katelyn Y. A. McKenna, and Grainne M. Fitzsimons, "Can You See the Real Me? Activation and Expression of the 'True Self' on the Internet," *Journal of Social Issues* 58, no. 1 (January 2002): 33–48; Koles and Nagy, "Who Is Portrayed."

35. Ellison, Steinfield, and Lampe, "Benefits of Facebook," 1145–48; Kavanaugh and Patterson, "Impact of Community Computer," 496–500; Kavanaugh et al., "Community Networks"; Wellman et al., "Does the Internet," 436–55; Williams, "On and Off the 'Net."

36. Sara Green-Hamann, Kristen C. Eichhorn, and John C. Sherblom, "An Exploration of Why People Participate in Second Life Social Support Groups," *Journal of Computer-Mediated Communication* 16, no. 4 (July 2011): 465–91; Sanjeev Kumar, Jatin Chhugani, Changkyu Kim, Daehyun Kim, Anthony Nguyen, Pradeep Dubey, Christian Bienia, and Youngmin Kim, "Second Life and the New Generation of Virtual Worlds," *Computer* 41, no. 9 (September 2008): 46–53.

37. Smiljana Antonijevic, "From Text to Gesture Online: A Microethnographic Analysis of Nonverbal Communication in the Second Life Virtual Environment," *Information Communication and Society* 11, no. 2 (April 2008): 221–38; Gary Bente, Sabine Ruggenberg, Nicole C. Kramer, and Felix Eschenburg, "Avatar-Mediated Networking: Increasing Social Presence and Interpersonal Trust in Net-Based Collaborations," *Human Communication Research* 34, no. 2 (April 2008): 287–318; Koles and Nagy, "Who Is Portrayed."

38. Koles and Nagy, "Who Is Portrayed"; John C. Sherblom, "The Computer-Mediated Communication (CMC) Classroom: A Challenge of Medium, Pres-

ence, Interaction, Identity, and Relationship," *Communication Education* 59, no. 4 (October 2010): 497–523.

39. Bargh, McKenna, and Fitzsimons, "Can You See," 33–40.

40. Barney Glaser and Anselm Strauss, *The Discovery of Grounded Theory: Strategies for Qualitative Research* (Chicago: Aldine, 1967), 25–37; Anselm Strauss and Juliet Corbin, *Basics of Qualitative Research: Grounded Theory Procedures and Techniques* (Newbury Park, CA: Sage, 1990), 65–87.

41. Jan Colvin, Lillian Chenoweth, Mary Bold, and Cheryl Harding, "Caregivers of Older Adults: Advantages and Disadvantages of Internet-Based Social Support," *Family Relations* 53, no. 1 (January 2004): 55–58; Ian Dey, *Grounding Grounded Theory: Guidelines for Qualitative Inquiry* (New York: Academic Press, 1999) 2–25; Thomas R. Lindlof, *Qualitative Communication Research Methods* (Thousand Oaks, CA: Sage, 1995), 250–4.

42. Ellison, Steinfield, and Lampe, "Benefits of Facebook," 1145–48.

43. Kevin B. Wright and Sally B. Bell, "Health-Related Support Groups on the Internet: Linking Empirical Findings to Social Support and Computer-Mediated Communication Theory," *Journal of Health Psychology* 8, no. 1 (January 2003): 39–54.

44. Lin, "Building a Network," 28–33.

45. Steinkuehler and Williams, "Where Everybody Knows," 885–88.

Part 4

The Light and Dark Side of Impression Management

Chapter 10

Face Threatening Messages and Attraction in Social Networking Sites: Reconciling Strategic Self-Presentation with Negative Online Perceptions

Nicholas Brody and Jorge Peña

How do people communicate in social networking sites (SNS) and what are the relational effects of social media messages such as status updates, comments, etc.? Consider that, in contrast to technologies such as dating sites and online multiplayer video games, relational development among SNS users frequently flows from the offline to the online realm—individuals are often communicating online with people they met of-fline.[1] In addition, interactions carried out through SNS can also effect the impressions garnered from users. For instance, comments on a profile left by physically attractive individuals may increase the perceived phys-ical and social attractiveness of the profile owner.[2]

Although SNS have captured the attention of researchers and lay-people, few studies have investigated how the messages exchanged in these sites affect receivers' attributions of senders. How do different top-ics mentioned by message senders affect the attributions made by receiv-

ers? For example, what specific messages make senders seem less socially or physically attractive in the eyes of receivers? Additionally, studies
have not yet clarified what types of messages are most frequently relayed
in SNS. For instance, it is unclear whether SNS users exchange more
personal opinions or if they ask for favors or donations. Finally, how do
receivers attribute intentionality to senders' messages in online environments? Researchers so far have not examined to what extent receivers
believe that senders are conscious of the effects caused by their SNS
messages. For example, the types of SNS messages that are perceived as
more or less intentional have not yet been explored. This is important to
clarify because, in general, intentional hurtful messages can do more
damage to personal relationships than unintentional hurtful messages and
romantic partners who view a hurtful message as intentional are less satisfied with their relationship.[3]

This chapter addresses these questions by drawing from impression-
formation models in computer-mediated communication (CMC), politeness theory, and the concept of face threatening acts (FTA), the affordances of communicative settings, and from studies about attributions
of sender intentionality when hurting receivers' feelings.[4] A main assumption in this chapter is that, in spite of sender's strategic self presentation motives or careful attention and even positive intentions behind a
communicative act, SNS messages that show disregard for receiver's
attitudes and values (i.e., positive FTA) and messages that burden or impede receiver's freedom of action (i.e., negative FTA) will result in negative impressions of the sender. A second main assumption is that because
SNS users are often not copresent but instead geographically distant,
senders will produce positive face threats more frequently than negative
face threats. In other words, SNS messages are more likely to be interpreted as showing disregard for receivers' feelings instead of impeding
concrete actions from receivers. Finally, because this chapter assumes
that FTA in SNS are akin to *gaffes* or blunders in everyday talk, it is expected that positive FTA will be perceived as less intentional than negative FTA.[5] To substantiate these assumptions, the following section reviews impression-formation models in CMC and politeness theory's
classification of messages as threats to positive and negative face. This is
followed by an analysis of the effects of context on the interpretation of
messages, and a review of literature regarding attributions of message
sender intentionality.

Rationale

Impression-Formation in Computer-Mediated Communication

Several theories explain how individuals make sense of each other when communicating through computers. For example, early theories focused on the lack of cues in computer-mediated interactions relative to FtF encounters.[6]However, these perspectives have been widely challenged and were ultimately discarded in favor of different models.[7]

Social Information Processing Theory (SIPT) highlights the relational mechanisms that may occur as individuals communicate through computers. In particular, regardless of the channel of communication, individuals are motivated to affiliate, get things done, save face, dominate, etc. Despite the relative absence of cues in online environments relative to FtF, communicators adapt the content of their messages using the cues available.[8] In one study applying SIPT to impressions garnered from SNS profiles found that individuals with either very few friends or more friends than average were seen as less socially attractive than individuals with a moderate number of friends.[9] In sum, what individuals say and how they present themselves online affects impressions and, over time, online communicators are able to form impressions similar to those garnered in person.[10]

The hyperpersonal model addresses how individuals may form inflated impressions of relational partners. This model is a formal extension of SIPT, and it explains inflated impressions from partners based on (a) senders' optimized online self-presentation when in the context of reduced cues (i.e., senders' increased capacity to highlight desirable traits and conceal undesirable attributes), (b) receivers' idealized perception of senders, (c) reallocation of mental resources devoted to online message construction (i.e., senders enhanced capacity to craft and edit a witty email), (c) the alleviation of entrainment issues when communicating through computers (e.g., social networking site use does not require co-presence or making temporal commitments), and (d) a reciprocal feedback loop that strengthens the mutual impressions of senders and receivers.[11]

The hyperpersonal model has several shortcomings in spite of its influence. For instance, few studies have looked at how specific messages lead to inflated partner impressions.[12] Also, because of its focus on selective use of communication input and output information, the model seems to be more adept at explaining positive impression formation in controlled information environments.[13] Such a focus on positive relational outcomes has been a consistent research bias in the study of interpersonal and computer-mediated relationships.[14] Unfortunately, the hyperpersonal model also falls in this tradition.

In order to address this issue, Walther recommends that investigators ". . . must address the issue of what predictions may be offered in the case where a communicator does not wish to be friendly, competent, or otherwise stereotypically positive."[15] That being said, it is difficult to identify a social media context where individuals do not attempt to present more positively. Impression management theorists generally assume that individuals in public settings are concerned with highlighting positive attributes and concealing negative features.[16] In order to address how messages relayed through SNS may result in more negative impressions in spite of senders' best intentions, the next section reviews politeness theory and the concept of FTA.

Politeness Theory and Face Threatening Acts

Politeness theory explains why individuals do not always speak straightforwardly and examines the communicative strategies people employ to enact, support, and threat the *face* or public identity of self and partners.[17] Face refers to the positive social value that individuals claim for themselves when interacting socially and thus, it reflects individuals' self-esteem and the treatment expected from others.[18] Because most individuals are expected to have a sense of face or self-worth, politeness theory addresses both the ways in which individuals increase, threat, and "save" their own face but also how they do so in relation to partners' public identity. Politeness theory distinguishes between positive and negative face: Positive face refers to the self-image claimed by communicators, while negative face refers to individuals' freedom of choice and autonomy.[19] Note that this chapter focuses on receiver's impression of the sender of a face threatening SNS message, but it does not address of how senders' messages might have affected his or her own face.

Though studies have not examined the types of face threats exchanged by users of online social networks, politeness theorists have identified face threatening message categories that are common in offline social interaction and that may occur on SNS. According to Brown and Levinson, overemotional messages, messages about taboo topics, messages that denote that the sender is bragging or boasting, and non sequitur messages are threats to positive face because they can potentially affect the self-image of a message hearer.[20] For example, consider a Facebook user that posts a status update regarding a good grade he received on a test. Someone reading the status update may be impressed by his friend's intelligence. However, a different reader may not care of even be offended by the update. On the other hand, orders and requests, suggestions, reminders, and threatening messages can jeopardize negative face because they impede receiver's course of action. Facebook users may post requests for their social network to attend an event for a student organization, donate money for a cause, etc.—all actions that may cause receivers to feel that their freedom of choice has been infringed upon.

Few studies have examined politeness phenomena and FTA exchange when individuals communicate through computers. In one example, a longitudinal analysis of teleconference users found that face-saving strategies were prevalent in online interactions in ways similar to offline interactions, but that users were more prone to bald-on-record strategies (i.e., little effort to reduce the impact of an FTA on receivers) instead of off-the-record strategies (i.e., use of indirect language to alleviate the impact of FTA on receivers).[21] Also, requests or constraints to receivers' negative face, were rated as more polite when occurring via email than when they occur in a voicemail.[22] This is congruent with the hyperpersonal model's assumption that asynchronous media (e.g., email) allows senders to optimize their self-presentation compared to synchronous media (e.g., voicemail) because asynchrony grants more opportunities to edit a message and thus appear less threatening when making requests.

Overall, researchers have been concerned about how politeness is enacted when individuals communicate through teleconference systems, email, and voicemail. However, researchers have not yet examined the frequency and types of FTA in SNS, nor have looked into how FTA affect receivers' impressions of senders as suggested by the SIPT/Hyperpersonal approach. Note how politeness theory and, more specifically the concept of FTA, allow the SIPT/Hyperpersonal approach to identify messages in online social networks may adversely affect user's online persona.

Specifically, a wealth of research suggests that mention of taboo topics, or messages that talk about sex, politics, alcohol consumption, should have a significant impact on interpersonal perceptions (e.g., social attractiveness) and satisfaction with personal relationships. For instance, discussing taboo topics negatively correlates with relational outcomes in various personal contexts.[23] The occurrence of taboo topics within family relationships and dating relationships is also negatively related to relational satisfaction.[24] In conclusion, individuals that post taboo topics in SNS should be rated as less interpersonally attractive than posters of other face threat types. Combining the implications of the SIPT/Hyperpersonal approach with politeness theory results in the following hypotheses and research questions:

H1: Individuals who post about taboo topics will be rated as less socially attractive than other FTA types.

RQ1: How do other FTA affect perceptions of senders' social attractiveness?

The following section details how the communicative setting affects the content of social messages in an attempt to clarify what FTA messages will be recalled by receivers.

The Features of Communicative Settings and Language Use

Establishing the distributional structure of categorized acts is a consistent theme in computer-mediated communication research.[25] For example, it is worth asking whether SNS users exchange more personal opinions or too much emotion (i.e., possible FTA to receiver's positive face) or whether they send more commands or requests for concrete actions (i.e., a possible FTA to receiver's negative face). Consider that members of online social support communities were less likely to request tangible assistance from other members, presumably because communicators were not physically present in order to give help.[26]

Also, several studies show that computer-mediated interactions are rife with emotional exchanges. For instance, when posting asynchronous "away messages," IM users were prone to use more informative assertions and emotional expressions (e.g., "at the library," "I hate this weather") than verdictive and effective expressions (e.g., "you're fired," "strike!").[27]

According to language use theorists, the features of communication technologies can affect the frequency of specific communicative acts. In particular, copresence, recordability, visibility, and simultaneity, etc., should influence the content of communication and the process by which senders and receivers achieve mutual understanding of their intentions.[28] Consistent with this assumption, this chapter suggests that copresence is a key factor affecting the frequency of positive FTA relative to negative FTA. For instance, a request such as "pass me the salt" (i.e., a possible negative FTA) is more appropriate when senders and receivers are co-present and thus aware about common projects (e.g., having dinner) and visually salient objects (e.g., the salt box). This assumption is also congruent with Braithwaite and collaborators' reasoning that the lack of physical proximity made tangible aid more difficult to perform in online social support groups.[29]

Additionally, the purpose of the interaction reliably affects the structure of communicative acts.[30] For instance, SNS are often employed to self-express and to display a public persona and to express likes and dislikes regarding movies, books, music, etc.[31] Note that expressing personal likes and self-expressing, because of their potential to result in a negative assessment of a message receiver's personal taste, could be construed as positive instead of negative FTA.[32] In summary, because SNS users lack copresence and these sites are a forum for displaying personal opinions, it is expected that:

H2: Senders will post more positive FTA messages than negative FTA messages.

The next section describes how receivers attribute intentionality to online messages in an attempt to shed light on how the intentionality of the FTA message categories will be perceived.

Face Threats and Attributions of Sender Intentionality

One the most intriguing assumptions of politeness theory is that, while people are expected to self-present positively, their words and actions can unintentionally threaten self and partner's face. Consider

Goffman's classic observations about mishaps in everyday conversation.[33] Goffman identified several forms of mishaps or speech faults that may put in question sender's face. One such mishap—gaffes—refer to unintended and unknowing breaches in manners or some norm of good conduct. Common gaffes in everyday life include being immodest, indiscrete, tactless, irreverent, or intrusive. In Goffman's view gaffes show ignorance of what one would have to know about partners and context in order to conduct oneself.[34]

Though Goffman did not examine interaction in SNS, based on his ideas we hypothesize that some FTA are analog to gaffes or blunders in social media contexts. Gaffes are, by definition, unintended acts that negatively can affect the positive face of senders and receivers. On the other hand, asking for a favor (i.e., a negative FTA) can be perceived as a very intentional action. Thus:

H3: Positive FTA will be rated as less intentional than negative FTA.

RQ2: What are the attributions of intentionality related to different FTA types?

Method

Participants

The participants were students at a large southwestern university. Individuals ($N = 132$) were recruited through communication classes and offered extra credit for their participation. There were thirty-eight males and ninety-four females in the study. Participants' ages ranged from eighteen to thirty years ($M = 21.10$, $SD = 1.85$). Grade level breakdown of the participants was 3.9 percent freshmen, 12.7 percent sophomores, 44.9 percent juniors, and 38.3 percent seniors. A majority (63.3 percent) were Caucasian, followed by Asian (15.2 percent), Hispanic (14.7 percent), African American (3 percent) and "other" (2.9 percent) ethnic origin. Participants also reported how many years they had been using a computer ($M = 12.43$, $SD = 2.85$) and how many years they had been on Facebook or Twitter ($M = 4.06$, $SD = 1.01$).

Procedure and Materials

Each participant signed up for a data collection session. Each session contained a maximum of fifteen participants that met in a classroom. Participants arrived to the session, completed a consent form, and were assigned to an Internet-connected laptop computer. After all participants arrived, the nature of the task was explained.

Task

In each session, individual participants were asked to log onto their Facebook or Twitter account and retrieve five status updates or posts that fit into the FTA categories selected for this study. To ensure data independence, individuals were instructed that each of the five messages should come from a different sender. The types of FTA were listed on an instruction sheet for each participant. Each FTA included a brief explanation based on Brown and Levinson, along with examples of each message type collected by the authors (see Table 10.1).[35]

Table 10.1
Face Threat Categories Proposed by Brown and Levinson (1987) and Example Messages

FTA categories	Definition	Example
Overemotional Messages	Expression of violent or out of control emotions.	___ *is 2 seconds away from pulling my hair out.*
Mention of Taboo Topics	Mention of irreverent, taboo topics that may be inappropriate for the context.	*My apologies to those of you who received a 3 am, 4 am, or 5 am drunk dial . . . those of you who received a 2:59 or earlier call can go (expletive) to someone else*
Boasting/Bragging	Bringing about good	*A on my linguistics of*

	news about the message sender.	*lying test.*
Non Sequitur	Noncooperation, showing nonattention, a message that does not make sense.	*like the energizer bunny, it keeps going!*
Orders/Requests	Messages that request a task of some sort to be carried out.	*Please do not invite me to anymore happy hours/parties/social events until June 6th.*
Unwanted advice	Suggesting that a message receiver ought to do some act.	*every american should watch "jamie oliver's food revolution"*
Reminders	Suggesting that a message receiver ought to remember to do something.	*Longhornrun.com– sign up today!! You get a free tshirt when you run!!*
Threats	Instigates that message sender or someone else will instigate sanctions against someone unless some act is carried out.	*it's ozone season— alright I'm down with the environment but if an eco-freako hates on my Tahoe, they are doomed*

Threats to positive face included overemotional messages, taboo topics, boasting/bragging messages, and nonsequiturs. Threats to negative face were orders/requests, unwanted advice, reminders, or threats. Participants could also label a message "other" if it did not seem to fit into the categories provided. The order of the FTA on the instruction sheet was reversed for half the sample to avoid possible order effects. The participants had two options for retrieving messages: (a) they could recall a past message that fit into a FTA category and locate that message on the site, or (b) they could scroll through their Facebook or Twitter homepage to find messages that fit into the categories. After participants identified a message, they pasted it into a spreadsheet and evaluated both the message and the sender of the message. The participants evaluated each of the five messages they found along the following dimensions:

Coding

The coding was primarily completed by the study participants as they retrieved messages that fit into the provided categories, similar to previous studies that allow participant to self-code their data.[36] To ensure validity of the participants' codes, an independent coder, blind to the hypotheses, was trained on the coding scheme. The set of posts was randomized and 10 percent of the posts were selected ($n = 58$). Because they were not relevant to an examination of face threatening messages and only forty-four messages (6.7 percent) were coded as "other," messages coded as "other" were not included. From there, the coder analyzed each of the fifty-eight posts. A reliability check between the independent coder and the participants yielded a Krippendorff's alpha of 0.82.

Social Attractiveness

This factor was measured with McCroskey and McCain's instrument on a 7-point Likert-type scale (1 = strongly disagree, 7 = strongly agree).[36] Examples of the social attractiveness items include "he/she is a friend of mine," and "I enjoy having a friendly chat with him/her." Reliability for the social attraction scale was good ($\alpha = 0.88$).

Attributions of Sender Intentionality

Participants' attribution about the intentionality behind each message was measured with two items created for this study (1 = strongly disagree, 7 = strongly agree). The items were: "the person that posted this message was aware of the possible outcomes the message would create" and "the effects of this message were intentional." Reliability was acceptable ($\alpha = 0.75$).

Results

Perceptions of Attractiveness

Hypothesis 1 predicted that posting about taboo topics would reduce social attraction. The hypothesis was tested with a one-tailed, a priori contrast (-7, 1, 1, 1, 1, 1, 1, 1). The contrast was significant, $F(7, 608)$ = 2.07, $p < 0.05$, partial $x^2 = 0.02$, indicating that individuals that posted taboo topics were rated as less socially attractive. Thus, H1 was supported.

RQ1 examined whether other face threats differed in their ratings of social attractiveness. Because the RQ1 was exploratory, an LSD post-hoc test at $\alpha = 0.05$ was utilized to determine differences between specific categories of face threat. Figure 10.1 displays a graph of the means of each face threat category. Taboo topics ($M = 4.51$, $SD = 1.56$) were rated as significantly lower in social attractiveness than nonsequiturs ($M = 5.36$, $SD = 1.53$) and messages giving advice ($M = 5.28$, $SD = 1.45$). Additionally, nonsequitur messages resulted in significantly higher social attractiveness than overemotional messages ($M = 4.78$, $SD = 1.77$) and giving orders or requests ($M = 4.85$, $SD = 1.67$).

Frequency of FTA

Hypothesis 2 predicted that threats to receivers' positive face will be observed more frequently than messages categorized as threats to negative face. Chi-square analyses indicated differing frequencies for each of the categories was significant $x^2(8, 660) = 155.18$, $p < 0.001$. Overemotional messages ($N = 135$) were reported most frequently, followed by boasting/bragging messages ($N = 119$), nonsequitur/off-topic messages ($N = 98$), orders/requests ($N = 80$), reminders ($N = 59$), and mention of taboo topics ($N = 58$). Unwanted advice ($N = 47$), other ($N = 44$), and threats ($N = 20$) were all reported less frequently. When the categories were collapsed into type of FTA, threats to positive face ($N = 410$) were reported more frequently than threats to negative face ($N = 206$), $x^2(1, 616) = 67.56$, $p < 0.001$). Thus, H2 was supported.

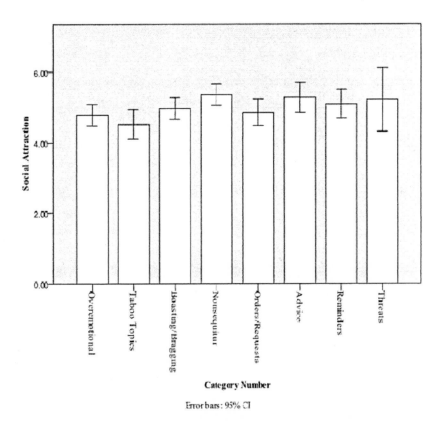

Figure 10.1 Perceptions of social attractiveness for each face threatening message category.

The Association between the FTA Message Coding and Intentionality

Hypothesis 3 predicted that threats to positive face would be perceived as less intentional than threats to negative face. The hypothesis was tested with an independent samples t-test. There was an effect for face threat type, $t(614) = -5.04$, $p < 0.001$, $d = -0.45$, as threats to positive face were rated as less intentional than threats to negative face. Thus H3 was confirmed.

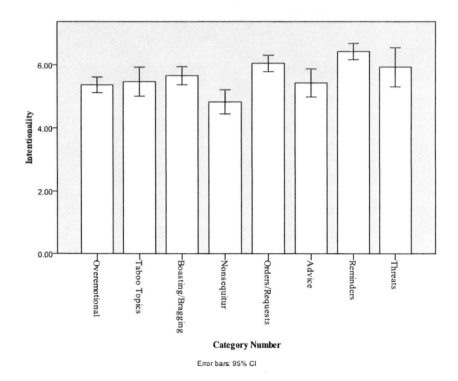

Figure 10.2 Attributions of intentionality for each face threatening message category.

RQ2 investigated how specific face threats would differ in their effects on perceived intentionality of a message. A GLM analysis uncovered significant differences between perceptions of intentionality based on the type of face threat posted, $F(7, 608) = 17.98$, $p < 0.001$, partial x^2 = 0.08, indicating that face threatening messages had a significant effect on perception of intentionality. Because the research question was exploratory, an LSD post-hoc test at $\alpha = 0.05$ was then conducted to determine differences between specific face threat categories. Figure 10.2 displays a graph of the means of each face threat category. Nonsequiturs (M = 4.83, SD = 1.89) were rated as significantly less intentional than each other face threat type, and reminders (M = 6.42, SD = .99) were rated as more intentional than every face threat type except for orders/requests and threats. Also, overemotional messages (M = 5.36, SD = 1.45) and taboo messages (M = 5.47, SD = 1.75) were each rated as significantly less intentional than orders/requests (M = 6.04, SD = 1.17). Orders/requests were considered significantly more intentional than unwanted advice (M = 5.43, SD = 1.51).

Discussion

Despite the surge of interest in the social and communicative implications of SNS, current studies have not investigated the effects of messages exchanged in these sites on receivers' attributions of senders. More specifically, in a response to calls for studies investigating situations in which individuals do not portray themselves in an overly positive fashion, the present study investigated SNS messages through the lens of SIPT/Hyperpersonal approach and politeness theory.[38] The features of SNS were also considered to predict which type of FTA occur most frequently in this communicative context. Additionally, the study examined how perceptions of message intentionality affected receiver's attributions.

One theoretical contribution of this chapter is extending the SIPT/Hyperpersonal approach to account for their lack of focus on negative impressions and the need to extend these approaches to situations in which communicators do not present themselves in an overly positive manner.[39] For example, the results illustrated how concepts such as face and FTA shed light on online behaviors that may result in unfavorable impressions despite senders' attempts to cause favorable impressions. In particular, mentioning taboo topics such as sex, politics, and religion had a distinct negative effect on perceptions of social attractiveness.

Face Threatening Acts and Perceptions of Social Attractiveness

As noted earlier, taboo messages reduced perceptions of senders' social attractiveness in comparison with the remaining FTA categories. Additionally, overemotional messages and orders/requests diminished senders' social attractiveness relative to nonsequitur messages. The results were consistent with previous findings on the effects of taboo topics on relationships. Although the nature and meaning of taboo topics depend on various factors, several studies have found links between discussing taboo topics and damaging relational outcomes. For instance, the frequency of discussions regarding taboo topics in dating relationships and family relationships is negatively associated with relational satisfaction.[40] In general, individuals avoid discussing taboo topics perhaps in an attempt to avoid the damaging effects of these controversial topics on their relationships.[41] Consistent with this, taboo topics were among the least frequently reported type of face threat, but they had a significant negative impact on perceptions of social attractiveness when they did occur. Researchers have struggled to identify instances where the SIPT/Hyperpersonal perspectives can be extended to instances where individuals do not portray themselves in an overly positive light. The results suggest that studying the mention of taboo topics and FTA in SNS is a fruitful avenue for investigating these theoretical questions.

Taken together, face threatening messages affected perceptions of social attractiveness. This suggests that SNS messages were more influential on how much an individual likes or feels similar to someone else, a finding consistent with SIPT. According to SIPT, individuals form impressions based on the content of messages.[42] The results of the present study support this prediction as perceptions of social attractiveness differed based on the type of FTA. In a context such as SNS where individuals are driven to strategically present themselves, negative impressions can still occur based on the context and content of a message.

Further research should evaluate change in attractiveness over time as SNS users are exposed to face threatening messages, and differences in attractiveness between online and offline contexts. Research can also build on these findings by measuring the relationship between degree of experienced face threat and outcomes such as interpersonal attraction. Furthermore, as face threats have been confirmed to occur within SNS, experimental studies can confirm and extend the measurement of face threat experienced by participants. For example, by utilizing the FTA categories used in this study, researchers can construct faux SNS profiles which contain face threatening messages, and measure social outcomes in experimental settings.[43]

The Features of SNS as a Communicative Setting and Face Threats

Face threat types were expected to occur with varying frequency consistent with the known goals and uses of SNS. In particular, this study hypothesized and confirmed that the lack of copresence on SNS should result in participants' reporting more positive than negative FTA. One explanation for this effect is that SNS are often used to display personal tastes in books, movies, music, activities, etc.[44] Expressing personal likes and dislikes tends to be construed as positive instead of negative FTA, while negative FTA include messages that infringe upon a receiver's course of action (e.g., a request or a reminder), and thus may be harder to enact online. In fact, emotional messages were reported more frequently than any other face threat type.[45] This resonates with previous studies showing that IM messages tend to feature more emotional expressions (i.e., positive FTA) than commands and effective expressions (i.e., negative FTA).[46] This finding is also consistent with research showing that asking and requesting tangible social support online is diminished by the lack of copresence between communicators.[47]

Future studies should extend the coding scheme to include the uses of politeness strategies that temper the impact of FTA or make receivers feel good. For example, if message senders are aware that they are posting a face threat on a SNS, which politeness strategies do they use to alleviate such face-threatening situation? What is the impact of the SNS audience (e.g., list of friends) on choosing a politeness strategy? Also, what are the effects of SNS messages expressing solidarity, optimism, and jokes? According to Brown and Levinson, such messages can have positive effects on receiver's perceptions.[48] A replication and extension of the coding scheme utilized in this study can address these questions.

Face Threats and Intentionality

The study also uncovered that nonsequiturs (i.e., off topic remarks, inside jokes, out of context quotations) were perceived as the least intentional FTA while reminders were rated as the most intentional FTA.

These findings support the assumption that online face threats are analog to Goffman's concept of gaffes in everyday conversation.[49] Gaffes occur when a message sender has little knowledge of their end audience or the potential impact of their message on the audience and thus represent ignorance of what one would have to know about the backgrounds, morals, and opinions of a message receiver and how they might react to certain messages.[50] Consider that the average Facebook user has over 100 friends, each which may read a particular status update.[51] Thus, status updates on Facebook are not one-to-one communication but instead are more akin to broadcasts or one-to-many communication. In this context, most SNS receivers might have not understood nonsequitur messages because decoding these comments requires substantial common ground with senders (e.g., likes, dislikes, wit, language codes). Thus, one interpretation is that nonsequiturs were rated as less intentional because they were not fully understood. On the other hand, reminders call attention to something the person has not done and, thus, put pressure on receiver's to perform an action.[52] Such a strong constraint to receivers' freedom of action was likely perceived as very intentional.

At a broader level, positive FTA were rated as less intentional than negative FTA. Although some message senders may merely intend to present their beliefs and convictions on a SNS by stating political opinions, such messages can be perceived as taboo and face threatening by at least a subset of the message audience, which, in the present study, resulted in lower reported social attractiveness and lower ratings of intentionality.[53] Also, positive FTA may be considered less intentional because they are gaffes resulting from a miscommunication between sender and receiver.[54] In this case, the sender had little knowledge of how the audience would perceive the message. Negative FTA may have been rated as more intentional because they were seen as concerted attempts to constrain the personal freedom of receivers.[55]

Limitations

The relatively small size of the findings may indicate that the message retrieval procedure used here did not tap some of the cues normally utilized to form impressions. For example, participants were allowed to retrieve messages from individuals of varying relational types and closeness levels. Future studies should analyze the impact of relational closeness and degree of face threat. Despite the limitation, the predictions from politeness theory were confirmed while statistically controlling for confounding variables such as relational closeness.

Conclusion

Though SNS have been widely adopted as a communication technology we know little about how messages exchanged through this channel results in negative impressions even when senders are motivated to present themselves in a positive light. By merging the assumptions of online impression formation models with politeness theory, the present study sheds some light on the role of online messages in the development of negative impressions. The study also illustrated how low copresense and the known uses of SNS may translate into the expression of more positive than negative FTA (e.g., stating likes instead of asking for favors). Overall, this study shows that while new channels of communication offer exciting possibilities for self-expression, age-old rules about politeness and gaffes still govern message perception in online social networks.

Notes

1. Cliff Lampe, Nicole Ellison, and Charles Steinfield, *A Familiar Face (Book): Profile Elements as Signals in an Online Social Network* (New York: ACM, 2007).

2. Joseph B. Walther, Brandon Van Der Heide, San-Yeon Kim, David Westerman, and Stephanie Tom Tong, "The Role of Friends Appearance and Behavior on Evaluations of Individuals on Facebook: Are We Known by the Company We Keep?" *Human Communication Research* 34, no. 1 (2008): 28–49.

3. Anita Vangelisti and Stacy Young, "When Words Hurt: The Effects of Perceived Intentionality on Interpersonal Relationships," *Journal of Social and Personal Relationships* 17, no. 3 (2000): 393–424.

4. Joseph B. Walther, "Interpersonal Effects in Computer-Mediated Interaction a Relational Perspective," *Communication Research* 19, no. 1 (1992): 52–90; Joseph B. Walther, "Computer-Mediated Communication: Impersonal, Interpersonal, and Hyperpersonal Interaction," *Communication Research* 23, no. 1 (1996): 3–43; Penelope Brown and Stephen C. Levinson, *Politeness: Some Universals in Language Usage*, Vol. 4. (Cambridge: Cambridge University Press, 1987); Herbert H. Clark, *Using Language*, Vol. 4 (Cambridge: Cambridge University Press, 1996); Herbert H. Clark and Susan E. Brennan, "Grounding in Communication," In *Perspectives on Socially Shared Cognition*, ed. Lauren B.

Resnick, John M. Levine, and Stephanie D. Teasley (Washington, D.C.: American Psychological Association, 1991), 127–49; Vangelisti and Young, "When Words Hurt," 393.

5. Erving Goffman, *Forms of Talk* (Philadelphia: University of Pennsylvania Press, 1981).

6. Sara Kiesler, Jane Siegel, and Timothy W. McGuire, "Social Psychological Aspects of Computer-Mediated Communication," *American Psychologist* 39, no. 10 (1984): 1123; John Short, Ederyn Williams, and Bruce Christie, *The Social Psychology of Telecommunications* (New York: Wiley, 1976).

7. Walther, "Interpersonal Effects," 52; Walther, "Computer-Mediated Communication," 30.

8. Walther, "Interpersonal Effects," 52.

9. Stephanie Tom Tong, Brandon Van Der Heide, Lindsey Langwell, and Joseph B. Walther, "Too Much of a Good Thing? The Relationship Between Number of Friends and Interpersonal Impressions on Facebook," *Journal of Computer Mediated Communication* 13, no. 3 (2008): 531–49.

10. Joseph B. Walther, "Impression Development in Computer Mediated Interaction," *Western Journal of Communication* 57, no. 4 (1993): 381–89.

11. Walther, "Computer-Mediated Communication," 3.

12. For an exception see Joseph B. Walther, "Selective Self-Presentation in Computer-Mediated Communication: Hyperpersonal Dimensions of Technology, Language, and Cognition," *Computers in Human Behavior* 23, no. 5 (2007): 2538–57.

13. Joseph B. Walther and Malcolm R. Parks, "Cues Filtered Out, Cues Filtered In: Computer-Mediated Communication and Relationships," in *Handbook of Interpersonal Communication*, eds. Mark Knapp and John Daly (Thousand Oaks, CA: Sage, 2002): 529–63.

14. Steve Duck, "Stratagems, Spoils, and a Serpent's Tooth: On the Delights and Dilemmas of Personal Relationships," in *The Dark Side of Interpersonal Communication,* eds. William R. Cupach and Brian H. Spitzberg, (Hillsdale, NJ: Lawrence Erlbaum, 1994): 3–24.

15. Walther, "Computer-Mediated Communication," 30.

16. Erving Goffman, "Alienation from Interaction," *Human Relations* 10, no. 1 (1957): 47–60; Mark Leary, *Self-Presentation: Impression Management and Interpersonal Behavior, Social Psychology Series* (Madison, WI: Brown and Benchmark, 1995).

17. Brown and Levinson, *Politeness.*

18. Erving Goffman, 'Face-Work,' An Analysis of Ritual Elements in Social Interaction," *Psychiatry: Journal for the Study of Interpersonal Processes* 18, no. 3 (1955): 213–31.

19. Brown and Levinson, *Politeness.*

20. Brown and Levinson, *Politeness.*

21. Glen Hiemstra, "Teleconferencing, Concern for Face, and Organizational Culture," *Communication Yearbook* 6, no. 6 (1982): 874–904.

22. Kirk W. Duthler, "The Politeness of Requests Made via Email and Voicemail: Support for the Hyperpersonal Model," *Journal of Computer Mediated Communication* 11, no. 2 (2006): 500–521.

23. Leslie A. Baxter, and William W. Wilmot, "Taboo Topics in Close Relationships," *Journal of Social and Personal Relationships* 2, no. 3 (1985): 253–69.

24. Anita Vangelisti, "Family Secrets: Forms, Functions, and Correlates," *Journal of Social and Personal Relationships* 11, no. 1 (1994): 113–35.

25. Dawn O. Braithwaite, Vincent R. Waldron, and Jerry Finn, "Communication of Social Support in Computer-Mediated Groups for People with Disabilities," *Health Communication* 11, no. 2 (1999): 123–51; Jacqueline Nastri, Jorge Peña, and Jeffrey T. Hancock, "The Construction of Away Messages: A Speech Act Analysis," *Journal of Computer Mediated Communication* 11, no. 4 (2006): 1025–45.

26. Braithwaite, Waldron, and Finn, "Social Support," 123.

27. Nastri, Peña, and Hancock, "Away Messages," 1025.

28. Herbert H. Clark, and Susan E. Brennan, "Grounding in Communication," in *Perspectives on Socially Shared Cognition,* eds. Lauren B. Resnick, John M. Levine, and Stephanie D. Teasley (Washington, DC: American Psychological Association, 1991), 127–49.

29. Braithwaite, Waldron, and Finn, "Social Support," 123.

30. Joseph E. McGrath, *Groups: Interaction and Performance* (Englewood Cliffs, NJ: Prentice Hall, 1984).

31. Hugo Liu, "Social Network Profiles as Taste Performance," *Journal of Computer-Mediated Communication* 13, no. 1 (2008): 252–75; danah boyd and Nicole B. Ellison, Social Network Sites: Definition, History, and Scholarship, *Journal of Computer Mediated Communication* 13, no. 1 (2008): 210–30.

32. Brown and Levinson, *Politeness.*

33. Erving Goffman, *Forms of Talk* (Philadelphia: University of Pennsylvania Press, 1981).

34. Goffman, *Forms of Talk,* 210–12.

35. Brown and Levinson, *Politeness.*

36. Sally Planalp, Dianne Rutherford, and James M. Honeycutt, "Events That Increase Uncertainty in Personal Relationships: Replication and Extension," *Human Communication Research* 14, no. 4 (1988): 516–47.

37. James McCroskey and Thomas McCain, "The Measurement of Interpersonal Attraction," *Communication Monographs* 41, no. 3 (1974): 261–66.

38. Walther, "Computer-Mediated Communication"; Walther, "Interpersonal Effects"; Brown and Levinson, *Politeness.*

39. Walther, "Computer-Mediated Communication."

40. Vangelisti, "Family Secrets"; Michael Roloff and Danette Ifert, "Antecedents and Consequences of Explicit Agreements to Declare a Topic Taboo in Dating Relationships," *Personal Relationships* 5, no. 2 (1998): 191–205.

41. Baxter and Wilmot, "Taboo Topics," 253–69.

42. Walther, "Interpersonal Effects."

43. Walther et al., "Friends Appearance and Behavior."

44. Liu, "Taste Performance."

45. Brown and Levinson, *Politeness*.

46. Nastri, Peña, and Hancock, "The Construction of Away Messages."

47. Braithwaite, Waldron, and Finn, "Communication of Social Support."

48. Brown and Levinson, *Politeness*.

49. Goffman, *Forms of Talk*.

50. Goffman, *Forms of Talk*.

51. Lars Backstrom, "Anatomy of Facebook," accessed April 15, 2012, www.facebook.com/note.php?note_id=10150388519243859.

52. Brown and Levinson, *Politeness*.

53. boyd and Ellison, "Social Network Sites."

54. Goffman, *Forms of Talk*.

55. Brown and Levinson, *Politeness*.

Chapter 11

Psychological Benefits and Costs: A Self-Affirmation Framework for Understanding the Effects of Facebook Self-Presentation

Catalina L. Toma

Self-presentation is a complex communicative process that involves selecting which aspects of self to disclose, which to conceal, and whether or not to use deception in the hopes of creating a desired impression in an audience.[1] In recent years, communication technologies have introduced new challenges and opportunities to the self-presentation process. In particular, social networking sites (SNS) invite users to construct self-presentations through online profiles—technological platforms with unique characteristics that affect the self-presentation process. For instance, SNS operate through articulating relationships between users and their "friends" within the system, thus demanding that users make "public displays of connection"; encourage, by design, the disclosure of vast arrays of personal information, ranging from politics and religion to favorite music and television shows; are accessible to large, and sometimes unknown audiences; are multimodal, allowing users to compose their personas through a multitude of tools, such as text, photographs, videos, and web links; and are recorded and archived, with self-presentational statements accruing over years of SNS use.[2] By bringing these new capabilities to the self-presentational process, SNS invite theoretical and empirical questions such as (1) what is the nature of SNS self-presentation?; (2) in what way do technological affordances and limitations shape SNS self-presentations?; and (3) what are the effects of SNS self-presentation on users' self-concepts?

This chapter approaches these questions by introducing a novel theoretical framework, self-affirmation theory, that explicates both the kinds of self-presentations that are likely to be constructed on Facebook (a quintessential SNS), given technological and social affordances, and the psychological effects of engaging with the version of self encapsulated in a Facebook profile.[3] In a nutshell, this chapter proposes that Facebook self-presentation, by virtue of being flattering, accurate, and indicative of meaningful aspects of self, such as social connectivity, represents an everyday venue for self-affirmation. As a self-affirming activity, Facebook profile self-presentation has considerable effects on how users view themselves and also on how they act in the world.

To support this line of argumentation, this chapter will proceed as follows. First, it will discuss the applicability of self-affirmation theory to Facebook self-presentation, by detailing how the latter fulfills the theoretical criteria for self-affirmation. Second, it will summarize empirical evidence from three studies that reveal the self-affirming properties of Facebook profiles on users' self-concept, self-esteem, and behavior. Finally, the chapter will discuss how the self-affirmation framework advances understanding of the causes and effects of Facebook use, and how it may be applicable to profile-based self-presentations beyond Facebook.

Facebook Self-Affirmation

One of the best documented findings in psychology is that people need to view themselves in a positive way, as "good" and "appropriate" individuals, although they are much more critical of others.[4] In order to maintain this positive self-image, they engage in a variety of defense mechanisms, such as dismissing, distorting, or avoiding information that threatens their elevated self-view. An additional strategy for satisfying the need for a positive self-image is self-affirmation, or the simple act of bringing to awareness defining aspects of self, such as treasured characteristics, values, and meaningful relationships.[5] According to self-affirmation theory, people are naturally drawn toward self-affirming information in the environment, seeking it because it reassures them of their positive qualities.

Additionally, people are particularly motivated to seek self-affirming information after their egos have been threatened in some way, such as by rejection, criticism, or failure, because they unconsciously try to repair their sense of self-worth. A related proposition of self-affirmation theory is that, after attending to self-affirming information, individuals' perception of self-worth is indeed enhanced, and they no longer need to protect themselves through other methods, such as defense mechanisms. Since affirmed individuals already feel secure in their self-worth, such defense tactics are superfluous.[6]

Let us now consider whether Facebook profile self-presentation is affirming, as per the dictates of self-affirmation theory. For information to be self-affirming, three criteria need to be met: the information needs to be personally meaningful, capturing defining aspects of self; it needs to be of a positive and flattering nature; and it needs to be accurate, because internal perceptions of self-worth cannot be boosted by information that the self-presenter knows to be untrue. In judging the applicability of these criteria to Facebook, special attention is paid to how the information Facebook profile self-presentation is affected by (1) technological factors, such as the design of the site and the ability to revise and record statements; and (2) social factors, such as the motivation to use the site, the presence of an audience and normative rules governing the site.

Consider first the criterion that Facebook self-presentation should revolve around personally meaningful aspects of self. Self-affirmation theory postulates that individuals' sense of self-worth is contingent on several key "domains" of self, namely social roles, personal relationships, treasured activities, values and beliefs.[7] In particular, close personal relationships with friends and family have been shown to be the most potent and widely used resource for self-affirmation.[8] An analysis of the design of Facebook profiles reveals that these key domains of self are prominently featured. First, personal relationships with "friends" are the raison d'être of Facebook. They are represented directly through lists of "friends" and links to family members and significant others, and indirectly through comments and "likes" posted by friends and visibly stored on the profiles. Second, users are prompted to reveal their social roles (i.e., friend, student) and membership into educational and local networks (e.g., University of Wisconsin-Madison; Madison, WI). These networks indicate belongingness in important, identity-defining groups. Third, users are prompted to explicitly state their values (i.e., religion, apolitical beliefs) and to display their treasured characteristics and activities (e.g., traveling, spending time with friends) through status updates and photo albums. Notably, Facebook self-presenters have developed social norms that mandate high degrees of disclosiveness, with users posting rich repositories of information about themselves.[9]To conclude, this analysis suggests that Facebook profile self-presentation is replete with personally meaningful information.

Importantly, technological affordances beyond the design of profiles enhance the value of this personally meaningful information. Specifically, recordability enables users to "collect" friends and tokens of friendships, such as wall postings, virtual gifts and photographs. These signals of connectivity accrue over time, and can act as powerful indicators of belongingness and close, meaningful relationships. This information is also tightly packaged and organized in an easily accessible online location. At the click of a button and hence with very little effort, users can enter a space where personally meaningful information abounds.

Let us now consider the second criterion for self-affirmation, namely that Facebook self-presentation is positive and flattering. Although no research has directly investigated this question to date, we may assume that Facebook self-presenters have both the motivation and the ability to compose flattering versions of themselves in their profiles. Research has established that publicness enhances self-presenters' motivation to come across positively.[10] Since Facebook profiles are highly public, with audiences often ranging in hundreds and even thousands of "friends," profile owners' motivation to create good impressions should be high. Additionally, many of these "friends" are consequential people (e.g., classmates, coworkers, supervisors) whom one is typically eager to impress. Facebook users should also be in the fortunate position of being able create optimal self-presentations, thanks to a constellation of technological affordances inherent to SNS. *Asynchronicity* allows them all the time they need to craft self-presentational statements—unlike FtF communicators, who must present themselves spontaneously. *Editability* allows them to revise their statements until they are optimal, an affordance that is also missing from FtF communication. Importantly, editability allows Facebook self-presenters to monitor and control friends' statements in addition to their own. Any undesirable postings (i.e., comments, photograph tags, events) left by friends can be easily removed. By the same token, friendship connections can be terminated (by removing friends) when they are no longer wanted. The *reallocation of cognitive resources* allows Facebook self-presenters to dedicate the entirety of their mental focus on the self-presentational task at hand, rather than to other environmental distractions. Together, asynchronicity, editability, and the reallocation of cognitive resources enable online communicators to engage in *selective self-presentation,* a type of self-presentation that is more controllable and aligned with communicators' goals than FtF self-presentation.[11] Selective self-presentation has been shown to operate in the cognate domain of online dating and it should similarly enable Facebook self-presenters to craft versions of self that are completely desirable and positive.[12]

Let us now consider the final criterion for self-affirming self-presentations: accuracy. As mentioned earlier, information that the self-presenters know to be false cannot boost their internal perceptions of self-worth. Online communication has great potential for deception, because it is disembodied (that is, it allows communicators to engage with each other without being physically present) and hence lacks the nonverbal cues that people usually employ to detect deception.[13] Nevertheless, there are characteristics of online communication that promote honesty, and some of these are featured on Facebook profiles. One such constraint against deception, conceptualized as a *warrant*, is the ability to link online with offline selves.[14] Warrants increase accuracy because they render online statements verifiable. For instance, research shows that online dating profiles are more accurate the more people from the online dater's social circle know about the existence of the profile.[15] In this case, these members of the dater's social circle act as a warrant, capable of verifying the veracity of profile claims. On Facebook, an even more potent warrant exists: the presence of an audience of friends, many of whom have had long-term, deep, offline relations with the self-presenters, and thus know them well enough to be able to spot deceptions. Facebook self-presenters should then construct accurate profiles, lest they should be caught red-handed by consequential people in their lives. An additional constraint against deception on Facebook is more technological in nature: the design of certain self-presentational elements. Specifically, claiming membership on certain restricted networks, such as colleges and universities, is contingent upon owning an active email account associated with that network. Similarly, self-presenters cannot claim friendship with other users, unless the latter confirm friendship requests. According to signaling theory, these cues are difficult and costly to fake, and hence they should be honest signals of social connectivity and group membership, respectively.[16] Finally, it is worth noting that Facebook profiles are co-constructed by profile owners and their friends. Information contributed by friends should be difficult to manufacture, and hence should be reliable.

Several studies to date provide indications for the accuracy of online profiles. Back and colleagues found that Facebook profiles are realistic enough for observers to form accurate impressions of profile owners' personality.[17] Additionally, as mentioned earlier, research on online dating, a similar SNS, found that deceptions are small and relatively benign.[18]

In conclusion, this theoretical analysis indicates that Facebook profiles self-presentation should indeed be self-affirming, by virtue of (1) their ability to capture meaningful aspects of self, (2) positivity, and (3) accuracy. The next section reviews a series of empirical studies testing this claim.

Overview of Empirical Studies

Three studies were conducted (currently under review at communication and psychology journals) to test the self-affirming properties of Facebook, and also illuminate how the self-affirming nature of Facebook may affect the causes and effects of Facebook use.

Study 1 asks the foundational question of whether Facebook profiles are self-affirming. In doing so, it employs a classic methodology, well-validated in the psychology literature, to establish whether a certain activity is self-affirming.[19] This methodology is based on the following logic. Because people have a fundamental need to view themselves positively, they tend to respond defensively when faced with threats to their egos, such as criticism, negative feedback, or rejection. However, if they are self-affirmed prior to facing the ego threat, they should no longer need to protect themselves in this defensive fashion, because their need for an elevated self-worth is already satisfied by the self-affirmation activity. Research shows quite conclusively that, when it comes to their sense of self-worth, people are satisficers rather than maximizers, meaning that they are content with a good-enough view of self, and don't take any opportunity available to make themselves feel good about themselves.[20] Given this pattern of response to ego threats, researchers can establish whether a certain activity is self-affirming by observing whether it elicits a decrease in defensiveness when interjected prior to the ego threat. If the activity produced less defensiveness, it means that it was able to satisfy people's need for self-worth in and of itself, rendering other defense tactics unnecessary. This reduced defensiveness is hence the hallmark of self-affirmation.

Implementing this defensiveness-reducing paradigm involves a three-step procedure: (1) participants are asked to engage in the activity believed to be self-affirming (in the treatment condition) or, for comparison purposes, to a control activity; (2) participants' egos are threatened; and (3) participants' defensive responses to the threat are measured. If defensive responses are lower in the experimental condition than in the control condition, it can be concluded that the activity in which participants engaged prior to the ego threat was self-affirming. Study 1 employed this methodology verbatim.

Study 2 built on Study 1 by testing a fundamental proposition of self-affirmation theory in the context of Facebook profile self-presentation. Specifically, self-affirmation theory posits that individuals unconsciously but predictably gravitate toward self-affirming venues after their egos had been threatened. Are Facebook users similarly attracted toward their profiles after suffering a blow to their egos? Do they tend to gravitate toward their Facebook profiles when they feel bad about themselves and need an ego boost? Hence, Study 2 had two important goals. First, it meant to establish not only whether Facebook profiles *can* act as venues for self-affirmation (when users are prompted to access them by an experimenter, as was the case in Study 1), but whether they *do* in fact act as such (when users access them of their own accord, without an experimental prompt). Second, Study 2 meant to illuminate some of the unconscious motivations of Facebook use—in other words, what *causes* users to spend time on Facebook.

Finally, the goal of Study 3 was to investigate the effects of Facebook profile self-presentation, through the lens of self-affirmation theory. How do users feel and act in the world after browsing their own Facebook profile self-presentation? Two categories of effects were considered: (1) intrapersonal effects on users' state self-esteem; and (2) behavioral effects on cognitive task performance (i.e., ability to perform well in a mental task). One important contribution of this study was its measurement of self-esteem, a construct that is highly susceptible to social desirability biases (i.e., participants reporting higher self-esteem than they actually possess in order to conform to social norms, whereby high self-esteem is a very desirable attribute).[21] To alleviate this concern, Study 3 used an implicit association test (IAT) procedure. IATs gauge unconsciously held attitudes, and has been applied to a wide range of attitudes where social desirability is a concern (e.g., religion, race, sex, politics). IATs operate by measuring the speed with which participants associate concepts with evaluative statements; the faster the association is made, the more strongly held the attitude. For the self-esteem IAT, the concepts are related to oneself, and the evaluative statements are "good" or "bad." Participants who quickly associate words related to themselves with good evaluations, but have a hard time associating words related to themselves with bad evaluations, have high implicit self-esteem. Conversely, participants who quickly associate words related to themselves with bad evaluations, but take longer to associate them with good evaluations, have low implicit self-esteem.[22]

Empirical Findings

Recall that the goal of Study 1 was to empirically establish whether Facebook profile self-presentation has self-affirmation value. Based on a theoretical analysis of the composition, valence, and accuracy of Facebook profile self-presentation, it was hypothesized that these profiles would be self-affirming in the sense of restoring users' perception of their own self-worth and self-integrity.

The defensiveness-reducing paradigm of self-affirmation effects was employed to determine whether Facebook profiles constitute a venue for self-affirmation, as follows.[23] Because self-affirmation operates at an unconscious level, participants were given a cover story about the purpose of the study, involving the Distance Learning Education Center at Cornell University and its efforts to develop an online version of the popular public speaking course. Participants were asked to pilot the viability of such a course by preparing a five-minute speech and delivering it live via videoconferencing technology to an evaluator. All participants received generic negative feedback on their speech performance, which constituted the ego threat. After receiving the feedback, participants were given an opportunity to evaluate the fairness and accuracy of the feedback, as well as the appropriateness of using videoconferencing for a public speaking course. This constituted an opportunity for participants to be defensive about the negative feedback they received, by either dismissing it as inaccurate, or dismissing the task as inappropriate.

The experimental manipulation was introduced prior to receiving the ego threat. In the treatment condition, the participants were asked to review their own Facebook profiles for five minutes, ostensibly as part of an unrelated study. In the control condition, participants were asked to review a stranger's Facebook profile. The stranger was in fact a participant in the treatment condition, who had permitted the research team to access his or her Facebook profile. Each participant in the experimental condition browsed the profile of the corresponding participant in the treatment condition. This yoked procedure ensured that participants in the control condition, as a group, viewed the exact same profiles as participants in the treatment condition—except they were not their own, and hence they could not be self-affirming.

Additionally, to ensure the validity of the results, Study 1 also directly compared the self-affirming power of Facebook to that of a well-established self-affirming activity: ranking and writing about one's most important values. This activity is the most widely used induction of self-affirmation in the literature and involves asking participants to rank a list of values (e.g., personal relationships, education, politics) in the order of personal importance and write a short essay about their highest ranked value and why it is important to them.[24]

The results were consistent with the hypotheses. As expected, participants who had browsed their own carefully constructed Facebook profiles were significantly less defensive when given negative feedback on their speech performance compared to participants in the control condition. After being exposed to this ego-boosting version of themselves, participants were less likely to derogate the negative feedback they received (by claiming it was inaccurate, or by claiming that the evaluator was incompetent) or the task (by claiming that videoconferencing is an inappropriate tool for teaching public speaking classes). This secure, accepting, nondefensive attitude is the hallmark of self-affirmation, and provides conclusive proof that one's own Facebook profile self-presentation is affirming. Additionally, participants who had been affirmed through their Facebook profiles were equally nondefensive as participants who had completed the classic values-essay self-affirmation induction, suggesting that Facebook self-affirmation is equally powerful as the most well-validated self-affirmation activity.

After spending time on their own Facebook profiles, participants also reported an increase in their positive affect compared to control participants. They felt more "loving," "joyful," "giving," "connected," "loved," "supported," "grateful," "proud," and "content." To summarize, Study 1 empirically demonstrated two categories of beneficial effects of attending to one's own flattering Facebook self-presentation: self-affirmation and a boost in positive affect.

Study 2 sought to determine whether Facebook users do in fact seek their profiles when their egos had been threatened, in an unconscious effort to restore their perceptions of self-worth and self-integrity. According to self-affirmation theory, people are expected to make use of self-affirming information in this manner, and if Facebook profiles are indeed self-affirming, they should be accessed more heavily in times of psychological need. To test this prediction, a similar methodology to Study 1 was employed. Participants were given the same cover story as in Study 1: They were requested to develop and deliver a short speech as a pilot test of the viability of a public speaking distance-education course. Half of the participants were given negative feedback on the speech and, for comparison purposes, the other half were given neutral feedback. Afterward, participants were invited to select another study out of ostensibly five different studies currently going on in the lab, in order to double their extra-credit compensation. These studies contained the self-affirming activity under investigation—browsing one's own Facebook profile, as well as four decoy activities designed to be as similar as possible to Facebook profile browsing, yet not self-affirming (i.e., listening to online music, playing online video games, watching videos on YouTube, and reading online news). Participants' selection of one of the five activities constituted the main dependent measure.

As predicted, participants in the control condition, whose egos were not threatened, selected the Facebook profile browsing activity at the same rate as would be expected by chance (30 percent). However, participants whose egos had been threatened by negative feedback gravitated toward Facebook at twice that rate (60 percent), and hence displayed a clear preference for Facebook profile browsing compared to all the other activities. Importantly, this pattern of preference emerged even when controlling for a host of variables that may have affected activity choice, such as level of familiarity with the activity, perceived effort in completing the activity, and how engaging and interesting participants perceived the activity to be. Hence, Study 2 shows that people do make use of Facebook in times of psychological need and, as will be discussed later, it illuminates an unconscious cause of Facebook use: replenishing one's reservoirs of self-worth.

Having established that Facebook profile self-presentation is self-affirming, Study 3 went on to investigate some of the effects of attending to this presentation. The self-affirmation literature has determined that self-affirming activities have a multitude of perceptual and behavioral effects. Two categories of effects were considered: on users' self-esteem, reliably measured through an implicit association test procedure, and on users' performance on a subsequent cognitive task. Participants were asked to examine their Facebook profile self-presentation for five minutes (in the treatment condition) or, following the yoking procedure employed in Study 1, a stranger's Facebook profile self-presentation (in the control condition). Immediately afterward, participants completed a computerized self-esteem IAT, and then a mental arithmetic task, involving rapid serial subtraction from a large number by intervals of seven. The serial subtraction task is a widely used measure of cognitive task performance.[25] Participants' task performance was operationalized in three ways: (1) the total number of subtractions they attempted; (2) the total number of correct subtractions they produced; and (3) their error rate, or the percentage of subtractions that were incorrectly performed out of the total number of attempted subtractions.

Results show that, after attending to the carefully crafted Facebook version of themselves, Facebook users experienced an increase in state self-esteem at a deep, unconscious level. This finding is consistent with the theoretical notion of selective self-presentation: If users do have the ability to compose highly flattering yet realistic self-presentations that can impress their audience, it stands to reason that attending to this version of themselves would boost their self-esteem. This psychological benefit was nevertheless accompanied by a psychological cost. After being self-affirmed through Facebook, participants' cognitive task performance deteriorated. They attempted fewer answers and produced fewer correct answers than participants in the control condition. Importantly, however, the error rate of affirmed participants was no different than that of control participants. This pattern of results suggests that self-affirmed participants' motivation, rather than ability, to perform well in the task was decreased. As such, results are consistent with self-affirmation theory. If participants' self-worth is already secured by the self-affirmation exercise, they no longer need to prove themselves by performing well in an unpleasant task.

Discussion: Causes and Effects of Facebook Use

The purpose of this chapter was to examine the nature of Facebook profile self-presentation, as well as its effects, through the prism of self-affirmation theory.[26] Self-affirmation claims that people have a fundamental need to view themselves as valuable, worthy, and good, and that they unconsciously scour the environment in search of information that can reassure them of their own self-worth. The research reported in this chapter examined whether SNS, specifically Facebook, play a role in these self-worth maintenances processes. Does Facebook self-presentation, by virtue of being carefully and thoughtfully crafted, re-store users' sense of self-worth and self-integrity? Does it then constitute an everyday venue of self-affirmation? If Facebook profiles do affirm their users, what are some of the perceptual and behavioral effects of becoming self-affirmed?

Results provide conclusive evidence that Facebook profile self-presentation is a self-affirming activity. After reviewing their own profile self-presentation, participants experienced a boost in their perceptions of self-worth, and this boost was of similar magnitude to the one provided by a well-established self-affirmation activity (Study 1). Furthermore, Facebook self-affirmation was actively, albeit unconsciously, sought after by users in times of psychological need (Study 2), indicating that Facebook profiles are used in everyday life as a comforting space, that can assuage feelings of distress. Consistent with the claims of self-affirmation theory, exposure to one's own Facebook profile also increases users' temporary self-esteem, and reduces their motivation to pursue other opportunities for self-affirmation, such as performing tasks where they can showcase their aptitudes (Study 3).

The fundamental premise underlying these findings, derived from the Hyperpersonal model of impression formation, is that Facebook profile self-presentation captures the self at its most desirable and socially attractive.[27] Indeed, according to the Hyperpersonal model, Facebook self-presenters have the ability to construct themselves in carefully orchestrated ways, and hence achieve their self-presentational goals, with more ease than FtF self-presenters. Additionally, the mission of SNS is to embed users in a network of social connections, and this mission is accomplished through a constellation of design choices, such as the ability to amass "friends," to link to friends' profiles, and collect comments and other tokens of connectivity from friends. Together, selective self-presentation and the embeddedness in a network of meaningful relationships (which most people consider to be the most treasured aspect of their lives), render Facebook profiles self-affirming.

This set of findings on the self-affirming properties of Facebook profile self-presentation add theoretical and empirical heft to a growing body of research on the uses and effects of Facebook. Following abundant speculation, usually pessimistic, in the media and popular discourse, academic research has only begun to illuminate the cases and effects of SNS use.[28] For instance, Facebook use has been shown to correlate with a boost in social capital, life satisfaction, social trust, civic engagement, and political participation; and college student motivation, affective learning, and positive classroom climate.[29] Research has also shown that participants identify as their primary motivation for using Facebook a desire to maintain their existing relationships with friends and family members.[30]

The studies reviewed in this chapter contribute to this literature by identifying a host of psychological effects and motivations for Facebook use. These studies are also some of the first experiments performed to examine Facebook uses and effects, and hence contribute increased confidence about causality to the correlational studies performed to date.

Consider first the psychological benefits that ensue from Facebook profile self-presentation. Following a brief exposure to this flattering and socially connected portrayal of self, participants experienced reduced defensiveness when confronted with an ego threat. Theoretically, this indicates that their perception of self-worth and self-integrity had been secured by the Facebook browsing activity. Facebook-induced self-affirmation produces an array of related psychological benefits, such as being more open-minded, secure, willing to take responsibility for failure in a task, and less likely to blame and derogate others. Although this idea was not directly tested in these studies, reduced defensiveness is an attitude that typically helps people to learn from their mistakes and to not ruminate about their failures.[31] Future research is invited to directly test these claims.

Psychological benefits beyond self-affirmation also emerged. Facebook profile self-presentation increased positive affect, both directed at oneself (i.e., feeling loved, content, proud, supported, connected) and at others (i.e., feeling loving, giving), and it also increased users' temporary self-esteem—that is, it led them to view themselves more favorably at a deep, unconscious level. Recall that the IAT procedure employed to measure self-esteem ensures that participants didn't fake or incorrectly report their self-esteem, hence providing highly reliable findings. Together, these psychological benefits suggest that Facebook profiles are psychologically comforting spaces that elicit both positive self-evaluations and prosocial sentiments. At a theoretical level, these findings provide indirect support for the notion of selective self-presentation and the Hyperpersonal model. As previously mentioned, the Hyperpersonal model predicts that Facebook self-presentation should be positive, flattering, and veridical, although no study to date has directly tested these claims. This type of self-presentation should indeed elicit the intrapersonal effects reported here. By observing the hypothesized effects, this study hence supports the contention of the Hyperpersonal model.

Precisely because Facebook profile self-presentation is psychologically rewarding, it was also hypothesized to be inviting and alluring to users. Study 2 provided support for this claim, with users becoming motivated to spend time on their Facebook profiles following a blog to the ego. This finding offers a new perspective on users' motivation to access SNS: Facebook use is seen as being prompted by unconscious goals and motivation (i.e., the need for self-worth) and by situational factors (threats to the ego that stem from sources external to the self). Viewing Facebook use as the product of unconscious needs and situational factors is a novel addition to the literature on motivations for SNS use, which has thus far relied on self-report methodologies to extract from users their conscious, explicit motivations.[32]

The self-affirmation framework may also provide a previously unexplored explanation for the overwhelming popularity of Facebook. If seeking positive self-regard is a fundamental human need, and Facebook profiles have the capacity to fulfill this need, it stands to reason that users will feel compelled to access these profiles. In particular, it is worth noting that social connectivity with friends and family is the most sought after type of self-affirmation and that Facebook excels precisely in capturing and offering reminders of this connectivity.[33] From this perspective, Facebook's success can be at least partially accounted by its ability to capture the most meaningful, self-affirming aspects of users' selves.

Consider next the psychological costs produced by Facebook profile self-presentation. One arguably negative outcome of the increase in self-worth induced by Facebook profile exposure was a reduction in users' motivation to perform well in a cognitive task of moderate difficulty (i.e., the serial subtraction task). Consistent with claims that people are content with a good-enough vision of themselves, participants who were induced to feel good about themselves by Facebook profile exposure did not take advantage of additional opportunities to increase their self-worth, such as performing well in an academic task. These findings are relevant to recent research that has proposed that Facebook use, broadly construed, hinders students' academic performance, by lowering their GPA.[34] The present research takes a narrower view on Facebook effects, by considering only one Facebook activity—own profile browsing, and one simple academically related task, mental arithmetic. The decrement in performance observed here can be explained in motivational terms, with users trying less hard to perform well (rather than being less *able* to do so). Thus, under limited conditions, Facebook use may indeed take a toll on scholastic performance. Future research, encompassing more diverse Facebook activities and performance metrics, is necessary to more fully understand Facebook's effect on school performance.

The final question that needs to be addressed is whether all profile-based SNS are self-affirming, and whether the effects outlined previously apply to all of them equally. In accordance with self-affirmation theory, SNS should be affirming to the extent that they provide users with the affordances to put their best "face" forward in a veridical way, and to embed themselves in a network of meaningful personal relationships. Future research is needed to gauge the applicability of self-affirmation theory to other SNS.

Conclusion

Self-presentation is a complex communicative activity that is deeply affected by technological affordances. Asynchronicity, editability, recordability, and access to an audience shape the kinds of images self-presenters construct. The research reviewed here proposed that Facebook self-presentation is typically flattering, veridical, and socially connected, as a result of these affordances. Once constructed, this unique version of oneself has profound intrapersonal and interpersonal effects that merit theoretical and empirical consideration.

Notes

1. Roy F. Baumeister, "A Self-Presentational View of Social Phenomena," *Psychological Bulletin* 91, no. 1 (1982): 3–26; Mark R. Leary, *Self-Presentation: Impression Management and Interpersonal Behavior, Social Psychology Series* (Madison, WI: Brown and Benchmark, 1995).

2. Judith Donath and danah boyd, "Public Displays of Connection," *BT Technology Journal* 22, no. 4 (October 2004): 71–82.

3. Claude M. Steele, "The Psychology of Self-Affirmation: Sustaining the Integrity of the Self," in *Advances in Experimental Social Psychology*, ed. Leonard Berkowtz, vol. 21 (San Diego, CA: Academic Press, 1988), 261–302; David K. Sherman and Geoffrey L. Cohen, "The Psychology of Self-Defense: Self-Affirmation Theory," in *Advances in Experimental Social Psychology* 38, ed. Mark P. Zanna (San Diego, CA: Academic Press, 2006), 183–242.

4. Abraham Tesser, "Toward a Self-Evaluation Maintenance Model of Social Behavior," in *Advances in Experimental Social Psychology*, ed. Leonard Berkowitz, vol. 21 (San Diego, CA: Academic Press, 1988), 181–227.

5. Sherman and Cohen, "The Psychology of Self-Defense"; Steele, "The Psychology of Self-Affirmation."

6. Steele, "The Psychology of Self-Affirmation."

7. Jennifer Crocker and Katherine M. Knight, "Contingencies of Self-Worth," *Current Directions in Psychological Science* 14, no. 4 (August 2005): 200–203.

8. Amy McQueen and William Klein, "Experimental Manipulations of Self-Affirmation: A Systematic Review," *Self and Identity* 5, no. 4 (October–December 2006): 289–354.

9. Ralph Gross and Alessandro Acquisti, "Information Revelation and Privacy in Online Social Networks," in *Proceedings of the 12th Annual Workshop on Privacy in the Electronic Society* (New York: ACM Press, 2005), 71–80; Cliff Lampe, Nicole Ellison, and Charles Steinfield, "A Familiar Face(book): Profile Elements as Signals in an Online Social Network," in *Proceedings of the SIGCHI Conference on Human Factors in Computing Systems,* (New York: ACM Press, 2007), 435–44; Zeynep Tufekci, "Can You See Me Now? Audience and Disclosure Regulation in Online Social Network Sites," *Bulletin of Science, Technology and Society* 28, no. 1 (February 2008): 20–36; Alyson L. Young and Anabel Quan-Haase, "Information Revelation and Internet Privacy Concerns on

Social Network Sites: A Case Study of Facebook," in *Proceedings of the Fourth International Conference on Communities and Technologies* (New York: ACM, 2009), 265–74.

10. Baumeister, "A Self-Presentational View."

11. Joseph B. Walther, "Selective Self-Presentation in Computer-Mediated Communication: Hyperpersonal Dimensions of Technology, Language, and Cognition," *Computers in Human Behavior* 23, no. 5 (2007): 2538–57.

12. Nicole Ellison, Rebecca Heino, and Jennifer Gibbs, "Managing Impressions Online: Self-Presentation Processes in the Online Dating Environment," *Journal of Computer- Mediated Communication* 11, 2006, accessed February 16, 2007, http://jcmc.indiana.edu/vol11/issue2/ellison.html; Catalina L. Toma and Jeffrey T. Hancock, "Looks and Lies: The Role of Physical Attractiveness in Online Dating Self-Presentation and Deception," *Communication Research* 37, no. 3 (2010): 335–51; Catalina L. Toma, Jeffrey T. Hancock, and Nicole Ellison, "Separating Fact from Fiction: Deceptive Self-Presentation in Online Dating Profiles," *Personality and Social Psychology Bulletin* 38, no. 8 (2008): 1023–36.

13. Jeffrey T. Hancock, "Digital Deception: From Ancient Empires to Internet Dating," in *Deception: Methods, Contexts and Consequences,* ed. Brooke Harrington (Palo Alto, CA: Stanford Press, 2007), 109–20.

14. Joseph B. Walther and Malcolm R. Parks, "Cues Filtered Out, Cues Filtered In: Computer-Mediated Communication and Relationships," in *Handbook of Interpersonal Communication* 3rd ed., eds. Mark L. Knapp and John A. Daly (Thousand Oaks, CA: Sage, 2002), 529–63; Joseph B. Walther, Brendan Van Der Heide, Lauren M. Hamel, Hilary C. Shulman, "Self-Generated Versus Other-Generated Statements and Impressions in Computer-Mediated Communication: A Test of Warranting Theory Using Facebook," *Communication Research* 36, no. 2 (2009): 229–53.

15. Toma, Hancock, and Ellison, "Separating Fact from Fiction."

16. Judith Donath, "Identity and Deception in the Virtual Community," in *Communities in Cyberspace*, eds. Marc Smith and Peter Kollock (New York: Routledge, 1999), 29–59.

17. Mitja Back, Juliane Stopfer, Simine Vazire, Sam Gaddis, Stefan C. Schmukle, Boris Egloff, and Samuel Gosling, "Facebook Profiles Reflect Actual Personality, Not Self-Idealization," *Psychological Science* 21, no. 3 (2010): 372–74.

18. Toma, Hancock, and Ellison, "Separating Fact from Fiction."

19. McQueen and Klein, "Experimental Manipulations"; Sherman and Cohen, "The Psychology of Self-Defense."

20. Abraham Tesser and David P. Cornell, "On the Confluence of Self Processes," *Journal of Experimental Social Psychology* 27, no. 6 (1991): 501–26.

21. Roy F. Baumeister, Dianne M. Tice, and Debra G. Hutton, "Self-Presentational Motivations and Personality Differences in Self-Esteem," *Journal of Personality* 57, no. 2 (1989): 547–79.

22. Anthony G. Greenwald and Mahzarin R. Banaji, "Implicit Social Cognition," *Psychological Review* 102, no. 1 (1995): 4–27.

23. McQueen and Klein, "Experimental Manipulations."

24. McQueen and Klein, "Experimental Manipulations."

25. Jamie Arndt, Jeff Schimel, Jeff Greenberg, and Tom Pyszczynski, "The Intrinsic Self and Defensiveness: Evidence That Activating the Intrinsic Self Reduces Self-Handicapping and Conformity," *Personality and Social Psychology Bulletin* 28, no. 5 (May 2002): 671–83; Jeff Schimel, Jeff Arndt, Katherine M. Banko, and Alison Cook, "Not All Self-Affirmations Were Created Equal: The Cognitive and Social Benefits of Affirming the Intrinsic (vs. Extrinsic) Self," *Social Cognition* 22, no. 1 (2004): 75–99; Joe Tomaka, Jim Blascovich, Jeffrey Kibler, John Ernst, "Cognitive and Physiological Antecedents of Threat and Challenge Appraisal," *Journal of Personality and Social Psychology* 73, no. 1 (1997): 63–72.

26. Steele, "The Psychology of Self-Affirmation"; Sherman and Cohen, "The Psychology of Self-Defense."

27. Joseph B. Walther, "Computer-Mediated Communication: Impersonal, Interpersonal, and Hyperpersonal Interaction," *Communication Research* 23, no. 1 (1996): 3–44; Walther, "Selective Self-Presentation."

28. Tom Hodgkinson, "With Friends Like These. . ." *The Guardian*, January 14, 2008, May 1, 2010, from http://www.guardian.co.uk/technology/2008/jan/14/facebook; Abbott Koloff, "States Push for Cyberbully Controls; But Efforts to Go Beyond Schools Raise Concerns Over Freedom of Speech, Privacy," *USA Today*, February 7, 2008, 3A; Brad Stone, "New Scrutiny for Facebook Predators," *New York Times*, July 30, 2007, May 1, 2010, fromhttp://www.nytimes.com/2007/07/30/business/media/30facebook.html.

29. Nicole B. Ellison, Charles Steinfield, and Cliff Lampe, "The Benefits of Facebook "Friends:" Social Capital and College Students' Use of Online Social Network Sites," *Journal of Computer-Mediated Communication* 12, no. 4 (July 2007): 1143–68; Sebastian Valenzuela, Namsu Park, and Kerk F. Kee, "Is There Social Capital in a Social Network Site? Facebook Use, and College Students' Life Satisfaction, Trust, and Participation," *Journal of Computer-Mediated Communication* 14, no. 4 (2009): 875–901; Joseph P. Mazer, Richard E. Murphy, and Cheri Simonds, "I'll See You on Facebook: The Effects of Computer-Mediated Self-Disclosure on Student Motivation, Affective Learning, and Classroom Climate," *Communication Education* 56, no. 1 (2007): 1–17.

30. Adam Joinson, "Looking At, Looking Up or Keeping Up With People? Motives and Use of Facebook," in *Proceedings of the 26 Annual Human Factors inComputing Systems Conference* (New York: ACM, 2008), 1027–36.

31. Sherman and Cohen, "The Psychology of Self-Defense."

32. Gross and Acquisti, "Information Revelation and Privacy"; Ellison, Steinfield and Lampe, "The Benefits of Facebook "Friends"; Joinson, "Looking at, Looking Up."

33. McQueen and Klein, "Experimental Manipulations."

34. Reynol Junco, "Too Much Face and Not Enough Books: The Relationship Between Multiple Indices of Facebook Use and Academic Performance," *Computers in Human Behavior* 28, no. 1 (2012): 187–98; Paul A. Kirschner and Aryn C. Karpinski, "Facebook and Academic Performance," *Computers in Human Behavior* 26, no. 6 (November 2010): 1237–45.

Chapter 12

What You Can Really Know about Someone from Their Facebook Profile (And Where You Should Look to Find Out)

Jeffrey A. Hall and Natalie Pennington

Few questions are as fascinating to lay and academic audiences alike as, "Who are you?" and "How do others see me?" Throughout the twentieth century, personality psychologists investigated how people are perceived via their nonverbal behavior and physical appearance. One model that stood out for its utility and intuitive design was the Brunswik lens model. This model became a dominant tool in person perception research for estimating personality at zero acquaintance and in understanding interpersonal rapport.[1] As the twentieth century became the twenty-first, the questions inherent to person perception research remained, but the context of inquiry changed from initial FtF (FtF) interactions to perceptions obtained from personal web pages and social networking sites (SNS).[2] As we increasingly use some form of digital mediation when forming impressions of strangers and new acquaintances, the questions, "Who are you?" and "How do others see me?" remain among our foremost concerns.[3]

The aim of this chapter is to answer the question, "How much can we really know about a person by viewing their Facebook (FB) profile page or personal web page?" In summarizing current research on online impression formation and management, two other important questions will also be answered: "Can some personality traits be more accurately perceived than others?" and "What types of cues tell us the most about the profile owner's personality?" This chapter will offer detailed and empirically driven answers to all these questions by summarizing several prominent studies using the Brunswik lens model and reporting the results of a major lens model investigation conducted by the chapter authors.[4]

Facebook Impressions

Social networking sites such as FB are "mediated publics," wherein users can "express themselves and learn from the reactions of others. [T]hey let people make certain acts or expressions 'real' by having witnesses acknowledge them."[5] Within FB, the profile owner's page is the mediated representation of communicator within the user-generated public made possible by the online platform. The specific features of the profile (e.g., status updates, photos) serve as *sign vehicles*, which are constructed to convey particular impressions.[6] Each activity on FB, whether the particular wording of a status update or the particular profile photo selected, is a self-presentational act to be witnessed by the user's mediated public.

Mediated self-presentation is important to and valued by SNS users. Indeed, Livingstone argues that the profile is an attempt to publicly answer central questions, such as "What matters to me?" and "Who am I?"[7] Answers to these questions become an "idealized representation" of the self, which is consequential not only within the online community, but can also spill over to offline impressions and interactions.[8] As research from online dating demonstrates, users' dispositions influence their online self-presentation.[9] In turn, users' online presentations influence future offline interactions.[10]

As SNS become further integrated into users' lives, they will become more important in both forming and managing impressions. This exacerbates perceivers' concerns about the veracity of users' profiles. Yet, despite temptations, most online users maintain a fairly accurate self-presentation on personal websites. That is, users' dispositions, as judged from a personal website alone, match up meaningfully with friends' judgments of users' offline dispositions.[11] Furthermore, dishonest presentations on FB are risky because so many FB friends are familiar with the user both online and offline. Misrepresentation on FB is often called out and castigated as hypocritical and untrustworthy.[12] Despite the tension between a desire to accurately know a person by only viewing their online profile and worry of misrepresentation, there is good reason to believe that we can accurately estimate users' personality from their FB profile alone. To form these online impressions, we look for credible warrants of users' dispositions and personalities.

Warranting Theory

Warranting theory has become a prevalent and valuable theory in generating predictions germane to online impression formation. Due to the disconnect between an offline and online self, warranting theory states that perceivers seek information that can establish trustworthy links between the two selves.[13] Past research using warranting theory in the context of FB has explored the relationship between the impressions formed about the user and the number of friends the user has, friends' comments about the user, user photos, and all three in combination.[14] These articles explore the relationship between particular FB cues on the profile page and the impressions of strangers. However, we believe that these studies only explore two of the three components of a warrant.

Of the three components of a warrant, the first is warrant credibility. This is the degree to which an aspect of an online self-presentation is immune to manipulation. We argue that warrant credibility should be restricted to the degree to which warrants are considered trustworthy or not easily manipulated. The second component of warranting theory is perceived warrant value. This is the degree to which perceivers actually use or are influenced by any particular cue when judging user personality. Walther et al. and Tong et al. all measure perceived warranting value by the variance explained in impressions formed.[15] Essentially, if one cue explains more variance in the impressions formed by strangers, then it has higher perceived warrant value. The degree to which cues are influential is not synonymous with the degree to which they are truthful or unable to be manipulated. This distinction separates perceived warrant value from warrant credibility.

The third concept, introduced in our chapter, is warrant diagnosticity, or the actual predictive value of a cue. Warrant diagnosticity is the degree to which cues used by perceivers to make judgments of users are actually related to users' characteristics. This is the accuracy of the cue. Although warranting theory has been used primarily to explore the perceived value of a warrant, we suggest that warranting theory also leaves space for exploring the veracity of a warrant. Although a cue could be thought trustworthy, a cue would not be diagnostic if it were not associated with the underlying personality of the target. To be able to fully apply this concept, researchers must know whether the cues used to make judgments are, in fact, related to user personality. The lens model can evaluate the perceived warrant value and the diagnosticity of any given cue simultaneously in a highly ecologically valid way.

The Lens Model

The lens model allows researchers to answer three questions: What cues are related to a target's actual personality traits (cue validity); what cues are being used by observers to judge a target's personality (cue utilization); and to what degree are these cues in agreement (diagnostic warrants). The lens model has also been applied to personality in a range of contexts, including targets' physical environments, such as bedrooms and offices.[16] Although the target is not physically present when observers judge their personality, Gosling et al. suggest that targets leave behind *behavioral residue*, which offers others clues about targets' underlying dispositions.[17] Similarly, although a SNS profile owner may not be logged on, the profile reveals information about its owner in the form of updates, comments by friends, pictures, and details about tastes and beliefs. Recent research using the lens model, including our project, has extended the lens model into personal web pages and FB profile pages.[18]

The lens model can determine which FB cues are associated with FB users' underlying personality, which cues are used by strangers to form impressions of users, and the agreement between the two. To determine which cues are associated with users' personality, FB users' personalities are self-reported and the content of their profile pages are broken down into discrete cues through content analysis. Users' personalities are then correlated with the content of their profile pages. These correlations are the cue validity side of the lens model. Then, strangers, whose job it is to estimate the personality of the profile owner by only evaluating their profile page, examine targets' profile pages. Aggregate stranger estimates of each FB user's personality are correlated with the content of each of the user's profile pages. These correlations are the cue utilization side of the lens model. The matches between the two sets of correlations are called cues in agreement or diagnostic warrants.

Hall, Pennington, and Lueder's FB Lens Model Project

We conducted an extensive lens model investigation, reported in Hall et al. Thirty-five observers were given screen shots of one hundred users' FB profile pages in PDF format, including the main profile page, the eight most recent profile pictures, recent news feed, and the entire Info page. Observers, who were strangers to the profile owners, estimated all one hundred targets' personalities from this information alone. Personality was measured using the Big Five Factor inventory.[19] In addition, humor orientation and narcissism were evaluated.[20] Importantly, over two-thirds of the final sample came from a community snowball sample, not college undergraduates. This quota sample was drawn to be a representative sample of all users on FB in 2010.[21]

A total of fifty-five cues from each target's FB profile page were coded by up to four independent coders. First, attributes of the profile picture (e.g., attractiveness) and features of friends in targets' photos (e.g., number of friends) were coded. Second, objective measures of the status update text (e.g., word count) were coded using the linguistic analysis program Diction, while subjective measures from status updates (e.g., positive affect, humor use) were coded by independent coders.[22] Third, the Info section on the profile was coded for information that may contribute to personality judgments (e.g., hobbies, quotes). Finally, three cues generated by users' FB friends were coded (i.e., number of likes and comments on status updates, number of unique friends commenting on status updates).

Accuracy

Although an ancillary question to warranting theory, the lens model offers a clear answer to a question central to this chapter, "What personality traits can we accurately know by examining a users' FB profile page or personal web page alone?" To provide the best possible answer, we combined the accuracy results found in all known publications using the lens model on personal web pages and FB. Because personality is the most common set of traits used in lens model research, our summary will focus on the Big Five (i.e., extraversion, agreeableness, conscientiousness, neuroticism, and openness). We will also share results from our project not reported elsewhere on narcissism and humor orientation.

Accuracy

The lens model allows researchers to determine the accuracy of observers' estimates of targets' personality. Accuracy is calculated by correlating the self-reported personality of the user with the aggregate personality estimates of all observers. When accuracy is significant, the trait can be estimated above what might be expected by mere chance alone. The results of four past investigations with five samples judging five personality traits are shown in the Figure 12.1. We performed a mini-meta-analysis of the effect sizes drawn from these five samples to determine an overall accuracy rate for each personality trait across all five samples.

As this figure shows, while differences existed between studies, extraversion, openness, and conscientiousness can be judged accurately through an online self-representation. However, estimating neuroticism is quite difficult, which is also the case in estimating neuroticism during FtF interactions.[23] The results of the mini-meta-analysis found that the average neuroticism estimate was $r = 0.13$, which was not significantly different from zero. By comparison, the mini-meta-analysis showed that both openness, $r = 0.31, p < 0.001$, and extraversion, $r = 0.25, p < 0.001$, were accurately estimated on FB and personal websites. According to the mini-meta-analysis, the two remaining traits were somewhere in the middle: conscientiousness was significantly accurately estimated, $r = 0.21, p < 0.01$, while agreeableness was in the right direction, $r = 0.14$, but accuracy was not significant.

Figure 12.1. Accuracy Rates by Trait and Study

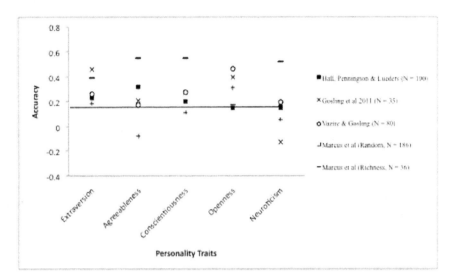

Personal Web Pages vs. Facebook

The figure demonstrates that some personality traits are easier to diagnose on FB and some are more easily judged on personal web pages. While observers examining personal web pages struggled to diagnose agreeableness accurately studies using a FB profile were more accurate.[24] By way of comparison, the opposite was true for openness: it was more accurately judged from personal web pages than FB profiles.

What explains the differences between personal web pages and FB profiles? One likely reason is there are many cues that are readily available on FB that are not available on personal web pages. There is good reason to believe that rich and interactive SNS platforms may improve observer accuracy. As noted in Figure 12.1, Marcus et al. relied on two separate samples: a random selection of personal web pages and a sample that was handpicked for richness and interactivity.[25] In the case of the random sample, agreeableness and conscientiousness could not be accurately estimated, whereas in the rich sample they both were. Perhaps SNS that are more rich and interactive can lead to more accurate judgments than thin or static personal profiles.

Another difference between personal web pages and FB pages that might influence the accuracy of observers is photos. FB profiles prominently display photos. Indeed, an entire subsection of the profile is dedicated to photos. These photos might help observers more accurately judge certain personality traits. Borkenau and Liebler's study of person perception using the lens model suggested that conscientiousness and extraversion could be accurately judged from a still photo alone.[26]

By contrast, openness can be more accurately estimated from personal web pages than FB profiles. Looking to the cues used by observers to estimate openness (e.g., musical and artistic tastes) shows that many of them are found within the subsections rather than the primary view of the FB profile. If observers' attention was inappropriately placed on nondiagnostic and misleading cues when examining a FB profile, it could have led to a less accurate estimate of personality.

Humor

One personality trait analyzed in our study, but not explored in past research, was humor orientation, or the ability to produce humor.[27] In our study, humor orientation achieved a significant level of accuracy, $r(99) = 0.22$, $p < 0.01$. The accuracy rate was comparable to extraversion and conscientiousness. This suggests that FB users' sense of humor comes through on their profiles in a way that is accurate and meaningful to strangers.

Narcissism

Another trait unique to our study was narcissism. We found that narcissism was similar to neuroticism in the sense that it could not be accurately estimated, $r(99) = 0.05$, $p = ns$. One interpretation of this finding is that less desirable traits, such as narcissism, are hard to detect or more easily hidden on FB. However, without establishing that you can accurately estimate a person's narcissism FtF but not via FB profiles, this explanation awaits further study.

More Information, More Accuracy?

Both Marcus et al. and Gosling et al. suggest that providing more information on a web page or FB profile will improve the accuracy of observers.[28] When the information on a SNS profile page is disjointed, minimal, or rarely used, observers may have a hard time figuring out what the profile owner is really like.

We decided to test this hypothesis using our study data. We identified thirteen of our fifty-five cues that measured FB use in some way, including number of posts, number of comments on others' posts, number of pictures posted, number of friends, number of words in posts, number of media shared, the total number of quotes on the Info page, and seven other cues. These cues were all converted into z-scores to standardize the amount each was used among the one hundred profiles. Then, we made a composite z-score from those thirteen cues for each target. For the Big Five personality traits, we found a weak and nonsignificant correlation between total FB use and accuracy, $r(99) = -0.084$, $p = ns$, range = $-0.23 - 0.03$.

There are two likely reasons for the lack of support for the conclusions of Marcus et al. and Gosling et al.[29] Although it seems reasonable that more rich and interactive information gives strangers a better impression of the profile owner, simply *more* information may not improve accuracy. As Gosling suggests, although extraverts may use FB more, it does not suggest that more use provides better information about the users' extraversion, unless that information is diagnostically linked to the trait. Therefore, Gosling's significant correlation between use and extraversion may have been simply because extraverted FB users have more friends, which we also found to be a diagnostic cue for extraversion.

Are Some People More Accurate Guessers?

Yes, they are. The lens model allows researchers to estimate observers' individual accuracy rates. Similar to past research reporting individual differences in judging interpersonal rapport, roughly half (seventeen of thirty-five) of our observers had a mean accuracy across all five personality traits that was significantly higher than what would be expected from chance alone.[30] Simply put, some observers are more talented than others in estimating user personality from a FB profile page.

Diagnostic Cues

What particular FB cues are most useful when attempting to judge a users' personality? To answer this question, we combed through eleven studies on FB and personal websites. In the four studies of online communication that used the lens model, we used the three studies that reported diagnostic warrants, which were cues that matched profile owners' personality to observers' impressions of profile owners' personality. We also included one past study using the lens model on individuals' photos since photos are a key FB profile feature, and one past lens model study on bedrooms and offices for cues related to music and media.[31] We included three studies that explored perceivers' impressions of users' personality from their FB page.[32] Finally, we included three studies that explored the relationship between user personality and FB use.[33] From these studies, we can offer a clear picture of what particular cues are diagnostic or likely to be diagnostic for each trait, what cues observers should use but do not, and what cues are used by observers but shouldn't be. Additionally, we will share the results of our lens model investigation regarding humor and narcissism (see Table 12.1).

Diagnostic Cues on Facebook

Openness

Someone who is high in openness is likely to include artistic information on their FB profile web page, including links to web pages about the arts, books, and music, song lyrics, and quotes from authors and musicians. All of these cues are examples of behavioral residue of openness, or someone who is open to cultural and artistic experiences by disposition. Strangers also used these cues to estimate users' openness, thereby creating a diagnostic match between users' self-presentation and strangers' estimates of their personality.

Extraversion

The two cues most consistently related to FB user extraversion and strangers' perception of extraversion are social in nature: having more FB friends and having more people in photos.[34] These two cues meaningfully represent what makes a person extraverted—being social and outgoing. In addition, our investigation suggests that expressing more positive emotions in status updates and manipulating text on status updates to express positive emotions are also diagnostic indicators of extraversion. We found that the use of extended letters (e.g., "heyyyyy" and "yayyyy") in status updates was diagnostic of an extraverted personality. While other studies did not find this match when it came to text manipulation, it was probably because these textual features were only introduced to FB

Table 12.1: *Cues Used to Form and Manage Impressions across Studies*

	Extraver-sion	Agreea-bleness	Conscien-tiousness	Neuroti-cism	Open-ness
Diag-nostic Cues	More FB Friends[1, 2, 6, 7, 8, 11]	Picture Friendli-ness[1, 10]			Books Listed[1, 3, 9]
	More Friends in Photos[1, 2, 3]				Music Listed[1, 3, 9]
	Positive Emotional Expression[1, 3, 7]				Media Sharer[1, 3]
Possibly Diag-nostic Cues	More Use of FB [2, 5, 11]	Less FB Use in General[1]	Concrete Info vs. Playful, Humorous[1, 3]	Less per-sonal or emotional expression infor-mation[1,3]	Discuss-ing Poli-tics[1, 3]
		Sharing Media[1]	More agree-ment with posts by FB friends[1]	Fewer pictures of self on profile[1, 3]	More Expres-sion of Beliefs[1, 3, 5, 8]
Cues - Should be Used		Comments and/or Viewing Other Profiles[1, 2]	Family Talk and/or Photos[1, 3]		Photos of User Alone[1, 3]
Cues - Should not be Used	Friend's Expressive-ness[1, 3, 4]	Attractive Photo[1, 10]	Political Talk[1, 3]	Less ac-tive use of FB[1, 3, 5]	

Other's Comments/ Actions[1,3]	Family Talk and/or Family Photos[1,3]	Less Friendly Photos[1,10]

Notes: 1 = Hall et al., in press; 2 = Gosling et al., 2011; 3 = Marcus et al., 2006; 4 = Utz, 2010; 5 = Ross et al., 2009; 6 = Tong et al., 2008; 7 = Antheunis and Schouten; 8 = Amichai-Hamburger and Vinizky; 9 = Gosling et al., 2002; 10 = Borkenau and Leibler, 1992; 11 = Ong et al., 2011

after 2007 and not explored in past FB research. We believe expressing positive emotions on FB status updates is probably diagnostic of extraversion.

Agreeableness

Surprisingly, two separate studies suggested that having a friendly looking photo was diagnostic of agreeableness. This finding had good empirical support due to the fact our investigation focused on FB and Borkenau and Leibler studied still photos of participants in an early lens model study, yet both studies found friendly photos to be related to user agreeableness and observer estimates of agreeableness.[35]

Likely Diagnostic Matches—Further Study

Some cues matched user and observers impressions in some studies but not others, and some cues were coded or analyzed in similar yet not wholly comparable forms. We believe these cues *might* be diagnostic of personality, but are in need of further study.

Openness

There are two cues that *might* be diagnostic of openness: discussing politics and increased personal expression. We found that a user who posts status updates and media to initiate political discussions is more open and perceived as more open, and Marcus et al. found that more links to political and nonprofit websites was a diagnostic sign of openness. In addition, multiple studies suggest that expression of personal beliefs might be diagnostic of openness.[36] We believe that greater expressions of personal beliefs or attitudes might be diagnostic of openness on FB as well, but since each prior study explored this concept in a slightly different way, the evidence is still inconclusive.

Extraversion

There is some evidence that increased FB use overall *might* be diagnostic of extraversion. Past research has found that greater FB use is both used by others to judge extraversion and is related to self-reported extraversion.[37] Gosling et al. report that users with a high number of photos, friends, and group membership self-reported being extraverted and were perceived to be more extraverted by strangers.[38] However, we would caution combining all indicators of FB use into a single measure if we wish to know which discrete cues are most diagnostic of the trait. Each FB cue may have unique warranting value in estimating personality.

Conscientiousness

Although there was insufficient evidence to say that any particular cues are truly diagnostic of conscientiousness, there are some promising cues that await further study. More conscientious users may share more hard and concrete facts about themselves (i.e., past experiences and history, a CV, or resume) and less conscientious users may be more playful and humorous in pictures, status updates, and quotes.[39] This dichotomy between factual/concrete and playful/humorous has not been explored in past studies in a consistent manner. However, it stands to reason that more factual information might be diagnostic of a user who wants things to be more organized and less frivolous on their online presentation of self.

In our study, we also found one other-generated cue that was diagnostic of conscientiousness: other FB friends' agreement with users' posts. While a FB user had no control over FB friends' support and agreement, strangers still used these comments to estimate user conscientiousness. We feel that this cue should inspire further study particularly because the role others' online behavior plays in forming impressions is a nascent but important topic of research.[40]

Agreeableness

There are two cues that might be diagnostic of a more agreeable FB user: less FB use in general, particularly less sharing of media. In our study, we found diagnostic matches between writing fewer status updates and posting less frequently and higher agreeableness. That is, the more you post on FB the less agreeable you are and are perceived to be. While this match was not found in other FB studies, we believe this is largely due to developing FB norms and the relative newness of status updates. Ours is the only study to-date that looks for diagnostic cues within FB status updates. The FB newsfeed is the place where all status updates are sent when you are friends with someone. We believe that frequent FB posters are viewed as "clogging" the newsfeed and are seen as annoying or intrusive (i.e., less agreeable). Additionally, our study found that sharing a variety of different media (e.g., books, music, news) was diagnostic of a less agreeable FB user, we suspect for similar reasons as more posts in general.

Neuroticism

There are no cues that show clear empirical evidence of being diagnostically related to neuroticism, but we found two that hold promise for future investigation. User neuroticism *might* be accurately known by witnessing a *lack* of emotional expression and through a *lack* of pictures of the self on the profile (e.g., a picture of a sunset, pictures of pets).[41] Insofar as a neurotic user is less willing to share personal and/or emotional information through images or text, the lack of personal information could also be a good clue for judging this trait.

Humor

One personality trait explored uniquely in our research that has not been developed in past research is humor orientation. Therefore, we treat the diagnostic cues from our study as promising, while not certain, diagnostic matches. Attempts at humor in status updates, pictures, or quotes on the Info page were found to be diagnostic of humor orientation. Although we did not measure whether these attempts at humor were objectively funny or not, it makes sense that attempting humor in several places within the FB profile is highly consistent with a person with a high humor orientation. We think it is quite likely that widespread humor use is related to a person's underlying sense of humor.

Other cues that were diagnostic of humor orientation in our study were status updates with relational talk, status updates with political talk (negatively related), and having pictures with friendly looking friends in them. Finally, the number of likes in response to a status update and the number of unique friends who commented were both related to user humor orientation and used by strangers to estimate humor orientation. It makes sense that a social behavior such as humor would be warranted by positive responses from friends. Since ours is the first study to use the lens model to estimate humor orientation on FB, more study is needed to confirm the diagnostic value of these cues.

Narcissism

Narcissism is a trait associated with a grandiose and inflated sense of ability and importance and the use of self-presentation strategies to enhance this self-view.[42] FB provides an excellent platform for narcissists because it allows nearly full control over one's self-presentation.[43] In our lens model analysis, we found that only one cue was related to profile owners' narcissism and used by observers to estimate narcissism: having a sexually provocative profile picture. Displaying profile pictures that show more skin or are in a more sexualized pose is consistent with the narcissistic desire for exhibitionism and their inflated estimation of their own physical attractiveness.[44] The emerging interest in narcissism on FB warrants further study.

Unused Cues to Attend To

There are cues used on FB that are related to a user's personality, but observers do not always pick up on. For example, both our project and Gosling et al found that increased use of FB is negatively related with conscientiousness, but observers did not use that cue to estimate conscientiousness.[45] In addition, our study suggests that family talk on status updates and Marcus et al. found that sharing pictures of family are related to increased conscientiousness, but perceivers did not catch those cues when forming impressions of users' conscientiousness. As such, perceivers should use these cues when estimating users' conscientiousness.

There are cues that perceivers should use to determine agreeableness and openness. As found both in our study and past research viewing and/or commenting on other people's pages is indicative of being an agreeable person, while having pictures on your profile of just you by yourself is indicative of openness.[46]

In the case of narcissism, it *might* be useful to attend to whether or not a user seeks out instrumental support through status updates. Narcissistic individuals tend to have an exaggerated sense of ability, and are unlikely to expose publicaly their need for assistance on FB. According to our research, the more a person seeks out instrumental aid on FB, the less narcissistic they are.

Misdiagnostic Cues

Just as in detecting deception, people often rely upon information that has no relationship with the actual personality of the target. Although one might believe that lying is best detected in a person's face, their voice and body are much better indicators of deception.[47] Therefore, cues that show a mismatch between an online self-presentation and the impressions formed by others is a way to document misperception. For example, if strangers consistently use a specific cue to form an impression of a user that is not related to the user's true personality, it will lead to a misdiagnosis of personality.

In the case of judging extraversion on FB, only self-generated cues are diagnostic. While past research on observers' impressions of extraversion has included other-generated cues, those cues do not appear to be associated with users' actual extraversion.[48] This is a case in which perceived warrant value was high, but actual predictive value was low. Other-generated information is simply not useful when judging extraversion.

There are other examples of misperception. Observers perceive users who engage in political discussions to be more conscientious, but no diagnostic match was found to confirm that perception. Additionally, strangers think that having an attractive photo and talking about family in status updates are signs that a user is more agreeable, but no match has been found to show that this is an accurate cue.

One trait where observers rely heavily on cues that were not related to user personality was neuroticism. Indeed, observers often perceive a user to be neurotic if they have less active use of FB and fewer photos, but these cues are not related to neuroticism. Observers also believe having less friendly photos makes one more neurotic, but no diagnostic match for that cue was found. This points to the overall difficulty in accurately perceiving neuroticism through SNS.

When observers judge profile owners' humor orientation, they relied heavily on cues associated with extraversion or sociability: having more FB friends, having more friendly profile pictures with more friendly looking friends in them, having active hobbies and having more pictures in sociable locations. However, none of these cues are actually indicative of a profile owner's humor orientation. This is a clear case of using an inexact heuristic when forming impressions.

Similarly, observers' estimations of narcissism used a similar set of cues as humor to misperceive that trait: more FB friends, having more friendly profile pictures with more friendly looking, and attractive friends in them. Past research has suggested that profile owners' self-reported profile attractiveness and the number of friends are related to narcissism, we found that these are indeed traits associated with perceptions of narcissism, but not to profile owners' actual narcissism.[49]

Conclusions

The Good Judge, Target, Trait, and Information

David Funder, a prominent researcher of person perception, identified four moderators of observer accuracy: good judge, good target, good trait, and good information.[50] Each of these moderators applies to online impressions as well. Although we have established that some of the observers in lens model studies are more befitting the title of *good judge* than others (about one-half in our estimation), what exactly makes a person a good judge of online profiles is unknown. Another prominent lens model researcher, Frank Bernieri, conducted a study on perceivers to determine if any individual difference, including personality, empathy, social acuity, or intelligence, was a characteristic of being a good judge.[51] None of those individual differences were correlated with accurate judgments of interpersonal rapport. What exactly makes a good judge a good judge in online impression formation is an exciting direction for future research.

A *good target* would be an online profile from which the target's personality is more easily read. In our study, some targets' profiles were more transparent, while others were nearly illegible. We agree with Marcus et al. that more interactive and rich profiles might be more transparent, but increased use of FB alone does not seem to correlate with greater perceiver accuracy.[52] It certainly is the case that the presence (rather than absence) of diagnostic cues will make a profile transparent. For example, because musical and literary tastes diagnose openness, the mere presence of these cues should improve perceiver accuracy of openness. Because having more FB friends is diagnostic of extraversion, this alone should improve accuracy of extraversion. Beyond these evidence-based observations, future research should explore what makes FB profiles more readable than others.

Funder notes that, "a *good trait* (i.e., the kind of trait that is easiest to judge accurately) generally refers to overt and visible behavior and is not strongly loaded with social desirability considerations."[53] We found that undesirable traits, like narcissism and neuroticism, were difficult to judge from FB pages, as they are in FtF settings. Given the number of cues that observers use to judge neuroticism and narcissism, it is clear that strangers make strong, albeit inaccurate, judgments from a FB profile. This helps to make the distinction between *impressions given off* and diagnostic matches. That is, less desirable traits may be *bad* traits for making accurate judgments, yet strangers are still forming strong impressions of users.

Finally, *good information* comes in two forms: quantity and quality. The extensions of warranting theory examined here and the list of particular cues on FB provided in Table 12.1 provide examples of both. In terms of quantity, more information is only better when that information is diagnostic. As for quality, certain parts of the FB profile contain key information about openness (i.e., the Info page) or conscientiousness (i.e., friends' behavior). In addition, platforms differ in their utility for estimating personality, wherein FB is better for agreeability and personal web pages are better for openness. This chapter provides a useful summary to help guide future research on the impact of particular cues on impressions. However, we caution that it may be that only when those cues are represented in the context of an entire FB profile can their significance be seen. Simply one cue in isolation of the whole profile may not strongly impact the impression formation processes.

Mediated Publics and Other-Generated Cues

Much of the appeal of SNS like FB lies in learning what friends' are doing and sharing, which is enhanced by the interactivity of comments and "likes" in response to status updates. As a newer feature to FB, many early studies of self-generated cues available on social media do not account for status updates. What this chapter shows is that friends' actions not only enhance the pleasure of using FB, but also influence the impressions we make and we give off to others.

Walther and Parks original warranting principle suggests that self-generated cues have lower warrant credibility because they are more open to manipulation than other-generated cues.[54] Our research and that of others would conclude this is not a matter of either-or, rather it is both-and. Particularly in the case of conscientiousness, the actions of FB friends matter greatly for both managing impressions and forming them. Why this occurs is an exciting topic of future research. Why do conscientious FB users have friends who actively support or agree with the profile owners' status updates? Is it something about what the profile owner says or something about the type of friends they make? Why do strangers use this information to form accurate judgments of conscientiousness? Is there something about certain traits that directs our attention to the actions of friends more than to the actions of the profile owner? How these truly social interactive processes influence impressions management and formation are topics that hold tremendous promise to integrating past communication theories and findings that were primarily explored FtF with the new world of SNS.

We also believe that further exploration of the relationship between warrant credibility, perceived warrant value, and actual warrant value (i.e., diagnosticity) is a potentially fruitful topic of inquiry. Can we better know someone because we know what cues we ought be trusting or avoiding (i.e., we put Table 12.1 to good use)? What role does experience with an online community play in this? Do you need to have some base-level knowledge to be an accurate estimator of the personality of users of that platform? Although questions of person perception are ancient, new media provides new and exciting opportunities to pursue answers.

Notes

1. Peter Borkenau and Anette Liebler, "Trait Inferences: Sources of Validity at Zero Acquaintance," *Journal of Personality and Social Psychology* 62, no. 4 (1992): 645–57; Robert Gifford, "A Lens Mapping Framework for Understanding the Encoding and Decoding of Interpersonal Dispositions in Nonverbal Behavior," *Journal of Personality and Social Psychology* 66, no. 2 (February 1994): 398–412; Frank J. Bernieri and John S. Gillis, "Personality Correlates of Accuracy in a Social Perception Task," *Perceptual and Motor Skills* 81, no. 1 (August 1995): 168–70.

2. Bernd Marcus, Franz Machilek, and Astrid Schütz, "Personality in Cyberspace: Personal Websites as Media for Personality Expressions and Impressions," *Journal of Personality and Social Psychology* 90, no. 6 (June 2006): 1014–31; Samuel D. Gosling, Adam A. Augustine, Simine Vazire, Nicholas Holtzman, and Sam Gaddis, "Manifestations of Personality in Online Social Networks: Self-Reported Facebook-Related Behaviors and Observable Profile Information," *Cyberpsychology, Behavior, and Social Networks* 14, no. 9 (September 2011): 483–88.

3. David Westerman, Brandon Van Der Heide, Katherine A. Klein and Joseph B. Walther, "How Do People Really Seek Information about Others?: Information Seeking across Internet and Traditional Communication Channels," *Journal of Computer-Mediated Communication* 13, no. 3 (April 2008): 751–67.

4. Jeffrey A. Hall, Natalie Pennington and Allyn Lueders, "Impression Creation and Formation on Facebook: A Lens Model Approach," *Journal of Communication,* still in press.

5. danah boyd, "Friendship," in *Hanging Out, Messing Around, and Geeking Out: Kids Living and Learning with New Media,* ed. Mizuko Ito (Cambridge, MA: MIT Press, 2010), 79–115.

6. Erving Goffman, *The Presentation of Self in Everyday Life* (Garden City, NY: Doubleday, 1959).

7. Sonia Livingstone, "Taking Risky Opportunities in Youthful Content Creation: Teenagers' Use of Social Networking Sites for Intimacy, Privacy and Self-Expression," *New Media and Society* 10, no. 3 (June 2008): 393–411.

8. Amy L. Gonzales and Jeffrey T. Hancock, "Identity Shift in Computer-Mediated Environments," *Media Psychology* 11 (2008): 180.

9. Jeffrey A. Hall, Namkee Park, Hayeon Song and Michael J. Cody, "Strategic Misrepresentation in Online Dating: The Effects of Gender, Self-Monitoring, and Personality Traits," *Journal of Social and Personal Relationships* 27, no. 1 (February 2010): 117–35.

10. Jennifer L. Gibbs, Nicole B. Ellison, and Rebecca D. Heino, "Self-Presentation in Online Personals: The Role of Anticipated Future Interaction, Self-Disclosure, and Perceived Success in Internet Dating," *Communication Research* 33, no. 2 (April 2006): 1–26.

11. Simine Vazire and Samuel D. Gosling, "E-Perceptions: Personality Impressions Based on Personal Websites," *Journal of Personality and Social Psychology* 87, no. 1 (2004): 123–32.

12. David C. DeAndrea and Joseph B. Walther, "Attributions for Inconsistencies between Online and Offline Self-Presentations," *Communication Research* 38, no. 6 (January 2011): 805–25.

13. Allucquere R. Stone, *The War of Desire and Technology at the Close of the Mechanical Age* (Cambridge, MA: MIT Press, 1995); Joseph B. Walther and Malcolm R. Parks, "Cues Filtered Out, Cues Filtered In: Computer-Mediated Communication and Relationships," in *Handbook of Interpersonal Communica-*

tion, edited by Mark L. Knapp and John A. Daly (Thousand Oaks, CA: Sage, 2002), 529–63.

14. Stephanie T. Tong, Brandon Van Der Heide, Lindsey Langwell and Joseph B. Walther, "Too Much of a Good Thing? The Relationship Between Number of Friends and Interpersonal Impressions on Facebook," *Journal of Computer-Mediated Communication* 13, no. 3 (April 2008): 531–49; Joseph B. Walther, Brandon Van Der Heide, Lauren M. Hamel and Hillary C. Shulman, "Self-Generated Versus Other-Generated Statements and Impressions in Computer-Mediated Communication: A Test of Warranting Theory Using Facebook," *Communication Research* 36, no. 2 (2009): 229–53; Sonja Utz, "Show Me Your Friends and I Will Tell You What Type of a Person You Are: How One's Profile, Number of Friends, and Type of Friends Influence Impression Formation on Social Network Sites," *Journal of Computer-Mediated Communication* 15, no. 2 (January 2010): 314–35; Marjolijn L. Antheunis and Alexander P. Schouten, "The Effects of Other-Generated and System-Generated Cues on Adolescents' Perceived Attractiveness on Social Network Sites," *Journal of Computer-Mediated Communication* 16, no. 3 (April 2011): 391–406.

15. Joseph B. Walther, Brandon Van Der Heide, Sang Yeon Kim, David Westerman, and Stephanie T. Tong, "The Role of Friends' Appearance and Behavior on Evaluations of Individuals on Facebook: Are We Known by the Company We Keep?" *Human Communication Research* 34 (2008): 28–49; Walther, Van Der Heide, Hamel and Shulman, "Self-Generated Versus"; Tong,Van Der Heide, Langwell and Walther, "Too Much of a Good Thing?"

16. Gosling et al, "Manifestations of Personality."

17. Samuel D. Gosling, Sei J. Ko, Thomas Mannarelli, and Margaret E. Morris, "Room with a Cue: Personality Judgments Based on Offices and Bedrooms," *Journal of Personality and Social Psychology* 82, no. 3 (March 2002): 379–98.

18. Hall, Pennington and Lueders, "Impression Creation"; Marcus, Machilek and Schütz, "Personality in Cyberspace"; Gosling et al., "Manifestations of Personality."

19. Oliver P. John, Laura P. Naumann, and Christopher J. Soto, "Paradigm Shift to the Integrative Big-Five Trait Taxonomy: History, Measurement, and Conceptual Issues," in *Handbook of Personality*, edited by Oliver P. John, Richard W. Robins, and Lawrence A. Pervin (New York: Guilford Press, 2008), 114–58.

20. Steve Booth-Butterfield and Melanie Booth-Butterfield, "The Communication of Humor in Everyday Life: The Use of Humorous Messages," *Southern Communication Journal* 56 (1991): 205–18; Daniel R. Ames, Paul Rose and Cameron P. Anderson, "The NPI-16 as a Short Measure of Narcissism," *Journal of Research in Personality* 40 (2006): 440–50.

21. Justin Smith, "Fastest Growing Demographic on Facebook: Women over 55," *Inside Facebook*, 2009, accessed April 12, 2010, http://www.inside facebook.com/2009/02/02/fastest-growing-demographic-on-facebook-women-over-55/.

22. Roderick P. Hart and Craig Carol, *Diction* (Thousand Oaks, CA: Sage, 2011).

23. David A. Kenny, *Interpersonal Perception* (New York: Guilford Press, 1994).

24. Marcus, Machilek, and Schütz, "Personality in Cyberspace"; Vazire and Gosling, "E-Perceptions"; Gosling et al., "Manifestations of Personality"; Hall, Pennington and Lueders, "Impression Creation."

25. Marcus, Machilek, and Schütz, "Personality in Cyberspace."

26. Peter Borkenau and Anette Liebler, "Trait Inferences: Sources of Validity at Zero Acquaintance," *Journal of Personality and Social Psychology* 62, no. 4 (1992): 645–57.

27. Booth-Butterfield and Booth-Butterfield, "The Communication of Humor."

28. Marcus, Machilek, and Schütz, "Personality in Cyberspace"; Gosling et al., "Manifestations of Personality."

29. Marcus, Machilek, and Schütz, "Personality in Cyberspace"; Gosling et al., "Manifestations of Personality."

30. Frank Bernieri, John S. Gillis, Janet M. Davis, and Jon E. Grahe, "Dyad Rapport and the Accuracy of Its Judgment across Situations: A Lens Model Analysis," *Journal of Personality and Social Psychology* 71, no. 1 (July 1996): 110–29.

31. Borkenau and Liebler, "Trait Inferences"; Gosling, Ko, Mannarelli, and Morris, "Room with a Cue."

32. Antheunis and Schouten, "The Effects of Other-Generated"; Tong et al., "Too Much of a Good Thing?"; Utz, "Show Me Your Friends."

33. Yair Amichai-Hamburger and Gideon Vinizky, "Social Network Use and Personality," *Computers in Human Behavior* 26, no. 6 (November 2010): 1289–95; Craig Ross, Emily S. Orr, Mia Sisic, Jamie M. Arseneault, Mary G. Simmering, and Robert R. Orr, "Personality and Motivations Associated with Facebook Use," *Computers in Human Behavior* 25, no. 2 (March 2009): 578–86.

34. Gosling et al., "Manifestations of Personality"; Hall, Pennington, and Lueders, "Impression Creation"; Anthenuis and Schouten, "The Effects of Other-Generated"; Tong et al., "Too Much of a Good Thing?"

35. Borkenau and Liebler, "Trait Inferences."

36. Amichai-Hamburger and Vinizky. "Social Network Use and Personality"; Hall, Pennington, and Lueders, "Impression Creation"; Marcus, Machilek, and Schütz, "Personality in Cyberspace"; Ross et al., "Personality and Motivations."

37. Gosling et al., "Manifestations of Personality"; Ross et al., "Personality and Motivations."

38. Gosling et al., "Manifestations of Personality."

39. Hall, Pennington, and Lueders, "Impression Creation"; Marcus, Machilek and Schütz, "Personality in Cyberspace"; Ross, et al., "Personality and Motivations."

40. Hall, Pennington, and Lueders, "Impression Creation"; Marcus, Machilek and Schütz, "Personality in Cyberspace."

41. Federick Rhodewalt and Benjamin Peterson, "Narcissism," in *Handbook of Individual Differences in Social Behavior*, edited by Mark R. Leary and Rick H. Hoyle (New York: The Guilford Press, 2009), 547–60.

42. Laura E. Buffardi and W. Keith Campbell, "Narcissism and Social Networking Sites," *Personality and Social Psychology Bulletin* 34, no. 10 (2008): 1303–14.

43. Buffardi and Campbell, "Narcissim and Social Networking Sites."

44. Hall, Pennington, and Lueders, "Impression Creation"; Marcus, Machilek, and Schütz, "Personality in Cyberspace."

45. Gosling et al., "Manifestations of Personality."

46. Gosling et al., "Manifestations of Personality"; Ong et al., "Narcissism, Extraversion."

47. Buffardi and Campbell, "Narcissim and Social Networking Sites."

48. Utz, "Show Me Your Friends."

49. Buffardi and Campbell, "Narcissim and Social Networking Sites"; Walther et al., "Self-Generated."

50. David C. Funder, "Accuracy in Personality Judgment: Research and Theory Concerning an Obvious Question," in *Personality Psychology in the Workplace*, edited by Brent W. Roberts and Robert Hogan (Washington, DC: APA, 2001), 121–40.

51. Bernieri and Gillis, "Personality Correlates of Accuracy."

52. Hall, Pennington, and Lueders, "Impression Creation"; Marcus et al., "Personality in Cyberspace."

53. Funder, "Accuracy in Personality Judgment," 133.

54. Walther and Parks, "Cues Filtered Out."

Bibliography

Adiche, Chimamanda. "The Dangers of a Single Story." TED video, 18:49. Posted October 2009. http://www.ted.com/talks/chimamanda _adichie_the_ danger_of_a_single_story.html.

Akleman, Ergun, James Palmer, and Ryan Logan. "Making Extreme Caricatures with a New Interactive 2d Deformation Technique with Simplicial Complexes." In *Visual 2000 Proceedings*, 100–105, 2000.

Alexander, Bryant Keith, *Performing Black Masculinities: Race, Culture, and Queer Identity*. Lanham, MD: AltaMira Press, 2006.

Alexander, Bryant Keith and John T. Warren. "The Materiality of Bodies: Critical Reflections on Pedagogy, Politics and Positionality." *Communication Quarterly* 50, no. 3 (Summer 2002): 328–43.

Allen, Myria W. and Rachel H. Caillouet. "Legitimation Endeavors: Impression Management Strategies Used by an Organization in Crisis." *Communication Monographs* 61, no. 1 (March 1994): 44–62.

Altheide, David L. "Identity and the Definition of the Situation in a Mass-Mediated Context." *Symbolic Interaction* 23, no. 1 (May 2000): 1–27.

Althusser, Louis. "Ideology and Ideological State Apparatuses: Notes Towards an Investigation." In *Lenin and Philosophy and Other Essays: Louis Althusser*. Translated by Ben Brewster, 85–126. New York: Monthly Review Press, 1971.

Altman, Irwin, and Dalmas Taylor. *Social Penetration: The Development of Interpersonal Relationships*. New York: Rinehart and Winston, 1973.

American Civil Liberties Union of Maryland. "Testimony for the Senate Finance Committee. SB 971—Labor and Employment—User Name and Password Privacy Protection," accessed February 10, 2011, http://www.aclu-md.org/aLegislative/2011/SB971_social_media.pdf.

Ames, Daniel R., Paul Rose, and Cameron P. Anderson. "The NPI-16 as a Short Measuer of Narcissicism." *Journal of Resarch in Personality* 40 (2006): 440–50.

Amaichai-Hamburger, Yair, and Gideon Vinizky. "Social Network Use and Personality." *Computers in Human Behavior* 26, no. 6 (November 2010): 1289–95.

An, Yun-Jo, and Theodore Frick. "Student Perceptions of Asynchronous Computer-Mediated Communication in Face-to-Face Courses." *Journal of Computer-Mediated Communication* 11 (2006): 485–99.

Anderson, Craig A., and Brad J. Bushman. "Effects of Violent Video Games on Aggressive Behavior, Aggressive Cognition, Aggressive Affect, Physiological Arousal, and Prosocial Behavior: A Meta-Analytic Review of Scientific Literature." *Psychological Science* 12, no. 5 (September 2001): 353–59.

Antheunis, Marjolijn L. and Alexander P. Schouten. "The Effects of Other-Generated and System-Generated Cues on Adolescents' Perceived Attractiveness on Social Network Sites." *Journal of Computer-Mediated Communication* 16, no. 3 (April 2011): 391–406.

"Antoine Dodson Warns PERP on LIVE TV! (Original)." YouTube video, 2:03. Posted by "CrazyLaughAction," April 11, 2012, http://www.youtube.com/watch?v=EzNhaLUT520.

"Antoine Dodson's Chimney Intruder Song." YouTube video, 5:46. Posted by "Lovelyti2002," December 23, 2010. http://www.youtube.com/watch?v=xCHvDML0IYU.

"Antoine Dodson's Commercial for the Sex Offender Tracker App." YouTube video, 1:13. Posted by "Hoodtzm5's," October 28, 2010. http://www.youtube.com/watch?v=L2uJyCPCy5w.

"Antoine Dodson-Woman Wakes Up to Find an Intruder in Her Bed (Parody)." YouTube video, 2:02. Posted by "ShortFunnyAsian," August 4, 2010. http://www.youtube.com/watch?v=VP38qBAXpAk.

Antonijevic, Smiljana. "From Text to Gesture Online: A Microethnographic Analysis of Nonverbal Communication in the Second Life Virtual Environment." *Information, Communication and Society* 11, no. 2 (April 2008): 221–38.

Aragon, Steven. "Creating Social Presence in Online Environments." *New Directions for Adult and Continuing Education* 100 (Winter 2003): 57–68.

Arndt, Jamie, Jeff Schimel, Jeff Greenberg, and Tom Pyszczynski. "The Intrinsic Self and Defensiveness: Evidence That Activating the Intrinsic Self Reduces Self-Handicapping and Conformity." *Personality and Social Psychology Bulletin* 28, no. 5 (May 2002): 671–83.

Associated Press. "Survey: 97 Percent of American Youth Play Video Games." *CNN.* Accessed September 16, 2008. http://www.cnn.com/2008/TECH/ptech/09/16/videogames.survey.ap/index.html

Axon, Samuel. "Five Ways Facebook Changed Dating (for the Worse)." *Mashable.com.* Last updated April 10, 2010. http://mashable.com/2010/04/10/facebook-dating/.

Back, Mitja D., Juliane M. Stopfer, Simine Vazire, Sam Gaddis, Stefan C. Schmukle, Boris Egloff, and Samuel D. Gosling. "Facebook Profiles Reflect Actual Personality, Not Self-Idealization." *Psychological Science* 21, no. 3 (March 2010): 372–74.

Backstrom, Lars, "Anatomy of Facebook," accessed April 15, 2012, www.facebook.com/note.php?note_id=10150388519243859.

Ballard, Mary E., and J. R. Wiest. "Mortal Kombat™: The Effects of Violent Videogame Play on Males' Hostility and Cardiovascular Responding." *Journal of Applied Social Psychology* 26, no. 8 (April 1996): 717–30.

Balmer, John. "Explicating Corporate Brands and Their Management: Reflections and Directions from 1995." *Brand Management* 18, no. 3 (December 2010): 180–96.

Barash, Vladimir, Nicolas Ducheneaut, Ellen Isaacs, and Victoria Bellotti. "Faceplant: Impression (Mis)Management in Facebook Status Updates." *Proceedings of the 4th International Association for the Advancement of Artificial Intelligence Conference on Weblogs and Social Media,* 207–10. New York: ACM, 2010.

Bargh, John A., "Beyond Simple Truths: The Human-Internet Interaction." *Journal of Social Issues* 58, no. 1 (2002): 1–8.

Bargh, John A. and Katelyn Y. A. McKenna. "The Internet and Social Life." *Annual Review of Psychology* 55, no. 1 (January 2004): 573–90.

Bargh, John A., Katelyn Y. A. McKenna, and Grainne M. Fitzsimons. "Can You See the Real Me? Activation and Expression of the 'True Self' on the Internet." *Journal of Social Issues* 58, no. 1 (January 2002): 33–48.

Barnes, Susan A. "A Privacy Paradox: Social Networking in the United States." *First Monday* 11, no. 9 (September 4, 2006): article 5.

Baumeister, Roy F. "A Self-Presentational View of Social Phenomena." *Psychology Bulletin* 91, no. 1 (January 1982): 3–26.

————. "Self-Esteem, Self-Presentation, and Future Interaction: A Dilemma of Reputation." *Journal of Personality* 50, no. 1 (March 1982): 29–45.

Baumeister, Roy F., Dianne M. Tice, and Debra G. Hutton. "Self-Presentational Motivations and Personality Differences in Self-Esteem." *Journal of Personality* 57, no. 2 (1989): 547–79. doi:10.1111/j.1467-6494.1989.tb02384.x.

Baxter, Leslie A., and William W. Wilmot. "Taboo Topics in Close Relationships." *Journal of Social and Personal Relationships* 2, no. 3 (1985): 253–69.

Becker, Jennifer A., and Glen H. Stamp. "Impression Management in Chat Rooms: A Grounded Theory Model." *Communication Studies* 56, no. 3 (September 2005): 243–60. doi:10.1080/10510970500181264.

"The Bed Intruder Song!!! (Now on iTunes)." YouTube video, 2:08. Posted by "schmoyoho," July 31, 2010. http://www.youtube.com/watch?v=hMtZfW2z9dw.

Bell, David. *An Introduction to Cybercultures.* London: Routledge, 2001.

Bente, Gary, Sabine Ruggenberg, Nicole C. Kramer, and Felix Eschenburg. "Avatar-Mediated Networking: Increasing Social Presence and Interpersonal Trust in Net-Based Collaborations." *Human Communication Research* 34, no. 2 (April 2008): 287–318.

Berger, Charles, and Richard J. Calabrese. "Some Explorations in Initial Interaction and Beyond: Toward a Developmental Theory of Interpersonal Communication." *Human Communication Research* 1, no. 2 (1975): 99–112. doi:10.1111/j.1468-2958.1975.tb00258.x.

Berger, Peter, and Thomas Luckmann. *The Social Construction of Reality: A Treatise in the Sociology of Knowledge.* New York: Anchor Books, 1967.

Bergman, Shawn M., Matthew E. Fearrington, Shaun W. Davenport, and Jacqueline Z. Bergman. "Millennials, Narcissism, and Social Networking: What Narcissist Do on Social Networking Sites and Why." *Personality and Individual Differences* 50 (January 2011): 706–11.

Bernieri, Frank, and John S. Gillis. "Personality Correlates of Accuracy in a Social Perception Task." *Perceptual and Motor Skills* 81, no. 1 (August 1995): 168–70.

Bernieri, Frank, John S. Gillis, Janet M. Davis, and Jon E. Grahe. "Dyad Rapport and the Accuracy of Its Judgment across Situations: A Lens Model Analysis." *Journal of Personality and Social Psychology* 71, no. 1 (July 1996): 110–29.

Bers, Marina U., Laura M. Beals, Clement Chau, Keiko Satoh, Elizabeth D. Blume, David Ray DeMaso, and Joseph Gonzalez-Heydrich. "Use of a Virtual Community as a Psychosocial Support System in Pediatric Transplantation." *Pediatric Transplantation* 14, no. 2 (March 2010): 261–67.

Bhattacharya, C. B. and Sankar Sen. "Consumer-Company Identification: A Framework for Understanding Consumers' Relationships with Companies." *Journal of Marketing* 67, no. 2 (2003): 76–88.

"Black Man Angry at Antoine Dodson." YouTube video, 8:13. Posted by "dcigs," December 11, 2010. http://www.youtube.com/watch?v= YJQRX6gg3pA.

Black, Laura, Jennifer J. Bute, and Laura D. Russell. "'The Secret Is Out!': Supporting Weight Loss through Online Interaction." In *Cases on Online Discussion and Interaction: Experiences and Outcomes*, edited by Leonard Shedletsky and Joan E. Aiken, 351–68. Hershey, PA: IGI Global, 2010.

"BlackBerry Service Updated," accessed May 4, 2012, http://www.rim.com/newsroom/service-update.shtml.

Blumer, Herbert. *Symbolic Interactionism: Perspective and Method.* Englewood Cliffs, NJ: Prentice Hall, 1969.

Bolino, Mark C., and William H. Turnley. "Measuring Impression Management in Organizations: A Scale Development Based on the Jones and Pittman Taxonomy." *Organizational Research Methods* 2, no. 187 (April 1999): 187–206.

Booth-Butterfield, Steve, and Melanie Booth-Butterfield. "The Communication of Humor in Everyday Life: The Use of Humorous Messages." *Southern Communication Journal* 56 (1991): 205–18.

Borkenau, Peter, and Anette Liebler. "Trait Inferences: Sources of Validity at Zero Acquaintance." *Journal of Personality and Social Psychology* 62, no. 4 (1992): 645–57.

Bowleg, Lisa. "When Black Plus Lesbian Plus Woman Does Not Equal Black Lesbian Woman: The Methodological Challenges of Qualitative and Quantitative Intersectionality Research." *Sex Roles* 59, no. 5-6 (September 2008): 312–25. doi:10.1007/s11199-008-9400-z.

boyd, danah. "Friendship." In *Hanging Out, Messing Around and Geeking Out: Kids Living and Learning with New Media*, edited by Mizuko Ito, 79–115. Cambridge, MA: MIT Press, 2007.

———. "Social Network Sites as Networked Publics: Dynamics, and Implications." In *A Networked Self: Identity, Community, and Culture on Social Network Sites*, edited by Zizi Papacharissi, 39–58. New York: Routledge, 2011.

boyd, danah, and Nicole B. Ellison. "Social Network Sites: Definition, History, and Scholarship." *Journal of Computer-Mediated Communication* 13, no. 1 (October 2007): 210–30.

boyd, danah, and Jeffrey Heer. "Profiles as Conversation: Networked Identity Performance on Friendster." In *Proceedings of the Hawaii International Conference on System Sciences*. Kauai, HI, 2006.

Boyle, Kris, and Thomas J. Johnson. " MySpace Is Your Space? Examining Self-Presentation of MySpace Users." *Computers in Human Behavior* 26, no. 6 (November 2010): 1392–99.

Bradley, Tony. "Facebook Privacy Is a Balancing Act," *PC World*, May 17, 2010, accessed May 17, 2010, http://www.pcworld.com/businesscenter/article/196431/facebook_pri vacy_is_a_balancing_act.html.

Braithwaite, Dawn O., Vincent R. Waldron, and Jerry Finn. "Communication of Social Support in Computer-Mediated Groups for People with Disabilities." *Health Communication* 11, no. 2 (1999): 123–51.

Brandenburg, Carly. "The Newest Way to Screen Job Applicants: A Social Networker's Nightmare." *Federal Communications Law Journal* 60, no. 3 (2008): 597–626.

Brown, Penelope, and Stephen C. Levinson. *Politeness: Some Universals in Language Usage*. Vol. 4. Cambridge: Cambridge University Press, 1987.

Brown, Tom J., Peter A. Dacin, Michael G. Pratt, and David A. Whetten. "Identity, Intended Image, Construed Image, and Reputation: An Interdisciplinary Framework and Suggested Terminology." *Journal of* the *Academy of Marketing Science* 34, no. 2 (Spring 2006): 99–106. doi:10.1177/0092070305284969.

Brunswik, Egon. *Perception and the Representative Design of Psychological Experiments*. Berkeley,CA: University of California Press, 1956.

Buffardi, Laura E., and W. Keith Campbell. "Narcissism and Social Netowrking Sites." *Personality and Social Psychology Bulletin* 34, no. 10 (2008): 1303–14.

Bull, Sheana S., Lindsey T. Breslin, Erin E. Wright, Sandra R. Black, Deborah Levine, and John S. Santelli. "Case Study: An Ethics Case Study of HIV Prevention Research on Facebook: The Just/Us Study" *Journal of Pediatric Psychology* 36, no. 10 (November/December 2011): 1082–92.

Bungie. "One Billion Served and Counting." Bungie, accessed June 20, 2012, http://www.bungie.net/news/content.aspx?type=topnews& link=CGHV33KGD2R9D3W9V4QY7MF9Q.

Butler, Judith. *Bodies That Matter*. New York: Routledge, 1993.

——. "Burning Acts: Injurious Speech." In *Performativity and Performance*, edited by Andrew Parker and Eve Kosofsky Sedgwick, 197–227. New York: Routledge, 1995.

——. "Performative Acts and Gender Constitution: An Essay in Phenomenology and Feminist Theory." In *The Performance Studies Reader*, edited by Henry Bial. 2nd ed. 187–99. New York: Routledge, 2007.

——. "Performative Acts and Gender Constitution: An Essay on Phenomenology and Feminist Theory." In *Performing Feminism: Feminist Critical Theory and Theatre*, edited by Sue Ellen Case, 270–82. Baltimore, MD: Johns Hopkins University Press, 1990.

Byrne, Dara N. " Public Discourse, Community Concerns, and Civic Engagement: Exploring Black Social Networking Traditions on BlackPlanet.Com." *Journal of Computer-Mediated Communication* 13, no. 1 (October 2007): 319–40.

Campbell, Alex. "The Search for Authenticity: An Exploration of an Online Skinhead Newsgroup." *New Media and Society* 8, no. 2 (April 2006): 269–94. doi:101177/1461444806059675.

Carnagey, Nicholas L., Craig A. Anderson, and Brad J. Bushman. "The Effect of Video Game Violence on Physiological Desensitization to

Real-Life Violence." *Journal of Experimental Social Psychology* 43, no. 3 (May 2007): 489–96. doi:10.1016/j.jesp.2006.05.003.

Cass, Vivienne C. "Homosexual Identity: A Concept in Need of a Definition." *Journal of Homosexuality* 9 (1983/1984): 105–26.

"CBS Interview with Shira Lizar." YouTube video, 9:59 Posted by "antoinedodson24," August 18, 2010. http://www.youtube.com/watch?v=Jb-ewYxdLJ4.

Cerulo, Karen. "Identity Construction: New Issues, New Directions." *Annual Review of Sociology* 23 (August 1997): 385–409.

Charmaz, Kathy. *Constructing Grounded Theory: A Practical Guide through Qualitative* Analysis. Thousand Oaks, CA: Sage, 2006.

Chen, Yi-Ning Katherine. "Examining the Presentation of Self in Popular Blogs: A Cultural Perspective." *Chinese Journal of Communication* 3, no. 1 (March 2010): 28–41.

Christofides, Emily, Amy Muise, and Serge Desmarais. "Information Disclosure and Control on Facebook: Are They Two Sides of the Same Coin or Two Different Processes?" *Cyberpsychologyand Behavior* 12, no. 3 (June 2009): 341–45.

Cicchirillo, Vincent and Rebecca Chory-Assad. "Effects of Affective Orientation and Video Game Play on Aggressive Thoughts and Behaviors." *Journal of Broadcasting and Electronic Media* 49, no. 4 (December 2005): 435–49. doi:10.1207/s15506878jobem4904_5.

Circle of Moms, "Toxins in Baby Shampoo." Accessed October 20, 2012. http://www.circleofmoms.com/parenting-debates-hot-topics/toxins-in-baby-shampoo-671679?.

Clampitt, Phillip G., Robert J. DeKoch, and Thomas Cashman. "A Strategy for Communicating about Uncertainty." *The Academy of Management Executive* 14, no. 4 (November 2000): 41–57.

Clark, Herbert H. *Using Language.* Vol. 4. Cambridge: Cambridge University Press, 1996.

Clark, Herbert H., and Susan E. Brennan. "Grounding in Communication." In *Perspectives on Socially Shared Cognition,* edited by Lauren B. Resnick, John M. Levine, and Stephanie D. Teasley, 127–49. Washington, DC: American Psychological Association, 1991.

Cole, Elizabeth R., and Abigail J. Stewart. "Invidious Comparisons: Imagining a Psychology of Race and Gender Beyond Differences." *Political Psychology* 22, no. 2 (June 2001): 293–308.

Coleridge, Samuel. *Biographical Sketches of My Literary Life and Opinions.* New York: Fenner, 1817.

Colvin, Jan, Lillian Chenoweth, Mary Bold, and Cheryl Harding. "Caregivers of Older Adults: Advantages and Disadvantages of Internet-Based Social Support." *Family Relations* 53, no. 1 (January 2004): 49–60.

Comscore, "It's a Social World: Top 10 Need-to-Knows about Social Networking and Where It's Headed." December 21, 2011. Accessed August 8, 2012, http://www.comscore.com/Press_Events/ Presentations_Whitepapers/2011/it_is_a_social_world_top_10_need-to-knows_about_social_networking.

"Coon." Urban Dictionary, accessed October 28, 2010, http://www.urbandictionary.com/define.php?term=coon.

Cooper, Joel, and Diane Mackie. "Video Games and Aggression in Children." *Journal of Applied Social Psychology* 16, no. 8 (1986): 726–44.

Cornelissen, Joep P., S. Alexander Haslam, and John M. T. Balmer. "Social Identity, Organizational Identity, and Corporate Identity: Towards an Integrated Understanding of Processes, Patternings, and Products." *British Journal of Management* 18, no. s1 (March 2007): 1–16.

Cory, Daniel Webster. *The Homosexual in America*. New York: Greenberg, 1951.

Crenshaw, Kimberle. "Mapping the Margins: Intersectionality, Identity Politics, and Violence against Women of Color." *Stanford Law Review* 43, no. 6 (July 1991): 1241–99.

Crocker, Jennifer, and Katherine M. Knight. "Contingencies of Self-Worth." *Current Directions in Psychological Science* 14, no. 4 (August 2005): 200–203. doi:10.1111/j.0963-7214.2005.00364.x.

Crossley, Adam, and Darren Langdridge. "Perceived Sources of Happiness: A Network Analysis." *Journal of Happiness Studies* 6, no. 2 (2005): 107–35.

Daft, Richard L., and Robert H. Lengel. "Information Richness: A New Approach to Managerial Behavior and Organizational Design." In *Research in Organizational Behavior*, edited by Barry M. Staw and Larry L. Cummings. Vol. 6. 191–233. Greenwich, CT: JAI Press, 1985.

Dank, Barry. "Coming Out in the Gay World." *Psychiatry* 34 (1971): 180–97.

Davis, Aaron. "Maryland Corrections Department Suspends Facebook Policy for Prospective Hires." *Washington Post,* February 22, 2011.

Davison, Kathryn P., and James W. Pennebaker. "Who Talks? The Social Psychology of Illness Support Groups." *American Psychologist* 55, no. 2 (February 2000): 205–17.

DeAndrea, David C., and Joseph B. Walther. "Attributions for Inconsistencies between Online and Offline Self-Presentations." *Communication Research* 38, no. 6 (January 2011): 805–25.

Deetz, Stanley. *Democracy in an Age of Corporate Colonization: Developments in Communication and the Politics of Everyday Life.* Albany, NY: State University of New York Press, 1992.

Dey, Ian. *Grounding Grounded Theory: Guidelines for Qualitative Inquiry.* New York: Academic Press, 1999.

DiMicco, Joan Morris, and David R. Millen. "Identity Management: Multiple Presentations of Self in Facebook." In *Proceedings of the 2007 International ACM Conference on Supporting Group Work,* 383–86. New York: ACM, 2007.

Divol, Roxanne, David Edelman, and Hugo Sarrazin. "Demystifying Social Media." *McKinsey Quarterly,* April, 2012, accessed August 5, 2012, http://www.mckinseyquarterly.com/Demystifying_social_media_2958.

Doherty, Kevin and Barry R. Schlenker. "Self-Consciousness and Strategic Self-Presentation." *Journal of Personality* 59, no. 1 (March 1991): 1–18.

Dominick, Joseph R. "Who Do You Think You are? Personal Home Pages and Self-Presentation on the World Wide Web." *Journalism & Mass Communication Quarterly* 76, no. 4 (December 1999): 646–58. doi:10.1177/107769909907600403.

Donaldson, Jam. "Antoine Dodson: Why He Makes Us Laugh and Uncomfortable." *Black Voices,* accessed October 22, 2010, http://www.bvBlackspin.com/2010/08/04/antoine-dodson.

Donath, Judith. "Identity and Deception in the Virtual Community." In *Communities in Cyberspace,* edited by Marc Smith and Peter Kollock, 29–59. New York: Routledge, 1999.

Donath, Judith, and danah boyd. "Public Displays of Connection." *BT Technology Journal* 22, no. 4 (October 2004): 71–82.

Douglas, Karen M., and Craig McGarty. "Identifiability and Self-Presentation: Computer-Mediated Communication and Intergroup

Interaction." *British Journal of Social Psychology* 40, no. 3 (September 2001): 399–416.

Dubrofsky, Rachel E. "Surveillance on Reality Television and Facebook: From Authenticity to Flowing Data." *Communication Theory* 21, no. 2 (May 2011): 111–29.

Duck, Steve. "Stratagems, Spoils, and a Serpent's Tooth: On the Delights and Dilemmas of Personal Relationships." In *The Dark Side of Interpersonal Communication,* edited by William R. Cupach and Brian H. Spitzberg, 3–24. Hillsdale, NJ: Lawrence Erlbaum, 1994.

Dunkels, Elza, Gun-Marie Frånberg, and Camilla Hällgren. *Youth Culture and Net Culture: Online Social Practices.* Hershey, PA: Information Science Reference, 2011.

Duthler, Kirk W. "The Politeness of Requests Made via Email and Voicemail: Support for the Hyperpersonal Model." *Journal of Computer-Mediated Communication* 11, no. 2 (2006): 500–521.

Eadie, William. "Action, Interaction, and Transaction: Three Means of Viewing the Communication World." Paper presented at the annual meeting of the Speech Communication Association, New York: November 1973.

Eastin, Matthew S. "Video Game Violence and the Female Game Player: Self and Opponent Gender Effects on Presence and Aggressive Thoughts." *Human Communication Research* 32, no. 3 (July 2006): 351–72. doi:10.1111/j.1468-2958.2006.00279.x.

Ehlers, Nadine. "Hidden in Plain Sight: Defying Juridical Racialization in *Rhinelander v. Rhinelander.*" *Communication and Critical/Cultural Studies* 1, no. 4 (December 2004): 313–34. doi:10.1080/1479142042000270458.

Ellison, Nicole B., Rebecca Heino, and Jennifer Gibbs. "Managing Impressions Online: Self-Presentation Processes in the Online Dating Environment." *Journal of Computer-Mediated Communication* 11, no. 2 (January 2006): 415–41.

Ellison, Nicole B., Charles Steinfield, and Cliff Lampe. "The Benefits of Facebook 'Friends': Social Capital and College Students' Use of Online Social Network Sites." *Journal of Computer-Mediated Communication* 12, no. 4 (July 2007): 1143–68.

Epstein, Steven. "Gay Politics, Ethnic Identity: The Limits of Social Constructionism." *Socialist Review* 93/94 (1987): 9–54.

Erickson, Thomas. "From PIM to GIM: Personal Information Management in Group Contexts." *Communications of the ACM* 49 (January 2006): 74–75.

Ethisphere. Accessed August 8, 2012. http://ethisphere.com/wme/.

Evans, Martin. "Sex Predator May Have Groomed Over 1,000 Schoolgirls." *The Daily Telegraph,* May 19, 2012, 1.

"Facebook. "Key Facts," accessed May 4, 2012, http://newsroom.fb.com/content/default.aspx?NewsAreaId=22.

Facebook, "Statistics," *Facebook Statistics* 2012, accessed June 21, 2012, http://newsroom.fb.com/Key-Facts/Statistics-8b.aspx.

Factor, Rhonda J., and Esther D. Rothblum. "A Study of Transgender Adults and Their Non-Transgender Siblings on Demographic Characteristics, Social Support, and Experience of Violence." *Journal of LGBT Health Research* 3, no. 3 (2008): 11–30.

FatSecret. "About Us." FatSecret, accessed June 20, 2012, www.fatsecret.com/Default.aspx?pa=a.

Ferris, Lucy. "Antoine Saves My Class." *The Chronicle of Higher Education,* September 7, 2011, accessed March 14, 2012, http://chronicle.com/blogs/linguafranca/2011/09/07/antoine-dodson-saves-my-class/.

Finneran, Kevin. "To Blog, or Not to Blog." *Issues in Science and Technology* 22, no. 2 (Winter 2006): 23–24.

Fombrun, Charles, and Violina Rindova. "The Road to Transparency: Reputation Management at Royal Dutch/Shell." In *The Expressive Organization*, edited by Majken Schultz, Mary Jo Hatch, and Mogens H. Larsen, 78–96. Oxford University Press: Oxford, 2000.

Foucault, Michel. *Discipline and Punish: The Birth of a Prison.* New York: Random House, 1975.

Funder, David C. "Accuracy in Personality Judgment Research and Theory Concerning an Obvious Question." In *Personality Psychology in the Workplace*, edited by Brent W. Roberts and Robert Hogan, 121–40. Washington, DC: APA, 2001.

Gagne, Patricia, and Richard Tewksbury. "Conformity Pressures and Gender Resistance among Transgendered Individuals." *Social Problems* 45, no. 1 (February 1998): 81–101.

Garber, Megan. "Who You Are on Facebook Is Probably Pretty Much Who You Are." *The Atlantic*, January/February 2012, accessed January 13, 2012, www.theatlantic.com/technology/archive /2012/01/

who-you-are-on-facebook-is-probably-pretty-much-who-you-are/251318.

Gefen, David, and Detmar W. Straub. "Gender Difference in the Perception and Use of E-Mail." *MIS Quarterly* 21, no. 4 (December 1997): 389–400.

Gergen, Kenneth. *The Saturated Self: Dilemmas of Identity in Contemporary Life*. New York: Basic Books, 1991.

Gibbs, Jennifer, Nicole B. Ellison, and Rebecca Heino. "Self-Presentation in Online Personals: The Role of Anticipated Future Interaction, Self-Disclosure, and Perceived Success in Internet Dating." *Communication Research* 33, no. 2 (April 2006): 1–26.

Gifford, Robert. "A Lens Mapping Framework for Understanding the Encoding and Decoding of Interpersonal Dispositions in Nonverbal Behavior." *Journal of Personality and Social Psychology* 66, no. 2 (February 1994): 398–412.

Gilpin, Dawn. "Organizational Image Construction in a Fragmented Online Media Environment." *Journal of Public Relations Research* 22, no. 3 (July 2010): 265–87. doi:10.1080/10627261003614393.

Gini, Al. *My Job, My Self: Work and the Creation of the Modern Individual*. New York: Routledge, 2000.

Glaser, Barney G. "The Constant Comparative Method of Qualitative Analysis." *Social Problems* 12, no. 4 (1965): 436–45.

Glaser, Barney, and Anselm Strauss. *The Discovery of Grounded Theory: Strategies for Qualitative Research*. Chicago: Aldine, 1967.

Gleason, Philip. "Identifying Identity: A Semantic History." *Journal of American History* 69, no. 4 (March 1983): 910–31.

Goffman, Erving. "Alienation from Interaction." *Human Relations* 10, no. 1 (1957): 47–60.

———. 'Face-Work,' An Analysis of Ritual Elements in Social Interaction." *Psychiatry: Journal for the Study of Interpersonal Processes* 18, no. 3 (1955): 213–31.

———. *The Presentation of Self in Everyday Life*. New York: Anchor Books, 1959.

———. *Forms of Talk*. Philadelphia: University of Pennsylvania Press, 1981.

Goleman, Daniel. "Can You Tell When Someone Is Lying to You?" In *Nonverbal Communication Reader*, edited by Laura K. Guerrer, and Michael L. Hecht, 421–32. Long Grove, IL: Waveland Press, 2008.

Gonzales, Amy L., and Jeffrey T. Hancock. "Identity Shift in Computer-Mediated Environments." *Media Psychology* 11 (2008): 167–85.

Gosling, Samuel D., Adam A. Augustine, Simine Vazire, Nicholas Holtzman, and Sam Gaddis. "Manifestations of Personality in Online Social Networks: Self-Reported Facebook-Related Behaviors and Observable Profile Information." *Cyberpsychology, Behavior, and Social Networking* 14, no. 9 (September 2011): 483–88.

Gosling, Samuel D., Sei J. Ko, Thomas Mannarelli, and Margaret E. Morris. "Room with a Cue: Personality Judgments Based on Offices and Bedrooms." *Journal of Personality and Social Psychology* 82, no. 3 (March 2002): 379–98.

Grasmuck, Sherri, Jason Martin, and Shanyang Zhao. "Ethno-Racial Identity Displays on Facebook." *Journal of Computer-Mediated Communication* 15, no. 1 (October 2009): 158–88. doi:10.1111/j.1083-6101.2009.01498.x.

Greenbaum, Thomas L. *Moderating Focus Groups. A Practical Guide for Group Facilitation.* Thousand Oaks, CA: Sage, 2000.

Green-Hamman, Sara, Kristen C. Eichhorn, and John C. Sherblom. "An Exploration of Why People Participate in Second Life Social Support Groups." *Journal of Computer-Mediated Communication* 16, no. 4 (July 2011): 465–91.

Greenwald, Anthony G., and Mahzarin R. Banaji. "Implicit Social Cognition: Attitudes, Self-Esteem, and Stereotypes." *Psychological Review* 102, no. 1 (1995): 4–27. doi:10.1037/0033-295X.102.1.4.

Gross, Ralph, and Alessandro Acquisti. "Information Revelation and Privacy in Online Social Networks." *Proceedings of the 2005 ACM Workshop on Privacy in the Electronic* Society, 71–80. New York, ACM, 2005.

Grossman, Lev. "How to Become Famous in 30 Seconds." *Time Magazine*, April 24, 2006, accessed October 22, 2010, http://www.time.com/time/magazine/article/0,9171,1184060,00.html.

Hall, Jeffrey A., Natalie Pennington, and Allyn Lueders. "Impression Creation and Formation on Facebook: A Lens Model Approach." *Journal of Communication*, in press.

Hall, Jeffrey A., Namkee Park, Hayeon Song, and Michael J. Cody. "Strategic Misrepresentation in Online Dating: The Effects of Gender, Self-Monitoring, and Personality Traits." *Journal of Social and Personal Relationships* 27, no. 1 (February 2010): 117–35.

Hall, Stuart. *Representation: Cultural Representations and Signifying Practices*. Thousand Oaks, CA: Sage, 2000.

Hampton, Keith, Lauren Sessions, Goulet, Lee Rainie, and Kristen Purcell. "Social Networking Sites and our Lives." Pew Internet & American Life Project, accessed June 6, 2012, http://www.pewinternet. org/Reports/2011/Technology-and-social-networks.aspx.

Hancock, Ange-Marie. "When Multiplication Doesn't Equal Quick Addition: Examining Intersectionality as a Research Paradigm." *Perspectives on Politics* 5, no. 1 (2007): 63–79.

Hancock, Jeffrey T. "Digital Deception: From Ancient Empires to Internet Dating." In *Deception: Methods, Contexts and Consequences*, edited by Brooke Harrington, 109–20. Palo Alto, CA: Stanford University Press, 2007.

Harquail, Celia V. "Re-Creating Reputation through Authentic Interaction: Using Social Media to Connect with Individual Stakeholders." In *Corporate Reputation: Managing Opportunities and Threats*, edited by Ronald J Burke, Cary L. Cooper and Graeme Martin, 245–66. United Kingdom: Gower Publishing Ltd., 2011.

Hars, Alexander, and Shaosong Ou. "Working for Free? Motivations of Participating in Open Source Projects." *International Journal of Electronic Commerce* 6, no. 3 (April 2002): 25–39.

Hart, Roderick and Craig Carol. *Diction*. Thousand Oaks, CA: Sage, 2011.

Hawkesworth, Mary. "Congressional Enactments of Race-Gender: Toward a Theory of Race-Gendered Institutions." *American Political Science Review* 97, no. 4 (November 2003): 529–50.

Hemming, Jon. "British Spy Chief's Cover Blown on Facebook," *Reuters News Wire* (London), July 4, 2009. http://www.reuters.com/.

Hennink, Monique M. *International Focus Group Research: A Handbook for the Health and Social Sciences*. Cambridge, UK: Cambridge University Press, 2007.

Herring, Susan C. "Introduction." In *Computer-Mediated Communication*, edited by Herring, Susan C., 1–13. Philadelphia, PA: John Benjamins Publishing Company, 1996.

Hewitt, Anne, and Andrea Forte. "Crossing Boundaries: Identity Management and Student/Faculty Relationships on Facebook." In *Proceedings of the ACM Conference on Computer-Supported Cooperative Work*. New York: ACM, 2006.

"Hideja Kids, It's Antoine Dodson." YouTube video, 4:49. Posted by "Fdeez," October 27, 2010. http://www.youtube.com/watch?v=yxTPKQ_sv98.

Higgins, Edward. "Self-Discrepancy: A Theory Relating Self and Affect." *Psychological Review* 94, no. 3 (July 1987): 319–40.

Hiemstra, Glen. "Teleconferencing, Concern for Face, and Organizational Culture." *Communication Yearbook* 6, no. 6 (1982): 874–904.

Hodgkinson, Tom. "With Friends Like These . . ." *The Guardian,* January 13, 2008, accessed May 1, 2010, http://www.guardian.co.uk/technology/2008/jan/14/facebook.

Holland, Dorothy, William Lachiotte Jr., Debra Skinner, and Carole Cain. *Identity and Agency in Cultural Worlds*. Cambridge, MA: Harvard University Press, 1998.

Hooker, Evelyn. "Male Homosexuality in the Rorschach." *Journal of Projective Techniques* 22 (1958): 33–54.

Horn, Leslie. "7.5 Million Facebook Users Are Below the Minimum Age." *PC Magazine*, May 10, 2011, accessed May 5, 2011, http://www.pcmag.com/article2/0,2817,2385122,00.asp.

Horton, Paula. "Two Washington Officers Fired over Facebook Indiscretions." *The Tri-City Herald,* 2009, accessed February 2, 2011, http://www.policeone.com/police-technology/articles/1776582-Two-Wash-officers-fired-over-Facebook-indiscretions/.

Huffaker, David. "The Educated Blogger: Using Weblogs to Promote Literacy in the Classroom." *Association for the Advancement of Computing in Education Journal* 13, no. 2 (April 2005): 91–98.

Humphreys, Laud. *Out of the Closets: The Sociology of Homosexual Liberation*. Englewood Cliffs: NJ, Prentice-Hall, 1972.

Hutchinson, Earl Ofari. "My Gay Problem, Your Black Problem." In *The Greatest Taboo: Homosexuality in Black Communities*, edited by Delroy Constantine-Simms, 2-6. Los Angeles: Alyson Books, 2000.

Iedema, Jurjen, and Matthijs Poppe. "The Effect of Self-Presentation on Social Value Orientation." *The Journal of Social Psychology* 134, no. 6 (1994): 771–82.

Jelinek, Pauline. "Pentagon Reviews Social Networking on Computers." *Associated Press Wire,* August 4, 2009, accessed August 4, 2009, http://www.policeone.com/police-technology/articles/1776582-Two-Wash-officers-fired-over-Facebook-indiscretions/.

Jenkins, Henry. *Convergence Culture: Where Old and New Media Collide*. New York: New York University Press, 2006.

John, Oliver P., Laura P. Naumann, and Christopher J. Soto. "Paradigm Shift to the Integrative Big-Five Trait Taxonomy: History, Measurement, and Conceptual Issues." In *Handbook of Personality*, edited by Oliver P. John, Richard W. Robins, and Lawrence A. Pervin, 114–58. New York: Guilford Press, 2008.

Johnson and Johnson. "About Us." Last modified April 27, 2012. Accessed August 8, 2012. http://www.jnjcanada.com/our-values.aspx.

Johnson, E. Patrick. *Appropriating Blackness: Performance and the Politics of Authenticity*. Durham, NC: Duke University Press, 2003.

———. "'Quare' Studies, or (Almost) Everything I Know about Queer Studies I Learned from My Grandmother." In *Black Queer Studies: A Critical Anthology*, edited by E. Patrick Johnson and Mae G. Henderson, 124–57. Durham, NC: Duke University Press, 2005.

Johnson, Thomas J., and Barbara K. Kaye. "Wag the Blog: How Reliance on Traditional Media and the Internet Influence Credibility Perceptions of Weblogs among Blog Users." *Journalism and Mass Communication Quarterly* 81, no. 3 (September 2004): 622–42.

Joinson, Adam J. "Looking At, Looking Up or Keeping Up with People?: Motives and Use of Facebook." In *Proceedings of the SIGCHI Conference on Human Factors in Computing Systems*, 1027–36. New York: ACM, 2008.

Joinson, Adam N. "Self-Disclosure in Computer-Mediated Communication: The Role of Self-Awareness and Visual Anonymity." *European Journal of Social Psychology* 31, no. 2 (March/April 2001): 177–92. doi:10.1002/ejsp.36.

Jones, Edward E., and Thane S. Pittman. "Toward a General Theory of Strategic Self-Presentation." In *Psychological Perspectives on the Self*, edited by Jerry M. Suls, 231–61. Hillsdale, NJ: Erlbaum, 1982.

Junco, Reynol. "Too Much Face and Not Enough Books: The Relationship between Multiple Indices of Facebook Use and Academic Performance." *Computers in Human Behavior* 28, no. 1 (2012): 187–98.

Junco, Reynol, and Shelia R. Cotten. "No A 4 U: The Relationship between Multitasking and Academic Performance." *Computers & Education* 59, no. 2 (September 2012): 505–14. doi:10.1016/j.compedu.2011.12.023.

Juntunen, Mari, Salia Saraniemi, Milla Halttu, and Jaana Tahtinen. "Corporate Brand Building in Different Stages of Small Business Growth." *Brand Management* 18, no. 3 (2010): 115–33.

Kaiser Family Foundation. "Daily Media Use among Children and Teens Up Dramatically from Five Years Ago," accessed May 14, 2012, http://www.kff.org/entmedia/entmedia012010nr.cfm.

Katz, Daniel, and Robert Kahn. *The Social Psychology of Organizations.* New York: John Wiley and Sons, 1966.

Kavanaugh, Andrea L., John M. Carrol, Mary Beth Rosson, Than Than Zin, and Debbie Denise Reese. "Community Networks: Where Offline Communities Meet Online." *Journal of Computer-Mediated Communication* 10, no. 4 (2005): article 3. http://jcmc.indiana.edu/vol10/issue4/kavanaugh.html.

Kavanaugh, Andrea L., and Scott J. Patterson. "The Impact of Community Computer Networks on Social Capital and Community Involvement." *American Behavioral Scientist* 45, no. 3 (November 2001): 496–509.

Kelly, Anita E., and Robert R. Rodriguez. "Publicly Committing Oneself to an Identity." *Basic and Applied Social Psychology* 28, no. 2 (June 2006): 185–91. doi:10.1207/s15324834basp2802_8.

Kenny, David. *Interpersonal Perception.* New York: Guilford Press, 1994.

Kiesler, Sara, Jane Siegel, and Timothy W. McGuire. "Social Psychological Aspects of Computer-Mediated Communication." *American Psychologist* 39, no. 10 (1984): 1123–34.

Kirkpatrick, Daniel. *The Facebook Effect: The Inside Story of the Company That Is Connecting the World.* New York: Simon & Schuster, 2010.

Kirkpatrick, Marshall. "A Closer Look at Facebook's New Privacy Options," *ReadWriteWeb*, June 29, 2009, accessed June 20, 2012, http://www.readwriteweb.com/archives/a_closer_look_at_facebooks_new_privacy_options.php.

Kirschner, Paul A., and Aryn C. Karpinski. "Facebook and Academic Performance." *Computers in Human Behavior* 26, no. 6 (November 2010): 1237–45. doi:10.1016/j.chb.2010.03.024.

Kleck, Christine, Christen Reese, Dawn Behnken, and Shyam Sundar. "The Company You Keep and the Image You Project: Putting Your Best Face Forward in Online Social Networks." Paper presented at the annual meeting of the International Communication Association, San Francisco, CA, May 2007.

Kolbitsch, Josef, and Maurer Herman. "The Transformation of the Web: How Emerging Communities Shape the Information We Consume."

Journal of Universal Computer Science 12, no. 2 (February 2006): 187–213.

Koles, Bernadett, and Peter Nagy. "Who Is Portrayed in Second Life: Dr. Jekyll or Mr. Hyde? The Extent of Congruence between Real Life and Virtual Identity." *Journal of Virtual Worlds Research* 5, no. 1 (2012): 3–19.

Koloff, Abbott. "States Push for Cyberbully Controls: But Efforts to Go Beyond Schools Raise Concerns Over Freedom of Speech, Privacy." *USA Today,* February 7, 2008, 3A.

Kramer, Nicole C., and Stephan Winter. "Impression Management 2.0: The Relationships of Self-Esteem, Extraversion, Self-Efficacy, and Self-Presentation within Social Networking Sites." *Journal of Media Psychology* 20, no. 3 (2008): 106–16.

Kubiak, Anthony. "Splitting the Difference: Performance and Its Double in American Culture." *The Drama Review* 42, no. 4 (Winter 1998): 91–114.

Kumar, Sanjeev, Jatin Chhugani, Changkyu Kim, Daehyun Kim, Anthony Nguyen, Pradeep Dubey, Christian Bienia, and Youngmin Kim. "Second Life and the New Generation of Virtual Worlds." *Computer* 41, no. 9 (September, 2008): 46–53.

Lampe, Cliff, Nicole B. Ellison, and Charles Steinfield. "A Face(book) in the Crowd: Social Searching vs. Social Browsing." In *Proceedings of the 2006 20th Anniversary Conference on Computer Suppored Cooperative Work*, 167–70. New York: ACM Press, 2006.

———. "A Familiar Face(book): Profile Elements as Signals in an Online Social Network." In *Proceedings of the 2007 ACM Conference on Human Factors in Computing*, 425–44. New York: ACM, 2007.

———. "Change in Use and Perception of Facebook." Paper presented at the ACM conference on Computer Supported Cooperative Work, San Diego, CA, November 2008.

Lea, Martin, and Russell Spears. "Love at First Byte? Building Personal Relationships over Computer Networks." In *Understudied Relationships: Off the Beaten Track*, edited by Julia T. Wood and Steve W. Duck, 197–233. Newbury Park, CA: Sage, 1995.

Leary, Mark., *Self-Presentation: Impression Management and Interpersonal Behavior, Social Psychology Series*. Madison, WI: Brown and Benchmark, 1995.

Leary, Mark R. and Robin M. Kowalski. "Impression Management: A Literature Review and Two-Component Model." *Psychology Bulletin* 107, no. 1 (January 1990): 34–47.

Lee, Eun-Ju. "Effects of Visual Representation on Social Influence in Computer-Mediated Communication: Experimental Tests on the Social Identity Model of Deindividuation Effects." *Human Communication Research* 30, no. 2 (April 2004): 234–59.

Leitch, Shirley, and Sally Davenport. "Corporate Identity as an Enabler and Constraint on the Pursuit of Corporate Objectives." *European Journal of Marketing* 45, no. 9–10 (2011): 1501–20.

Lenzoff, Maurice, and William A. Westley. "The Homosexual Community." *Social Problems* 3 (1956): 257–63.

Lin, Nan. "Building a Network Theory of Social Capital." *Connections* 22, no. 1 (1999): 28–51.

Lindlof, Thomas R. *Qualitative Communication Research Methods.* Thousand Oaks, CA: Sage, 1995.

Liu, Hugo. "Social Network Profiles as Taste Performance." *Journal of Computer-Mediated Communication* 13, no. 1 (2008): 252–75.

Livingstone, Sonia. "Taking Risky Opportunities in Youthful Content Creation: Teenagers' Use of Social Networking Sites for Intimacy, Privacy and Self-Expression." *New Media and Society* 10, no. 3 (June 2008): 393–411.

Lombardi, Emilia L. "Integration within a Transgender Social Network and Its Effect upon Members' Social and Political Activity." *Journal of Homosexuality* 37, no. 1 (1999): 109–26.

Marcus, Bernd, Franz Machilek, and Astrid Schütz. "Personality in Cyberspace: Personal Websites as Media for Personality Expressions and Impressions." *Journal of Personality and Social Psychology* 90, no. 6 (June 2006): 1014–31.

Markovits, Henry, Joyce Beneson, and Susan White. "Gender and Priming Differences in Speed and Processing of Information Relating to Social Structure." *Journal of Experimental Social Psychology* 42, no. 5 (September 2006): 662–67.

Marwick, Alice E., and danah boyd. "I Tweet Honestly, I Tweet Passionately: Twitter Users, Context Collapse, and the Imagined Audience." *New Media and Society* 13, no. 1 (February 2011): 114–33.

Mazer, Joseph P., Richard E. Murphy, and Cheri J. Simonds. "I'll See You on "Facebook": The Effects of Computer-Mediated Teacher Self-Disclosure on Student Motivation, Affective Learning, and

Classroom Climate." *Communication Education* 56, no. 1 (January 2007): 1–17. doi:10.1080/03634520601009710.

McBride, Dwight. *Why I Hate Abercrombie and Fitch: Essays on Race and Sexuality.* New York: New York University Press, 2005.

McCall, Leslie. "The Complexity of Intersectionality." *Signs: Journal of Women in Culture and Society* 30, no. 3 (Summer 2005): 1771–1800.

McCroskey, James, and Thomas McCain. "The Measurement of Interpersonal Attraction." *Communication Monographs* 41, no. 3 (1974): 261–66.

McGrath, Joseph E. *Groups: Interaction and Performance.* Englewood Cliffs, NJ: Prentice Hall, 1984.

McIntosh, Mary. "The Homosexual Role." *Social Problems* 16 (1968): 182–92.

McKenna, Katelyn Y. A., Amie S. Green, and Marci E. Gleason. "Relationship Formation on the Internet: What's the Big Attraction?" *Journal of Social Issues* 58, no. 1 (Spring 2002): 9–31.

McKinney, Bruce C., Lynne Kelly, and Robert L. Duran. "Narcissism or Openness?: College Students' Use of Facebook and Twitter." *Communication Research Reports* 29, no. 2 (April 2012): 108–18. doi:10.1080/08824096.2012.666919.

McMillan, David W. and David M. Chavis. "Sense of Community: A Definition and Theory." *Journal of Community Psychology* 14, no. 1 (January 1986): 6–23.

McQueen, Amy, and William Klein. "Experimental Manipulations of Self-Affirmation: A Systematic Review." *Self and Identity* 5, no. 4 (October–December, 2006): 289–354..

Mead, George Herbert. *Mind, Self, and Society.* Chicago: University of Chicago Press, 1934.

Mehdizadeh, Soraya. "Self-Presentation 2.0: Narcissism and Self-Esteem on Facebook." *Cyberpsychology, Behavavior, and Social Networking* 13, no. 4 (August 2010): 357–64.

Merkle, Erich, and Rhonda Richardson. "Digital Dating and Virtual Relating: Conceptualizing Computer Mediated Romantic Relationships." *Family Relations: An Interdisciplinary Journal of Applied Family Studies* 49, no. 2 (April 2000): 187–92.

Mershon, Phil. "26 Promising Social Media Stats for Small Businesses," November 8, 2011, accessed August 8, 2012, http://www.socialmediaexaminer.com/26-promising-social-media-stats-for-small-businesses/.

"Microsoft's Halo 3 Registers Biggest Day in US Entertainment History with $170 Mln in Sales." Reuters, accessed June 20, 2012, www.reuters.com/article/2007/09/27/idUSIN20070927063131MSFT 20070927.

Miller, Hugh, and Jane Arnold. "Self in Web Home Pages: Gender, Identity, and Power in Cyberspace." In *Towards Cyberpsychology: Mind, Cognitions, and Society in the Internet Age*, edited by Giuseppe Riva and Carlo Galimberti, 73–94. Fairfax, VA: IOS Press, 2001.

Miron, Louis F., and Jonathan Xavier Inda. "Race as a Kind of Speech Act." *Cultural Studies: A Research Annual* 5 (2000): 85–107.

Mitchell, Colin. "Selling the Brand Inside." *Harvard Business Review* 80 (2002): 5–11.

Monberg, John. "Trajectories of Computer-Mediated Communication Research." *Southern Communication Journal* 70, no. 3 (Spring 2005): 181–86.

Mulyanegara, Riza C., Yelena Tsarenko, and Alastair Anderson. "The Big Five and Brand Personality: Investigating the Impact of Consumer Personality on Preferences Towards Particular Brand Personality." *Brand Management* 16, no. 4 (2009): 234–37.

Murray, Janet. *Hamlet on the Holodeck: The Future of Narrative in Cyberspace*. Cambridge, MA: MIT Press, 1999.

Myers, W. Benjamin, and Desireé Rowe. "The Critical Lede: New Media and Ecological Balance." *Text and Performance Quarterly* 32, no. 1 (January 2012): 73–77. doi:10.1080/10462937.2011.631404.

National Center for Transgender Equality. *Transgender Terminology*, 2009, accessed March 30, 2012, www.transequality.org/Resources/ NCTE_TransTerminology.pdf.

Nastri, Jacqueline, Jorge Peña, and Jeffrey T. Hancock. "The Construction of Away Messages: A Speech Act Analysis." *Journal of Computer Mediated Communication* 11, no. 4 (2006): 1025–45.

Nguyen, Nha, and Gaston Leblanc. "Corporate Image and Corporate Reputation in Customers' Retention Decisions in Services." *Journal of Retailing and Consumer Services* 8, no. 4 (July 2001): 227–36. doi:10.1016/S0969-6989(00)00029-1.

Nielsen Wire. "Social Media Report: Spending Time, Money, and Going Mobile," accessed May 14, 2012, http://blog.nielsen.com/

nielsenwire/online_mobile/social-media-report-spending-time-money-and-going-mobile/.

Nielsen, Carolyn. "Moving Mass Communication Scholarship beyond Binaries: A Call for Intersectionality." *Media Report to Women* 39, no. 1 (Winter 2011): 6–11.

Noah's Arc. DVD. Directed by Patrik-Ian Polk. Santa Monica, CA: MTV Studios, 2005.

Noveck, Jocelyn. "Gay Users Applaud Facebook Options." *Cincinnati Enquirer,* February 19, 2011, sec. A.

Nowak, Kristine L. "Sex Categorization in Computer-Mediated Communication (CMC): Exploring the Utopian Promise." *Media Psychology* 5, no. 1 (2003): 83–103.

NPR Staff. "Antoine Dodson: Riding YouTube Out of the 'Hood'." *National Public Radio,* August 23, 2010.

Null, Christopher. "No Such Thing as "Deleted" on the Internet." *Christopher Null: The Working Guy,* accessed May 22, 2009, http://www.anahuactexasindependence.com/NoSuchThingAsDeletedOnInternet.htm.

Oblinger, Diana and Brian Hawkins. "The Myth about Putting Information Online." *EDUCASE Review* 41, no. 5 (Sept./Oct. 2006): 14–15.

Obst, Patricia, and Jana Stafurik. "Online We Are All Able-Bodied: Online Psychological Sense of Community and Social Support Found through Membership of Disability-Specific Website Promotes Well-Being for People Living with a Physical Disability." *Journal of Community and Applied Psychology* 20, no. 6 (November/December 2010): 525–31.

Ong, Eileen Y. L., Rebecca P. Ang, Jim C. M. Ho, Joylynn C. Y. Lim, Dion H. Goh, Chei Sian Lee, and Alton Y. K. Chua. "Narcissism, Extraversion, and Adolescents' Self-Presentation on Facebook." *Personality and Individual Differences* 20, no. 2 (January 2011): 180–85.

Orgad, Shani. *Storytelling Online: Talking Breast Cancer on the Internet.* New York: Peter Lang, 2005.

O'Riordan, Kate, and David Phillips, eds. *Queer Online: Media, Technology and Sexuality.* New York: Peter Lang Publishing, 2007.

"The Original A&T Bed Intruder Song 8.11.2010." YouTube video, 3:26. Posted by "SpeechlessQue," August 12, 2010. http://www.youtube.com/watch?v=Q3UsvLyu3N0.

Ortutay, Barbara. "Facebook Adjusts Privacy Controls after Complaints." *Associated Press Wire,* May 26, 2006, accessed May 26, 2006, http://www.semissourian.com/story/1638005.html.

O'Sullivan, Patrick B. "Masspersonal Communication: Rethinking the Mass-Interpersonal Divide." Paper presented at annual meeting of the International Communication Association, New York, 2005.

———. "What You Don't Know Won't Hurt Me: Impression Management Functions of Communication Channels in Relationships." *Human Communication Research* 26, no. 3 (July 2000): 403–31.

Paisner, Jonathan. "Jump on the Blog Wagon." *Journal of Accountancy* 201, no. 6 (June 2006): 28.

Palmieri, Cynthia, Kristen Prestano, Rosalie Gandley, Emily Overton, and Qin Zhang. "The Facebook Phenomenon: Online Self-Disclosure and Uncertainty Reduction." *China Media Research* 8, no. 1 (January 2012): 48–53.

Papacharissi, Zizi. "Conclusion: A Networked Self." In *A Networked Self: Identity, Community, and Culture*, edited by Zizi Papacharissi, 304–17. New York: Routledge, 2011.

———. "The Presentation of Self in Virtual Life: Characteristics of Personal Home Pages." *Journalism and Mass Communication Quarterly* 79, no. 3 (Autumn 2002): 643–60.

———. "The Virtual Sphere: The Internet as a Public Sphere." *New Media and Society* 4, no. 1 (February 2002): 9–27.

———. "The Virtual Geographies of Social Networks: A Comparative Analysis of Facebook, LinkedIn and ASmallWorld." *New Media and Society* 11, no. 1–2 (February–March 2009): 199–220. doi:10.1177/1461444808099577.

Parks, Malcolm R., and Kory Floyd. "Making Friends in Cyberspace." *Journal of Communication* 46, no. 1 (Winter 1996): 80–97.

Paulhus, Delroy L., and Paul D. Trapnell. " Self-Presentation of Personality: An Agency-Communion Framework." In *Handbook of Personality*, edited by Oliver P. John, Richard W. Robins, and Lawrence A. Pervin, 492–517. New York: The Guilford Press, 2008.

Pearson, Erika. "All the World Wide Web's a Stage: The Performance of Identity in Online Social Networks." *First Monday* 14, no. 3 (March 2009): article 5.

Pempek, Tiffany A., Yevdokiya A. Yermolayeva, and Sandra L. Calvert. "College Students' Social Networking Experiences on Facebook," *Journal of Applied Developmental Psychology* 30 (2009): 227–38.

Petronio, Sandra. *Boundaries of Privacy: Dialectics of Disclosure.* Albany: State University New York Press, 2002.

Pew Internet and American Life Project. "Trend Data (Adults)." Pew Internet and American Life Project, accessed June 27, 2012, http://www.pewinternet.org/Trend-Data-(Adults)/Online-Activities-Daily.aspx.

Pizarro, Narciso. "Structural Identity and Equivalence of Individuals in Social Networks." *International Sociology* 22, no. 6 (November 2007): 767–92.

Planalp, Sally, Dianne Rutherford, and James M. Honeycutt. "Events That Increase Uncertainty in Personal Relationships: Replication and Extension." *Human Communication Research* 14, no. 4 (1988): 516–47.

Plummer, Kenneth. "Homosexual Categories: Some Research Problems in the Labeling Perspective of Homosexuality." In *The Making of the Modern Homosexual*, edited by Kenneth Plummer, 53–75. London: Hutchinson, 1981.

Plutchak, T. Scott. "I See Blog People." *Journal of the Medical Library Association* 93, no. 3 (July 2005): 305–7.

Ponse, Barbara. *Identities in the Lesbian World: The Social Construction of Self.* Westport, CT: Greenwood Press, 1978.

Postmes, Tom, Russell Spears, and Martin Lea. "The Formation of Group Norms in Computer-Mediated Communication." *Human Communication Research* 26, no. 3 (July 2000): 341–71.

Punyanunt-Carter, Narissa Maria. "An Analysis of College Students' Self-Disclosure Behaviors on the Internet." *College Student Journal* 40, no. 2 (June 2006): 329–31.

Rainie, Lee, Kristen Purcell, and Aaron Smith. *The Social Side of the Internet*, Pew Internet and American Life Project, 2011, accessed February 20, 2011, http://pewinternet.org/Reports/2011/The-Social-Side-of-the-Internet.aspx.

Ramirez, Artemio, Jr., and Judee K. Burgoon. "The Effect of Interactivity on Initial Interactions: The Influence of Information Valence and Modality and Information Richness on Computer-Mediated Interaction." *Communication Monographs* 71, no. 4 (2004): 422–47.

Rhodewalt, Federick, and Benjamin Peterson. "Narcissim." In *Handbook of Individual Differences in Social Behavior*, ed. Mark R. Leary and Rick H. Hoyle, 547–60. New York: The Guilford Press, 2009.

Riggs, Marlon. "Black Macho Revisited: Reflection of a Snap! Queen." In *Out in Culture: Gay, Lesbian and Queer Essays on Popular Culture*, edited by Cory K. Creeknur and Alexander Doty, 470–75. Durham, NC: Duke University Press, 1995.

Rogers, Everett. *A History of Communication Study: A Biographical Approach*. New York: The Free Press, 1994.

Rogers, Paul, and Martin Lea. "Social Presence in Distributed Group Environments: The Role of Social Identity." *Behavior and Information Technology* 24, no. 2 (2005): 151–58.

Roloff, Michael, and Danette Ifert. "Antecedents and Consequences of Explicit Agreements to Declare a Topic Taboo in Dating Relationships." *Personal Relationships* 5, no. 2 (1998): 191–205.

Rosenbaum, Judith E., Benjamin K. Johnson, Peter A. Stepman, and Koos C. M. Nuijten. "Just Being Themselves? Goals and Strategies for Self-Presentation on Facebook." Paper presented at the 80th annual conference of the Southern States Communication Association, Memphis, TN, April 2010.

Ross, Craig, Emily S. Orr, Mia Sisic, Jamie M. Arseneault, Mary G. Simmering, and Robert R. Orr. "Personality and Motivations Associated with Facebook Use." *Computers in Human Behavior* 25, no. 2 (March 2009): 578–86.

Rutledge, Amy. "Charity Worker Fired over Facebook Comments." *WGN News,* 2011, accessed February 2, 2011, www.wgntv.com/news/wgntv-man-fired-over-facebook-jan12,0,7228739.story.

Saccoccio, Sabrina. "The Facebook Generation: Changing the Meaning of Privacy." *CBC News,* May 24, 2007, accessed June 18, 2012, http://www.cbc.ca/news/background/tech/facebook-generation.html.

Saloman, David. *A Concise Introduction to Data Compression*. London: Springer-Verlag, 2008.

Sarfoh, Joseph A. "The West African Zongo and the American Ghetto." *Journal of Black Studies* 17, no. 1 (September 1986): 71–84. doi:10.1177/002193478601700105.

Schechner, Richard. *Between Theatre and Anthropology*. Philadelphia: University of Pennsylvania Press, 1985.

Schimel, Jeff, Jamie Arndt, Katherine M. Banko, and Alison Cook. "Not All Self-Affirmations Were Created Equal: The Cognitive and Social

Benefits of Affirming the Intrinsic (vs. Extrinsic) Self." *Social Cognition* 22, no. 1 (2004): 75–99.

Schlenker, Barry R. "Self-Presentation." In *Handbook of Self and Identity*, edited by Mark R. Leary and June Tangney, 492–519. New York: Guilford Press, 2003.

Schoenfeld, Adam. "Social Media for Business: 31 Stats and Anecdotes," accessed May 4, 2012, http://www.slideshare.net/schoeny/social-media-for-business-31-stats-and-anecdotes.

Schroeder, Jonathan E. and Miriam Salzer-Morling, eds. *Brand Culture*. New York: Routledge, 2006.

Sedgwick, Eve K. "Epistemology of the Closet." In *The Lesbian and Gay Studies Reader*, edited by Henry Abelove, Michele A. Barale, and David M. Halperin, 45–61. New York: Routledge, 1993.

Segerstad, Yiva, and Peter Ljungstrand. "Instant Messaging with Web-Who." *International Journal of Human-Computer Studies* 56, no. 1 (January 2002): 147–71.

Sevelius, Jae M., Adam Carrico, and Mallory O. Johnson. "Antiretroviral Therapy Adherence among Transgender Women Living with HIV." *Journal of the Association of Nurses in AIDS Care* 21, no. 3 (May–June 2010): 256–64.

Sherblom, John C. "The Computer-Mediated Communication (CMC) Classroom: A Challenge of Medium, Presence, Interaction, Identity, and Relationship." *Communication Education* 59, no. 4 (October 2010): 497–523.

Sherblom, John C., Lesley A. Withers, and Lynnette G. Leonard. "Communication Challenges and Opportunities for Educators Using Second Life." In *Higher Education in Virtual Worlds: Teaching and Learning in Second Life*, edited by Charles Wankel and Jan Kingsley, 29–46. Bingley, UK: Emerald, 2009.

Sherman, David K. and Geoffey L. Cohen. 'The Psychology of Self-Defense: Self-Affirmation Theory." In *Advances in Experimental Social Psychology*, edited by Mark P. Zanna, 183–242. San Diego: CA: Academic Press, 2006.

Shields, Stephanie A. "Gender: An Intersectionality Perspective." *Sex Roles* 59, no. 5 (September 2008): 301–11.

Short, John A., Ederyn Williams, and Bruce Christie. *The Social Psychology of Telecommunications*. London: Wiley, 1976.

Simões, Cláudia, Sally Dibb, and Raymond P. Fisk. "Managing Corporate Identity: An Internal Perspective." *Journal of the Academy of Marketing Science* 33, no. 2 (April 2005): 153–68. doi:10.1177/0092070304268920.

Skiba, Diane J. "WEB 2.0: Next Great Thing or Just Marketing Hype?" *Nursing Education Perspectives* 27, no. 4 (2006): 212–14.

Slinn, E. Warwick. "Poetry and Culture: Performativity and Critique." *New Literary History* 30, no. 1 (Winter 1999): 50–74.

———. "Fasting Growing Demographic on Facebook: Women over 55." *Inside Facebook,* accessed April 12, 2010, http://www.insidefacebook.com/2009/02/02/fastest-growing-demo graphic-on-facebook-women-over55/.

Smith, Aaron and Joanna Brenner. "Twitter Use 2012," Pew Internet and American Life Project, accessed June 6, 2012, http://pewinternet.org/Reports/2012/Twitter-Use-2012.aspx.

Smith, Stacy L., Ken Lachlan, and Ron Tamborini. "Popular Video Games: Quantifying the Presentation of Violence and Its Context." *Journal of Broadcasting and Electronic Media* 47, no. 1 (March 2003): 58–76.

Song, Felicia Wu. *Virtual Communities: Bowling Alone, Online Together.* New York: Peter Lang, 2009.

Spitzberg, Brian H. "Preliminary Development of a Model and Measure of Computer-Mediated Communication (CMC) Competence." *Journal of Computer-Mediated Communication* 11, no. 2 (January 2006): 629–66.

Sproull, Lee, and Sara Kiesler. "Reducing Social Context Cues: Electronic Mail in Organizational Communication." *Management Science* 32, no. 11 (November 1996): 1492–1512.

Steele, Claude M. "The Psychology of Self-Affirmation: Sustaining the Integrity of the Self." In *Advances in Experimental Social Psychology,* edited by Leonard Berkowitz. Vol. 21, 261–302. San Diego, CA: Academic Press, 1988.

Steinkuehler, Constance, and Dmitri Williams. "Where Everybody Knows Your (Screen) Name: Online Games as 'Third Places'." *Journal of Computer-Mediated Communication* 11, no. 4 (August 2006): 885–909.

Stern, Susannah. "Expressions of Identity Online: Prominent Features and Gender Differences in Adolescents' World Wide Web Home

Pages." *Journal of Broadcasting and Electronic Media* 48, no. 2 (2004): 218–43.

Stevens, Kyle. "Checking Your Face and Space: When Companies Look Outside the Interview." *Campus News*, February 11, 2008, http://uwmpost.com/article52/19/3039-Checking-your-face-and-space.

Stone, Allucquere R. *The War of Desire and Technology at the Close of the Mechanical Age.* Cambridge, MA: MIT Press, 1995.

Stone, Brad. "New Scrutiny for Facebook Predators." *The New York Times,* July 30, 2007, accessed May 1, 2010, http://www.nytimes.com/2007/07/30/business/media/30facebook.html.

Stone, Gregory P. "Appearance and the Self: A Slightly Revised Version." In *Social Psychology through Symbolic Interaction*, edited by Stone, Gregory P. and Harvey A. Farberman. 2nd ed., 187–202. New York: Wiley, 1981.

Strano, Michele M. "User Descriptions and Interpretations of Self-Presentation through Facebook Profile Images." *Cyberpsychology: Journal of Psychosocial Research* 2, no. 2 (2008): article 1.

Strauss, Anselm, and Juliet Corbin. *Basics of Qualitative Research: Grounded Theory Procedures and Techniques.* Newbury Park, CA: Sage, 1990.

Stripling, Jack. "Not So Private Professors." *Inside Higher Ed,* 2010, accessed October 3, 2010, http://www.insidehighered.com/news/2010/03/02/facebook.

Stryker, Susan. *Transgender History.* Berkeley, CA: Seal Press, 2008.

Sullivan, Nikki. *A Critical Introduction to Queer Theory.* New York: New York University Press, 2003.

Sung, Yongjun, and Keith Campbell. "Brand Commitment in Consumer-Brand Relationships: An Investment Model Approach." *Brand Management* 17, no. 2 (April 2009): 97–113.

Talamo, Alessandra, and Beatrice Ligorio. "Strategic Identities in Cyberspace." *Cyberpsychologyand Behavior* 4, no. 1 (February 2001): 109–22.

Tedeschi, James T., and Marc Riess, "Identities, the Phenomenal Self, and Laboratory Research." In *Impression Management Theory and Social Psychological Research*, edited by James T. Tedeschi, 3–22. New York: Academic Press, 1981.

Tesser, Abraham. "Toward a Self-Evaluation Maintenance Model of Social Behavior." In *Advances in Experimental Social Psychology*, edited by Leonard Berkowitz. Vol. 21, 181–227. San Diego, CA: Academic Press, 1988.

Tesser, Abraham, and David P. Cornell. "On the Confluence of Self Processes." *Journal of Experimental Social Psychology* 27, no. 6 (November 1991): 501–26. doi:10.1016/0022-1031(91)90023-Y.

Thelwall, Mike, and David Wilkinson. "Public Dialogs in Social Network Sites: What Is Their Purpose/" *Journal of the American Society for Information Science and Technology* 61, no. 2 (2009): 392–404.

Thompson, Don. "California Man Used Facebook to Hack Women's Emails." *Associated Press Wire,* January 14, 2011, http://www.cbsnews.com/2100-201_162-7247851.html

Thorndike, Edward. "A Constant Error in Psychological Ratings." *Journal of Applied Psychology* 4, no. 1 (March 1920): 25–29.

Tice, Dianne M., Jennifer L. Butler, Mark B. Muraven, and Arlene M. Stillwell. "When Modesty Prevails: Differential Favorability of Self-Presentation to Friends and Strangers." *Journal of Personality and Social Psychology* 69, no. 6 (December 1995): 1120–38.

Tidwell, Lisa C., and Joseph B. Walther. "Computer-Mediated Communication Effects on Disclosure, Impressions, and Interpersonal Evaluations: Getting to Know One Another a Bit at a Time." *Human Communication Research* 28, no. 3 (2002): 317–48.

Toma, Catalina L., and Jeffrey T. Hancock. "What Lies Beneath: The Linguistic Traces of Deception in Online Dating Profiles." *Journal of Communication* 62, no. 1 (February 2012): 78–97.

Toma, Catalina L., and Jeffrey T. Hancock. "Looks and Lies: The Role of Physical Attractiveness in Online Dating Self-Presentation and Deception." *Communication Research* 37, no. 3 (June 2010): 335–51. doi:10.1177/0093650209356437.

Toma, Catalina L., Jeffrey T. Hancock, and Nicole B. Ellison. "Separating Fact from Fiction: An Examination of Deceptive Self-Presentation in Online Dating Profiles." *Personality and Social Psychology Bulletin* 34, no. 8 (August 2008): 1023–36. doi:10.1177/0146167208318067.

Tomaka, Joe, Jim Blascovich, Jeffrey Kibler, and John M. Ernst. "Cognitive and Physiological Antecedents of Threat and Challenge Appraisal." *Journal of Personality and Social Psychology* 73, no. 1 (1997): 63–72. doi:10.1037/0022-3514.73.1.63.

Tong, Stephanie T., Brandon Van Der Heide, Lindsey Langwell, and Joseph B. Walther. "Too Much of a Good Thing? The Relationship between Number of Friends and Interpersonal Impressions on Facebook." *Journal of Computer-Mediated Communication* 13, no. 3 (April 2008): 531–49.

Tracy, Sarah Jane, and Angela Trethewey. "Fracturing the Real-Self-Fake-Self Dichotomy: Moving toward Crystallized Organizational Identities." *Communication Theory* 15, no. 2 (May 2005): 168–95.

Trepte, Sabine, Leonard Reincke, and Keno Juechems. "The Social Side of Gaming: How Playing Online Computer Games Creates Online and Offline Social Support." *Computers in Human Behavior* 28, no. 3 (May 2012): 832–39.

Troiden, Richard. *Gay and Lesbian Identity: A Sociological Analysis.* New York: General Hall, 1988.

True Blood. DVD. Directed by Allan Ball. Studio City, CA: HBO Studios, 2008.

Tufekci, Zeynep. "Can You See Me Now? Audience and Disclosure Regulation in Online Social Network Sites." *Bulletin of Science, Technology and Society* 28, no. 1 (February 2008): 20–36. doi:10.1177/0270467607311484.

Turkle, Sherry. *Alone Together: Why We Expect More from Technology and Less from Each Other.* New York: Basic Books, 2011.

———. *Life on the Screen: Identity in the Age of the Internet.* New York: Simon and Schuster, 1995.

Utz, Sonja. "Show Me Your Friends and I Will Tell You What Type of Person You Are: How One's Profile, Number of Friends, and Type of Friends Influence Impression Formation on Social Network Sites." *Journal of Computer-Mediated Communication* 15, no. 2 (January 2010): 314–35.

Utz, Sonja, and Nicole C. Krämer. "The Privacy Paradox on Social Network Sites Revisited: The Role of Individual Characteristics and Group Norms." *Cyberpsychology: Journal of Psychosocial Research on Cyberspace* 3, no. 2 (2009): article 1.

Valenzuela, Sebastián, Namsu Park, and Kerk F. Kee. "Is There Social Capital in a Social Network Site?: Facebook Use and College Students' Life Satisfaction, Trust, and Participation." *Journal of Computer-Mediated Communication* 14, no. 4 (2009): 875–901. doi:10.1111/j.1083-6101.2009.01474.x.

Valkenburg, Patti M., and Jochen Peter. "Social Consequences of the Internet for Adolescents." *Current Directions in Psychological Science* 18, no. 1 (February 2009): 1–5. doi:10.1111/j.1467-8721.2009.01595.x.

Van Der Heide, Brandon, Jonathan D. D'Angelo, and Erin M. Schumkaer. "The Effects of Verbal vs. Photographic Self-Presentation on Impression Formation in Facebook." *Journal of Communication* 62, no. 1 (February 2012): 98–116.

Vangelisti, Anita. "Family Secrets: Forms, Functions, and Correlates." *Journal of Social and Personal Relationships* 11, no. 1 (1994): 113–35.

Vangelisti, Anita, and Stacy Young. "When Words Hurt: The Effects of Perceived Intentionality on Interpersonal Relationships." *Journal of Social and Personal Relationships* 17, no. 3 (2000): 393–424.

Vazire, Simine, and Samuel D. Gosling. "E-Perceptions: Personality Impressions Based on Personal Websites." *Journal of Personality and Social Psychology* 87, no. 1 (2004): 123–32.

Veil, Shari R., Timothy L. Sellnow, and Elizabeth L. Petrun. "Hoaxes and the Paradoxical Challenges of Restoring Legitimacy." *Management Communication Quarterly* 26, no. 2 (May 2012): 322–45. doi:10.1177/0893318911426685.

Waisbord, Silvio. "When the Cart of Media Is Before the Horse of Identity: A Critique of Technology-Centered Views on Globalization." *Communication Research* 25, no. 4 (August 1998): 377–98.

Walther, Joseph B. "Computer-Mediated Communication: Impersonal, Interpersonal, and Hyperpersonal Interaction." *Communication Research* 23, no. 1 (February 1996): 3–43.

———. "Selective Self-Presentation in Computer-Mediated Communication: Hyperpersonal Dimensions of Technology, Language, and Cognition." *Computers in Human Behavior* 23, no. 5 (September 2007): 2538–57.

———. "Interpersonal Effects in Computer-Mediated Interaction: A Relational Perspective." *Communication Research* 19, no. 1 (February 1992): 52–90.

Walther, Joseph B., and Ulla Bunz. "The Rules of Virtual Groups: Trust, Liking, and Performance in Computer-Mediated Communication." *Journal of Communication* 55, no. 4 (December 2005): 828–46.

Walther, Joseph B., Caleb Carr, Sejung Choi, David DeAndrea, Stephanie Tom Tong, and Brandon Van Der Heide. "Interaction of Interpersonal, Peer, and Media Influence Sources Online: A Research Agenda for Technology Convergence." In *A Networked Self: Identity, Community, and Culture on Social Network Sites*, edited by Zizi Papacharissi, 17–38. New York: Routledge, 2011.

Walther, Joseph B., Yuhua Liang, David C. DeAndrea, Stephanie T. Tong, Caleb Carr, Erin L. Spottswood, and Yair Amaichai-Hamburger. "The Effect of Feedback on Identity Shift in Computer-Mediated Communication." *Media Psychology* 14, no. 1 (January 2011): 1–26.

Walther, Joseph B., and Malcolm R. Parks. "Cues Filtered Out, Cues Filtered in: Computer-Mediated Communication and Relationships." In *Handbook of Interpersonal Communication*, edited by Knapp, Mark L. and John A. Daly. 3rd ed., 529–63. Thousand Oaks, CA: Sage, 2002.

Walther, Joseph B., Brandon Van Der Heide, Lauren M. Hamel, and Hilary C. Shulman. "Self-Generated Versus Other-Generated Statements and Impressions in Computer-Mediated Communication: A Test of Warranting Theory Using Facebook." *Communication Research* 36, no. 2 (April 2009): 229–53.

Walther, Joseph B., Brandon Van Der Heide, Sang-Yeon Kim, David Westerman, and Stephanie Tom Tong. "The Role of Friends' Appearance and Behavior on Evaluations of Individuals on Facebook: Are We Known by the Company We Keep?" *Human Communication Research* 34, no. 1 (January 2008): 28–49.

Wartick, Steven L. "The Relationship between Intense Media Exposure and Change in Corporate Reputation." *Business and Society* 31, no. 1 (Spring 1992): 33–49. doi:10.1177/000765039203100104.

Watts, Eric King. "Border Patrolling and 'Passing' in Eminem's *8 Mile*." *Critical Studies in Media Communication* 22, no. 3 (August 2005): 187–206. doi:10.1080/07393180500201686.

Wehner, Mike. "Facebook Timeline Mandatory Rollout: You Have Seven Days to Scour Your Past." *Tecca,* January 24, 2012, http://news.yahoo.com/blogs/technology-blog/facebook-timeline-mandatory-rollout-7-days-scour-past-185456598.html.

Wellman, Barry, Anabel Quan Haase, James Witte, and Keith Hampton. "Does the Internet Increase, Decrease, or Supplement Social Capital?

Social Networks, Participation, and Community Commitment." *American Behavioral Scientist* 45, no. 3 (November 2001): 436–55.

Westerman, David, Brandon Van Der Heide, Katherine Klein, and Joseph B. Walther. "How Do People Really Seek Information about Others?: Information Seeking across Internet and Traditional Communication Channels." *Journal of Computer-Mediated Communication* 13, no. 3 (April 2008): 751–67.

Westwood, Gordon. *A Minority: A Report on the Life of the Male Homosexual in Great Britain*. London: Longmans, 1960.

Whitty, Monica. "Liar, Liar: An Examination of How Open, Supportive, and Honest People are in Chat Rooms." *Computers in Human Behavior* 18, no. 4 (July 2002): 343–52.

———. "Peering into Online Bedroom Windows: Considering the Ethical Implications." In *Readings in Virtual Research Ethics: Issues and Controversies*, edited by Elizabeth A. Buchanan, 203–19. Hershey Park, PA: Information Science Publishing, 2004.

Whitty, Monica, and Jeff Gavin. "Age/Sex/Location: Uncovering the Social Cues in the Development of Online Relationships." *Cyberpsychologyand Behavior* 4, no. 5 (October 2001): 623–30.

Wilcox, Dennis H., Glen T. Cameron, Bryan H. Reber, and Jae-Hwa Shin. *THINK Public Relations*. Boston: Allyn and Bacon, 2011.

Williams, Christopher. "BlackBerry Blackout Enters Day Three." *Telegraph,* 2011, accessed May 4, 2012, http://www.telegraph.co.uk/technology/blackberry/8821912/BlackBerry-blackout-enters-day-three.html.

Williams, Dmitri. "On and Off the 'Net': Scales for Social Capital in an Online Era." *Journal of Computer-Mediated Communication* 11, no. 2 (2006): 593–28.

Williamson, Catherine. "Providing Care to Transgender Persons: A Clinical Approach to Primary Care, Hormones and HIV Management." *Journal of the Association of Nurses in AIDS Care* 21, no. 3 (May–June 2010): 221–29.

Willson, Michele A. *Technically Together: Rethinking Community within Technosociety*. New York: Peter Lang, 2006.

"Woman Wakes Up to Find Intruder in Her Bed (SPOOF)." YouTube video, 0:45 Posted by "AfricanBoiShow," August 2, 2010. http://www.youtube.com/watch?v=tLgF_ZjFD9I.

Wright, Kevin B., and Sally B. Bell. "Health-Related Support Groups on the Internet: Linking Empirical Findings to Social Support and Computer-Mediated Communication Theory." *Journal of Health Psychology* 8, no. 1 (January 2003): 39–54.

WSBTV.com. "Former Teacher Sues for Being Fired for Facebook Pics," accessed October 3, 2010, http://www.wsbtv.com/news/news/former-teacher-sues-for-being-fired-for-facebook-p/nFCzs/.

Xavier, Jessica M. "The Washington Transgender Needs Assessment Survey." Accessed June 22, 2102. www.gender.org/vaults/wtnas.html.

Young, Alyson L., and Anabel Quan-Haase. "Information Revelation and Internet Privacy Concerns on Social Network Sites: A Case Study of Facebook." In *Proceedings of the Foruth International Conferene on Communities and Technologies*, 265–274. New York: ACM, 2009.

Yun-Jo An, and Theodore Frick. "Student Perceptions of Asynchronous Computer-Mediated Communication in Face-to-Face Courses." *Journal of Computer-Mediated Communication* 11, no. 2 (January 2006): 485–99. doi:10.1111/j.1083-6101.2006.00023.x.

The Wire. DVD. Directed by Alex Zakrzewski. Studio City: HBO Studios, 2002.

Zhao, Shangyang, Sherri Grasmuck, and Jason Martin. "Identity Construction on Facebook: Digital Empowerment in Anchored Relationships." *Computers in Human Behavior* 24, no. 5 (March 2008): 1816–36.

Zhao, Shanyang. "Do Internet Users Have More Social Ties? A Call for Differentiated Analyses of Internet Use." *Journal of Computer-Mediated Communication* 11, no. 3 (April 2006): 844–62.

Zuckerberg, Mark. "About Facebook." Facebook, accessed June 28, 2012, http://www.facebook.com/about.php.

Index

About the Contributors

Nicholas Brody is a PhD student at the Department of Communication Studies at the University of Texas at Austin. His research examines the interplay of mediated communication, technology, and personal relationships.

Carolyn Cunningham (PhD, University of Texas at Austin) is an assistant professor in the Master's Program in Communication and Leadership Studies at Gonzaga University. She researches the social impacts of new technologies, with a specific focus on gender and youth. She has authored several book chapters and her work has appeared in *New Media and Society.*

Daniel C. Davis (PhD, University of Southern California) studies human communication and how social cues facilitate social categorization as a means of reducing human energy outlay. He is a faculty member at Illinois State University's School of Communication.

Bruce E. Drushel is associate professor of media studies in the Department of Communication at Miami University. His work has appeared in *Journal of Homosexuality, Journal of Media Economics, European Financial Review,* and *FemSpec,* and in the recent volumes *LGBT Identity and New Media, LGBT Transnational Identity in Media, Collected Essays on Popular Culture,* and *Language, Symbols and the Media.*

Sara Green-Hamann (MA, University of Maine) is working on her PhD at the University of Maine. Her research interests include computer-mediated communication, health communication, public relations, and online social support. She has presented conference papers and published a recent article on communication in Second Life social support groups in the *Journal of Computer-Mediated Communication.*

Jeffrey A. Hall (PhD, University of Southern California) is assistant professor of communication studies at the University of Kansas. His research addresses how individuals' gender and self-identities influence their personal relationships in various contexts. Look for his recent publications in *Human Communication Research, Journal of Social and Personal Relationships, Sex Roles,* and *New Media and Society.*

Amber Johnson (PhD, The Pennsylvania State University) is an assistant professor of languages and communication at Prairie View A&M University. Her research trajectory merges qualitative and rhetorical research design in the areas of sexuality, social media, and performance. Her focus is on narratives of sexuality and intersections of race, class, geography, education, and beauty.

Benjamin K. Johnson is a doctoral student at the School of Communication, the Ohio State University. His research interests include selective exposure and media choice, along with impression management and social comparison in social media settings. He earned his MA in telecommunication, information studies, and media at Michigan State University.

Jeffrey H. Kuznekoff (PhD, Ohio University) is a graduate of the School of Communication Studies at Ohio University. His research addresses how new technology influences communication.

Corey Jay Liberman (PhD, Rutgers University) is assistant professor of communication arts at Marymount Manhattan College. His research interests include the effects of organizational identification on work processes and job satisfaction, organizational and societal communication networks, and social influence in interpersonal relationships.

Margeaux B. Lippman (MA, Pepperdine University) studies rhetorical elements of popular culture, persuasion, and feminist movements. She is currently a doctoral student at the University of Washington in rhetoric and critical/cultural studies.

Bree McEwan (PhD, Arizona State University) is assistant professor at Western Illinois University. Dr. McEwan's research work focuses on the development of social relationships and social communication skills both on- and offline.

Jennifer J. Mease (PhD, University of North Carolina at Chapel Hill) is a consultant at the Center for Intentional Leadership. Dr. Mease's academic work has focused on the influence of race and organizations on the construction and communication of identity.

Timothy W. Morris (BA, Marist College) is currently working with both audio and video editing, making short films/vlogs/montages, and helping to produce electronic music.

Koos C. M. Nuijten holds an MA in remedial education and a PhD in communication science. He contributed to this study while he was a senior lecturer and head of research at the International Center for Experimental and Media Effects Research (NHTV International University of Applied Sciences, Breda, The Netherlands). Currently, Nuijten performs as advisor for a PSB children's media project.

Jorge Peña (PhD, Cornell University) is assistant professor at the Department of Communication Studies at the University of Texas at Austin. His research focuses on cognitive, affective, and behavioral processes involved in online collaboration and play.

Natalie Pennington (MA, Kansas State University) is a PhD student at the University of Kansas in communication studies. Her work focuses on new media and interpersonal communication. Look for her work on grief communication and social media published in *Death Studies*, and in a forthcoming book chapter in *Mediating and Remediating Death*.

Judith E. Rosenbaum (PhD, Radboud University) is assistant professor at the Department of English, Modern Languages and Mass Communication, Albany State University. She has published in *Communications:*

The European Journal of Communication Research, Communication Yearbook, as well as various edited volumes.

John C. Sherblom (PhD, University of Maine) is professor of communication and journalism at the University of Maine and past of editor of *The Journal of Business Communication* and of *Communication Research Reports*. He has published refereed journal articles and book chapters on the use and influence of communication technology and a book on *Small Group and Team Communication*.

Peter A. Stepman (MA, University of Southern California) is currently lecturer at the Academy for Digital Entertainment, Breda University of Applied Sciences, The Netherlands. Stepman's research interests lie in looking at the entertainment side of social networks and computer mediated communication across a variety of device platforms.

Binod Sundararajan is assistant professor of management in the School of Business Administration at Dalhousie University, Halifax, Canada. His research is anchored in organizational and computer-mediated communication and social network analysis, and he researches their applications in immigrant entrepreneurship, teaching, collaborative work, learning, and historical networks.

Malavika Sundararajan is assistant professor of entrepreneurship in the School of Business at North Carolina Central University. In addition to research work in innovation, social, and immigrant entrepreneurship, her focus has been in the cognitive-emotional characteristics of entrepreneurs and its impact on local and global new venture success.

Catalina L. Toma (PhD, Cornell University) is assistant professor in the communication science department at the University of Wisconsin-Madison. Her work examines the psychological impact of communication technologies on relational processes. Her work has been published in the *Journal of Communication* and *Communication Research*.

Jessica A. Tougas (MA, Marquette University) studies health communication and currently works as a research analyst for Aurora Health Care in Milwaukee, Wisconsin. She conducts product development and market research for the organization. She received her Master's degree from

Marquette University and also holds a Bachelor's degree from Marist College.

Edwards Brothers Malloy
Thorofare, NJ USA
March 22, 2013